Chart
Toppers

A FIREFLY BOOK

Published by Firefly Books Ltd. 2009

First printing

Publisher Cataloging-in-Publication Data (U.S.)

Brunning, Bob, 1943-
   Chart toppers : the great performers of popular music over the last 50 years / Bob Brunning.
[364] p. : col. photos. ; cm.
Includes index.
Summary: An examination of some of the most popular and dynamic musical artists of the last fifty years, from genres including: 1960s Pop, 1970s Pop, 1980s Pop, 1990s Pop, Blues, Heavy Metal, Jazz, Reggae, Rock and Rap, Rock and Roll, Soul and World Music.
ISBN-13: 978-1-55407-496-9
ISBN-10: 1-55407-496-7
1. Musicians—Biography. 2. Popular music--History and criticism. I. Title.
 782.42164/0922 dc22   ML394.B866   2009

Library and Archives Canada Cataloguing in Publication
Brunning, Bob
     Chart toppers : the great performers of popular music over the last 50
years / Bob Brunning and James Pickering.
Includes an index.
ISBN-13: 978-1-55407-496-9
ISBN-10: 1-55407-496-7
     1. Musicians--Biography. 2. Popular music--History and criticism.
I. Pickering, James II. Title.
ML394.B897 2009   782.42164'0922   C2009-904164-2

Published in the United States by
Firefly Books (U.S.) Inc.
P.O. Box 1338, Ellicott Station
Buffalo, New York 14205

Published in Canada by
Firefly Books Ltd.
66 Leek Crescent
Richmond Hill, Ontario L4B 1H1

Printed in China

Chart Toppers

The Great Performers of Popular Music over the Last 50 Years

BOB BRUNNING AND JAMES PICKERING

FIREFLY BOOKS

CONTENTS

1960s Pop

CONTENTS

On these disks is a selection of the artists' recordings. Many of these albums are now available on CD and MP3. If they are not, many of the tracks from them can be found on compilations.

These boxes give you extra information about the artists and their times.

Some contain anecdotes about the artists themselves or about the people who helped their careers or, occasionally, about those who exploited them.

Others provide historical facts about the music, lifestyles, fans, fads and fashions of the day.

The Beatles

INTRODUCTION

During the 1960s there was an explosion of talent in the popular music front in the UK and U.S. Young people were enjoying a lot more freedom than their parents had ever experienced, and the aftermath of the late 50s rock 'n' roll influence encouraged many teenagers to start making their own music.

Bob Brunning (far left) with Five's Company, before going on to join Fleetwood Mac and Savoy Brown.

With a modest outlay, four young people found that they could make a wonderful noise with a set of drums, a bass, a guitar and a microphone. There were certainly plenty of heroes to emulate. The Rolling Stones, the Beatles, the Who, the Shadows, the Kinks and many others achieved phenomenal success in the early 60s and proved that if you had some basic talent, however raw, there was a real chance that you could achieve pop stardom.

In the U.S. the Beach Boys, Jimi Hendrix, the Supremes and Little Stevie Wonder were among the most successful performers of the decade. Many of the performers and musicians were becoming confident enough to write their own songs, something quite new. During the 50s very few performers thought of doing this and relied instead on established songwriters to provide them with suitable material.

The 60s opened the door for huge numbers of young musicians to display their talent, and we are still listening to the great music they produced today.

The BEACH BOYS

The name you choose when you embark on a career in the music business can be crucial. Would the Quarry Men (the Beatles), Harry Webb (Cliff Richard) and Robert Zimmerman (Bob Dylan) have become successful if they hadn't changed their names? In Los Angeles, three brothers formed a band. It was 1961. The band had various names until Brian, Dennis and Carl Wilson decided on one that reflected a passion shared by thousands of teenagers — surfing. Brought up next to California's golden beaches, the Wilsons understood the powerful thrill of challenging the biggest and the best waves. The new band name? The Beach Boys.

Surfin' Safari
1962
Pet Sounds
1966
Smiley Smile 1967
Sunflower 1970

The Very Best of the Beach Boys
1983
Good Vibrations: Thirty Years
Of The Beach Boys
1993

SURFING USA

The brothers invited their cousin Mike Love to join them. Al Jardine, a friend of Dennis, completed the Beach Boys' lineup.

The Wilson brothers had learned close harmony singing from their father, Murray. They put layers of harmony together with Chuck Berry-style guitar riffs and simple rhythms, and the "surfin'" sound was born. They nervously recorded their first single, "Surfing" for the tiny Candix record label. The record entered the U.S. Top 100. The huge Capitol record label soon spotted the potential of the Beach Boys. Several "surfin'" singles followed in quick succession.

Like many rock 'n' rollers before them, the Beach Boys recognized current teenage obsessions like surfing, the others being cars and girls. Brian Wilson's early lyrics dealt directly with these preoccupations.

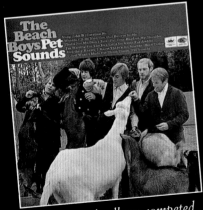

The Pet Sounds *album competed with the Beatles'* Sgt. Pepper.

THE WORLD

The Beach Boys had six singles and four albums in the U.S. charts before they achieved success in the UK. But in June 1964 "I Get Around" made the UK Top 10. Many albums and singles followed that were hits all over the world. By the mid-60s the Beach Boys were arguably the Beatles' main rivals.

But Brian Wilson hated performing and in 1965 gave it up to work in the studio. The band played on, performing and recording some of the finest music of the 60s.

TEENAGE REBELLION

There was a reason for the Beach Boys' first success, which paralleled the appeal of bands like the Beatles, the Rolling Stones and the Who on the other side of the Atlantic.

A huge change was taking place in the U.S. Young people were finding that they had power, socially and economically. They no longer had to mimic their parents, dress like them or listen to their kind of music.

On the West Coast the 60s surfing generation of teenagers lived for their dangerous sport, alarming their parents. The Beach Boys, representing this rebellious bunch, couldn't fail.

Murray Wilson (center) taught his sons to sing.

THIRTY YEARS ON

Over the next two decades, despite drug addiction and the need for years of therapy, Brian's musical genius and influence continued to shine. In 1998, 15 years after the death by drowning of his brother, Dennis, he died from cancer.

The innocence of the five beach bunnies singing about the pleasures of the sun, sea, surfing, girls, fast cars and rock 'n' roll has perhaps finally evaporated. But their legacy remains intact.

The lineup (from left to right) was Carl, Love, Jardine, Brian and Dennis.

The BEATLES

The Beatles are one of the best known groups in the history of popular music. They sold millions of records all over the world, and the songwriting team of John Lennon and Paul McCartney produced dozens of classics that have been recorded by many musicians.

The Beatles with wax look-alikes in London's Madame Tussaud's.

Please, Please Me 1963
A Hard Day's Night 1964
Help 1965
Sgt. Pepper's Lonely Hearts Club Band 1967
The Beatles 1962–1966 1973
The Beatles 1967–1970 1973
Live At The BBC 1994

EARLY DAYS

John, Paul, Ringo Starr and George Harrison sold out stadiums all over the world between 1962 and 66, but the original Beatles started out playing small clubs in the UK and Germany. Influenced by soul, rhythm and blues (R&B) and country and western (C&W) sounds from the U.S., John and Paul joined forces in 1956 in a skiffle group named the Quarry Men. In 1958 they were joined by guitarist George Harrison and later by Stuart Sutcliffe (who stayed less than a year) on bass. In 1959 they were the Silver Beatles; in 60 Pete Best joined the retitled Beatles.

UNDER THREAT

In 1966 the Beatles went to play at the Budokan stadium in Tokyo. A powerful student faction considered the site sacred and threatened to kill them if they played there — so the Beatles had to stay locked in their hotel.

The Beatles' next concert was in Manila, where they inadvertently snubbed Imelda Marcos by declining an invitation to lunch. The whole entourage was attacked and barely escaped the country with their lives.

The Beatles made headlines all over the world by speaking passionately about their beliefs.

SUCCESS

In 1961 the Beatles were spotted by Brian Epstein in their native Liverpool. He secured them a record contract with the EMI record label, and the Beatles started working with producer George Martin. During that same year, Pete Best was replaced by Ringo Starr.

Seized upon by a generation of teenagers who craved a culture they could call their own, the Beatles quickly became the heroes of the young. Their bluesy first single, "Love Me Do," entered the charts in 62.

Their second single, "Please, Please Me," zoomed to the top — the first of 17 number one hit records.

AMERICA BY STORM

The Beatles conquered the U.S. in early 1964, holding all five places at the top of the U.S. charts. Their film, *A Hard Day's Night* was released in 1964 and *Help* followed in 65. The Beatles tired of playing to hysterical, deafening audiences and stopped touring in 1966. They recorded many more albums and singles, including the innovative *Sergeant Pepper* in 1967, with its sitars, harpsichords and back-running tapes.

Ready, Steady, Go was the UK's weekly must-see pop music program on TV.

THE SPLIT

In 1968 the Beatles' manager, Brian Epstein, died, and the group began to drift apart, with its members each developing solo careers. After less than a decade of the world hanging on their every note, the Beatles officially split up on December 31, 1970.

Tragically, in 1980 John Lennon was murdered in New York, and George Harrison died of brain cancer in 2001. However, Paul McCartney and Ringo Starr are still working and producing music.

The influences of the Beatles' music can be found everywhere, even today.

Pop music had never sounded like this before. The incredible Sergeant Pepper *was the Beatles' acclaimed masterpiece concept album.*

BOB DYLAN

Robert Allan Zimmerman was born on May 24, 1941 in Duluth, Minnesota. He graduated from the University of Minnesota and began to establish a reputation for himself as an accomplished singer, writer and guitar player around the student bars and clubs in Minneapolis. The poignant and moving songs that "protest" singer Woody Guthrie had written and recorded had a profound effect on Zimmerman, and he managed to travel to New York to meet his hero just before he died. During the short time left to Guthrie, the two became friends.

PROTEST SONGS

A fan of Welsh poet Dylan Thomas, Robert Allan Zimmerman became plain Bob Dylan. Dylan wanted to carry on the tradition of protest songs established by his folk heroes. There was no shortage of causes. During the

Police attend an anti-Vietnam War protest at the Pentagon in 1967.

1960s, the civil rights movement was growing in the U.S., addressing the racism suffered by African-Americans and the deprivation of the poor. The threat posed to the Western world by nuclear weapons held by the U.S. and the then USSR was a source of real concern to many. Dylan wrote songs about it all.

The Freewheelin' Bob Dylan 1963
The Times They Are A-Changing 1964
Bringing It All Back Home 1965
Highway 61 Revisited 1965

Blonde on Blonde 1966
John Wesley Harding 1968
Blood on the Tracks 1975
Bob Dylan at Budokan 1979

RECORDING CONTRACT

The young Bob Dylan sang his heart out in the bars and coffee shops of Greenwich Village in New York's Manhattan. Word got around about his talent, and Dylan's astonishingly successful recording career commenced. Columbia Records executive John Hammond heard him playing.

He recognized Dylan's talent and organized the recording of his first album. Costing $402 to record (according to Hammond), *Bob Dylan* did not sell well. But Dylan's reputation as a protest singer was growing. He was confronting the issues that many Americans cared about.

In 1963 Dylan produced his first masterpiece. *The Freewheelin' Bob Dylan* album contained some classic songs, as did his 64 album, *The Times They Are A-Changing*. Dylan's reputation as the foremost protest writer of the 60s was established.

WORLD FAME

In 1965 *Subterranean Homesick Blues* put Dylan in the U.S. and UK charts for the first time. He performed the world over. Some of his earlier fans objected when he changed to an electric rhythm section using the versatile musicians, the Band, but still his popularity was high.

TWO YEARS OFF

In 1966 a serious motorcycle accident nearly killed Dylan, and his recuperation took months. After a reclusive two years, Dylan returned to work and released over 30 albums during the next 40 years. And he plays on, having embarked on a major concert tour in 2009 in support of his latest album, *Together Through Life*.

WOODY GUTHRIE

'Protest' songs have been written for centuries. Anger has inspired writers to express their feelings through songs and poetry. Fear of persecution often made writers subvert their messages so they were not obvious to the listener or reader.

In the 20th century writers had less to fear, and the 50s and 60s produced a crop of singers who used their songs to protest about what they saw as gross injustices.

During the 40s and 50s, the singer Woody Guthrie wrote and sang about the tens of thousands of Americans who had suffered appalling hardship during the Depression, a period when the economy crashed, creating mass unemployment. His work inspired many other singers.

Guthrie in the cap that Dylan imitated.

Dylan performs with the Band, an experienced and talented team.

JIMI HENDRIX

Johnny Allen Hendrix was born on November 27, 1942, in Seattle, Washington. His father renamed him James Marshall Hendrix when he was three years old and 13 years later bought him his first guitar. Left-handed, Hendrix reversed the strings and played it "upside down." Initially influenced by blues performers B.B. King, Muddy Waters, Chuck Berry and Robert Johnson, Hendrix soon developed his own style. After a short spell in the army, he moved to New York and played with many well-known rhythm and blues artists, including Little Richard, the Isley Brothers and Ike and Tina Turner. Hendrix's own bands were less successful.

SPOTTED

In 1966 Chas Chandler, the bass player with the well-known UK rhythm and blues band the Animals, saw Hendrix in New York. Astounded by his persona and technique, Chandler acted. He brought Hendrix, now Jimi, to the UK. (On Hendrix's very first night in London, Chandler took him to see the band Cream, which featured a young guitarist called Eric Clapton. Hendrix joined them on stage that night.) Chandler organized a rhythm section for Hendrix. It comprised Noel Redding on bass and Mitch Mitchell on drums. He also arranged a recording contract with Polydor.

Hendrix played to 250,000 at the Isle of Wight.

14

Are You Experienced
1967
Axis: Bold as Love
1967
Electric Ladyland
1968

The Ultimate Experience
1993
The Collection
1995

FIRST SINGLE CHARTS

Hendrix's first single, "Hey Joe," was released in December 1966 and went to number six in the UK charts. A label switch to Track followed, as did instant success. Hendrix was a creative songwriter, and the hit singles came thick and fast, propelling Hendrix toward world-wide recognition. In 1967 Hendrix played the U.S. for the first time at the Monterey Pop Festival, burning his guitar at the end of his act to the stunned amazement of the audience.

NEW GUITAR SOUNDS

Hendrix was a great performer, playing his guitar behind his neck and with his teeth, but, more than that, he experimented with the electric guitar as no one had before, using the amplifier, phaser, wah wah and chorus pedals and slide to amazing effect. The Jimi Hendrix Experience became one of the world's most popular bands, but by 1969 cracks were appearing. Mitchell and Redding were fired for personal and business reasons. Hendrix replaced them and earned his place in rock history with his performance of "Star Spangled Banner" at the most famous rock festival of all, Woodstock, in August 1969.

Hendrix wasn't the first to play with his teeth.

POP FESTIVALS

The emergence of huge outdoor rock music festivals in the 60s was linked to the development of modern PA systems. Before then no amplification setup could deliver a clear sound to large open-air arenas. The U.K. Windsor Jazz and Blues Festival, with its state-of-the-art Watkins PA system, led the way in 1966. As PA systems grew in power so did the size of the audiences. The famous Woodstock Festival in 1969 attracted 500,000 people, although its 10,000-watt PA system barely coped.

You had to be an enthusiast to enjoy the experience. Awful catering, inadequate toilet facilities, no shelter from the weather and the need for binoculars to see your favorite band were common problems at all the festivals!

Hendrix created a huge sensation at Woodstock.

JUST FOUR YEARS OF FAME

But tragedy was just around the corner. Hendrix played at the huge Isle of Wight Festival in August 1970. After a short European tour, he returned to London. Three years on the road, with all its temptations, caught up with Hendrix. He died on September 18, 1970, just 27 years old. He choked to death, probably as a result of drug and alcohol abuse.

The KINKS

In the early 60s many UK bands, such as the Rolling Stones, were being heavily influenced by the heady rhythm and blues music that was crossing the Atlantic. The Pretty Things, Manfred Mann, the Animals, the Yardbirds and the Beatles all featured rhythm and blues material in their recordings. North London group the Ramrods (later called the Ravers) were no exception, but they were failing to make an impact. Then they met entrepreneur Larry Page, who remolded their image, bizarrely dressing them in hunting jackets, and changed their name to the Kinks. "There's nothing kinky about us though," said Ray Davies, "Kinky is such a fashionable word we knew people would remember it."

CARNABY STREET

One of the Kinks' most successful singles was "Dedicated Follower of Fashion." It entered the UK Top 10 in February 1966, capturing the mood of the new generation of young people who had money to spend in the boom 60s (a time of full employment in the UK) and wanted to follow the fashions of the day.

London's Carnaby Street and the King's Road, Chelsea, were arguably the center of fashion in the 60s. Posing, strutting and flaunting your new "gear" was all-important. Bands, of course, followed suit and also tried to become innovators.

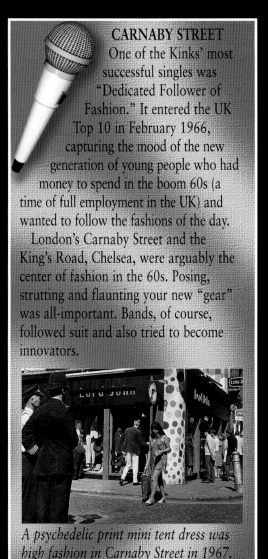

A psychedelic print mini tent dress was high fashion in Carnaby Street in 1967.

HIT SINGLES

Led by Ray and his brother, Dave, the Kinks signed a record contract with the UK label Pye. Their first two unsuccessful singles were by other writers, but the brothers discovered that they could write their own songs, and with great success. In 1964 "You Really Got Me," with its memorable guitar riff, went straight to the top of the charts. The Davies brothers were talented songwriters, and the hits followed. Over the next three years, they released a series of clever and amusing hit records that reflected their wry view of 60s England. Mostly written by Ray Davies, the lyrics of "Well Respected Man" (knocking the British class system), "Dedicated Follower of Fashion" (mocking 60s fashion fanatics), "Sunny Afternoon" (ruling class problems with the tax man) and "Waterloo Sunset" (even London can be picturesque) were direct and funny.

CONCEPT ALBUMS

A new idea was developing in the record industry in the 1960s — the "concept" album. A rock band would record a mini opera; not just a collection of unrelated songs, the album carried a story or devoted itself to developing a theme. The Stones, the Beatles, the Who and many others produced concept albums.

However, the Kinks' *The Kinks are The Village Green Preservation Society* and *Arthur (or the Decline and Fall of the British Empire)* were groundbreaking albums of their type. *Village Green* was Davies' tribute to England and the quirks of the English character. *Arthur* (1969) was originally commissioned as a play for TV, and its subject was an ordinary man reflecting on his life.

The Kinks' red hunting jacket phase did not last long.

FALLING OUT

Ray and Dave were growing apart by the late 60s and pursued solo careers in addition to their Kinks' involvement. They had created a rift with the other band members, Mick Avory (drums) and Pete Quaife (bass), who left. They carried on touring and recording with new musicians to the end of the 80s — and had the honor of being inducted into the Rock 'n' Roll Hall of Fame.

The Kinks
1964

The Kinks are the Village Green Preservation Society
1968

Arthur (or the Decline and Fall of the British Empire) 1969

The Ultimate Collection 1989

The Definitive Collection:
The Kinks' Greatest Hits
1993

PINK FLOYD

They started as the T-Set, became the Screaming Abdabs, then just the Abdabs. In 1965 George Waters, Rick Wright, Nick Mason and Roger Barrett took part of the name of a blues band called Pink Anderson and Floyd Council. They became the Pink Floyd Sound. They played rhythm and blues and gave powerful performances in London's clubs and pubs.

PSYCHEDELIC UNDERGROUND BAND

In 1966 they met Peter Jenner and Andrew King who became their managers. Their careers were about to take off. London was hosting a new "underground" music revolution, and audiences were eager to hear bands who were daringly experimental.

Now simply Pink Floyd, the band stopped playing rhythm and blues and concentrated on their own material — avant-garde, experimental, psychedelic rock written mainly by Roger, now Syd, Barrett. The band signed with the UK record label Columbia and released their first single "Arnold Layne," about a transvestite stealing women's underwear from clotheslines. It gave them their first Top-20 hit. The follow up single, "See Emily Play," was even more successful, and in August 1967 they released their first album, *The Piper at the Gates of Dawn*, named from the children's book, *The Wind in the Willows*, by Kenneth Graham.

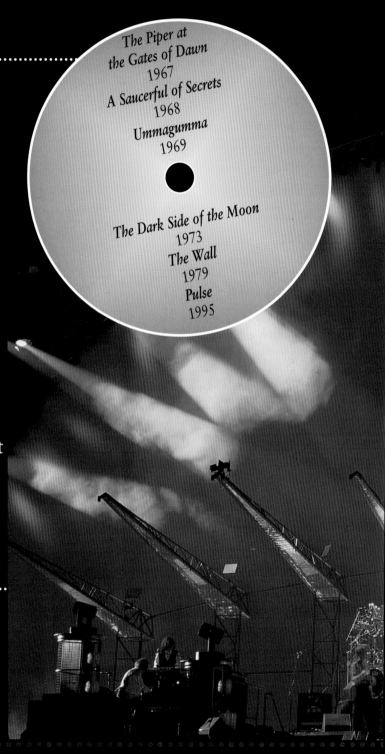

The Piper at
the Gates of Dawn
1967
A Saucerful of Secrets
1968
Ummagumma
1969

The Dark Side of the Moon
1973
The Wall
1979
Pulse
1995

BARRETT LEAVES

But soon there were problems within the band. Barrett's creativity was linked to his dependence on drugs. In time he could no longer function.

18

Dave Gilmour joined Pink Floyd and Barrett left. Barrett became extremely reclusive and never fully recovered from his drug addiction.

SUCCESS AND THE WALL

Pink Floyd became an "albums band" and one of the world's stadium-fillers. Their slow-moving songs could sometimes take as long as 20 minutes to develop and used unusual instruments and innovative sounds (such as the till ringing in "Money" and the clock sounds in "Time," both on the *Dark Side of the Moon* album). They used state-of-the-art lighting and complex stereo and quadrophonic sound systems.

In 1973 *Dark Side of the Moon*, with its theme of death and emotional breakdown, entered the UK and U.S. charts and stayed there for years. Two more successful albums, *Wish You Were Here* and *Animals* followed and then, in 1979, *The Wall*, almost certainly Pink Floyd's most famous work.

In the early 80s the band split. Happily its members continued to play and record the music loved by their millions of fans all over the world.

PSYCHEDELIC LIGHTS

The importance of lighting a stage to enhance drama has always been recognized, but pop groups discovered its power only relatively recently.

Major bands like the Rolling Stones and the Beatles started their careers illuminated by a couple of 150-watt light-bulbs. In the early 60s musicians realized that the "look" of the band was almost as important as its sound.

Not the first to use psychedelic lighting, Pink Floyd started with the simple projection of swirling images produced by heating specially oiled slides. By the late 80s they required 20 trucks to carry their lighting between concerts, and audiences were bowled over by the sheer spectacle.

Wright, Gilmour and Mason still used spectacular lighting in 1989.

The ROLLING STONES

In 1960 two students in their early 20s bumped into each other at a railway station in South London. They remembered playing together in their primary school ten years before. But what caught Michael's eye was Keith's armful of obscure rhythm and blues and and blues albums. It was a rare sight, and surprising to find someone else who was similarly passionate about his favorite music. And Keith was also a guitar player!

BLUES INCORPORATED

Michael invited Keith to join him and guitarist/bass player Dick Taylor in his amateur band, Little Boy Blue and the Blue Boys. All three often went to see the UK's first ever rhythm and blues band, Blues Incorporated, led by Alexis Korner at his London club. Sometimes the trio were invited to join Alexis on stage, a thrill for Mick and company. One night Brian Jones, a keen blues guitarist, was in the audience. He liked what he heard and joined the Blue Boys.

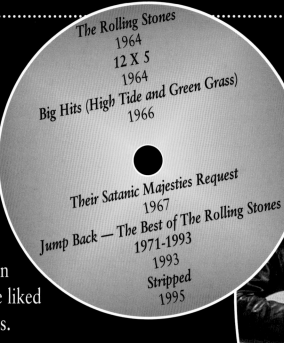

The Rolling Stones
1964
12 X 5
1964
Big Hits (High Tide and Green Grass)
1966

Their Satanic Majesties Request
1967
Jump Back — The Best of The Rolling Stones
1971-1993
1993
Stripped
1995

THE LINEUP

Mick Jagger, Keith Richards and Jones formed the embryonic Rolling Stones. The band wasn't yet complete. Bass player Taylor and drummer Richard Chapman left. Bill Perks was recruited as the bass player because he owned a brand new amplifier and a van! Jagger and Richards occasionally used drummer Charlie Watts. They pressured him to leave his day job to join the Rolling Stones. His comment? "What's my dad going to say?" Bill Perks became Bill Wyman, and the Rolling Stones were born.

20

IN THE BEGINNING

In 1962 the Stones piled into a van and drove from club to club. Andrew Loog Oldham spotted them and became their manager. He promoted them as scruffy, long-haired, dangerous-to-know bad boys — the opposite from the neat and suited Beatles. In 1962 parents did not want their daughters to marry a Rolling Stone!

By the end of 1963 the Stones had had two hit singles and their album, *The Rolling Stones*, released in 1964, was huge. Over 40 albums followed and 35 years later the Stones play on.

BRIAN JONES

By the late 60s Brian Jones was beginning to cause concern to those who knew him. He was becoming increasingly dependent on drugs and alcohol. His health deteriorated, and in 1969 the other members of the Stones had to dismiss him. On July 3rd in the same year he was found drowned in the pool of his luxurious Sussex home. The Rolling Stones paid a tribute to Jones during a huge open-air concert in London's Hyde Park a few days later.

Brian Jones' sad death was a reminder that, although the period known as the "Swinging 60s" was an exciting and liberating time for young people, there was a down side that should still serve as a warning.

The Stones play for Jones in Hyde Park in 1969.

NEVER ENDING

Self-styled "The Greatest Rock 'n' Roll Band in the World," in 2007 the Rolling Stones completed their A Bigger Bang world tour, filling stadiums and thrilling millions of fans with their spectacular stage shows. Nobody seemed to care that most of the band members were grandfathers!

A custard pie fight launches the Beggars Banquet *album.*

SIMON and GARFUNKEL

In October 1964 Tom and Jerry finally decided to use their own names and recorded their first album together, *Wednesday Morning 3AM*, as Simon and Garfunkel. It included their version of the song "The Sound of Silence." The album was not a success. Simon went to Britain to try out the growing folk club circuit, and Garfunkel went back to college. Under many different names, Simon and Garfunkel had released 18 singles between 1958 and 62 but had got only one into the U.S. charts — at number 49.

A HIT AT LAST

Producer Tom Wilson loved "The Sound of Silence." He remixed the song, adding a powerful rhythm section, and released it as a single. In December 1965 the record went straight to the top of the U.S. charts, and Paul Simon and Art Garfunkel got back together, quickly recording an album. It included an excellent song written by Simon on Widnes railway station in the UK. (There is now a plaque on the station to commemorate the fact.) "Homeward Bound" was the follow-up single and was successful on both sides of the Atlantic. "I Am A Rock" came next, and went into the Top 10 in both the U.S. and the UK.

The Sound of Silence
1966
Parsley, Sage Rosemary and Thyme
1966
Bookends
1968

Bridge Over Troubled Water
1970
The Simon and Garfunkel Collection
1981
The Concert in Central Park
1982

Their next successful album was *Parsley, Sage, Rosemary and Thyme*, which included "Scarborough Fair" and the witty "59th Bridge Street Song." Naturally, Simon and Garfunkel capitalised on their chart success, touring all over the world between 1966 and 70. Their

Hoffman starred as The Graduate.
The film's soundtrack was memorable.

Garfunkel appeared in many films,
including Catch 22 (above).

relationship on the road was occasionally uneasy, although they never resorted to the Everly Brothers' demands for separate hotels!

THE GRADUATE

In 1968 Dustin Hoffman starred in the controversial film *The Graduate*, the story of a university student seduced by an older woman, Mrs. Robinson. Simon and Garfunkel contributed to the soundtrack, and *Mrs. Robinson* was one of their biggest international successes.

Another successful album, *Bookends*, followed and in 1969 the single, "The Boxer" made the U.S. and UK Top 10. Although the end of their working relationship was in sight, Simon and Garfunkel's biggest commercial hit yet was imminent. "Bridge over Troubled Waters" made number one on both sides of the Atlantic, as did the album of the same name.

PARTING COMPANY

But Simon and Garfunkel wanted to go in different directions, and in 1970 they split up. Garfunkel pursued an acting career, and Simon carved his own impressive solo music career. They did get together again — for a concert in New York in 1981 and again for a series of concerts in 1993.

BACK TO SCHOOL

Paul Simon was keen to change the way he wrote and went back to school (to study songwriting!) after he and Garfunkel split up. Despite being one of the most successful songwriters in the U.S. at the time, he felt he had more to learn.

He wanted to research some very different music sources, and his post-Simon and Garfunkel work certainly incorporated elements of jazz, reggae and blues.

Simon's best-selling album, *Graceland*, strongly influenced by black South African music, reached number one in 1986, amid accusations of exploitation from the antiapartheid movement of South Africa.

Simon's Graceland *tour* included a large cast of South African musicians.

The SMALL FACES

For a short time during the mid 60s, a weekend ritual took place in some of the seaside resorts on the south coast of England. "Mods" and "rockers" would meet to do battle. The mods rode scooters and dressed in sharp, fashionable suits with button-down collared shirts. The rockers rode motorbikes and wore studded leather outfits. People got hurt sometimes, but it was as much about parading a fashion image as fighting a rival gang.

MODS

Fashion has always been closely allied to pop music. In 1965 one group of musicians exploited their mod image with great success. Steve Marriot, aged just 18, had already released two solo singles and had theater and TV success as a child actor. He joined Ronnie Lane, Kenney Jones and Jimmy Winston, and they named themselves the Small Faces. The name came from the term "faces," used for the most respected mods, and "small" because three of them were under 5 feet 3 inches tall!

Small Faces 1966
From the Beginning 1967
Ogdens' Nut Gone Flake 1968
Small Faces Collection 1985

The Singles As and Bs 1990
The Small Faces Boxed —
The Definitive Collection 1995
The Best of The Small Faces 1995

FIRST HIT SINGLE

Within weeks they had met their dynamic agent, Don Arden, and released the first of their Top 20 singles on the Decca label, "Watcha Gonna Do About It." By August 1965, organist Jimmy Winston (taller than the others) had left. Ian McLagan, an experienced organist and small in height, was the perfect replacement, and the Small Faces soon became a household name. Their extensive touring schedule, recording successes and TV appearances kept them in the spotlight, and thousands of teenage girls pursued them. From August 1965 to July 68, they had 13 singles in the UK charts, most of them written by Lane and Marriot. Influenced by rhythm and blues music, they were finding their own sound.

The first round album cover, it was designed to look like a tobacco tin.

OGDENS' NUT GONE FLAKE

The band switched to the Immediate label. In 1967 the single "Itchycoo Park" went to number three in the UK charts and was their only U.S. hit, reaching number 16. In 1968 they released their masterpiece album, *Ogdens' Nut Gone Flake*.

They took their music very seriously but were already becoming disillusioned with their pop-star lifestyle. By 1969 money and management problems caused tension in the band, and Marriot left to join Peter Frampton in Humble Pie.

MANAGERS' ROLE

Managers have always played a crucial role in the fortunes of bands. Talented musicians are not necessarily astute business people — a dynamic and knowledgeable manager can make all the difference between success and failure. Sadly, some managers take advantage of the naivete of their artists and tie them into unfair and unlucrative contracts with the promise of greater things to follow.

There is little doubt that many bands do not reap the financial rewards their success has earned. The Small Faces felt that they had been exploited, but lengthy litigation to pursue the back payment of record royalties failed to get them anywhere.

An infamous example of a manipulative manager was Colonel Tom Parker, Elvis Presley's manager. Elvis was not allowed to perform outside the U.S. Parker wouldn't let Elvis go alone and could not himself leave the U.S. since he was an illegal immigrant who may not have been allowed back in.

Mods in uniform parkas.

THE FACES

Rod Stewart and Ron Wood joined Lane, Jones and McLagan. Called the Faces, they toured UK clubs and universities for two years and had four hit singles. Lane left to start a solo career, and Wood became involved with the Rolling Stones. Stewart pursued his own solo career, and in 1975 the band split up.

Four years later Jones joined the Who. McLagan, too, still works as a musician. In 1991 Marriot died in a fire at his home in Essex. Lane died in 1997 from multiple sclerosis.

A designer hired the mod band for a fashion shoot.

The SUPREMES

To succeed in the music business you need to persevere. Diane Earle and the other members of the Detroit-based vocal group the Primettes did so. They talked themselves into the offices of the Motown record label, run by Berry Gordy, Jr., Diane worked there as a part-time secretary. The group's leader, Florence (Flo) Ballard, begged Gordy to sign up the girls. He agreed on condition that they change their name. They became the Supremes, and Diane Earle was renamed Diana Ross. It was 1960.

SLOW START

None of the Supreme's early singles on Motown were hits, but Ross, Ballard, Mary Wilson and Barbara Martin worked as backup singers. In 1962 Barbara Martin left, leaving a trio. After five flops in a row Gordy was about to give up, but he decided to give them one more chance. His highly successful song-writing and production team of Holland, Dozier and Holland were asked to find something for the Supremes. In 1963 "When The Lovelight Starts Shining Through My Eyes" entered the U.S. Top 40. But its follow-up, "Run, Run, Run," did no better than their previous single.

From the start the Supremes always wore glamorous matching costumes.

DIANA LEADS

Berry Gordy, Jr., looked hard at the Supremes and decided that they would have more chance of success if Ross became lead singer instead of Ballard. He also realized that they needed a lot more nationwide exposure.

So they appeared on the 1964 package tour *The Cavalcade of Stars*, for $500 per week.

In 1964 the Supremes went back into the studio for their seventh attempt at recording a hit single. "Where Did Our Love Go?" was released in August.

Meet The Supremes
1963

Where Did Our Love Go
1964

Love Child
1969

Compact Command Performances —
Twenty Greatest Hits
1986

THE HITS START

The Supremes had at last found the magic. The single went to number one in the U.S. and number three in the UK. With the support of the powerful Motown team, the Supremes were on their way. They were the first artists to have five of their singles top the U.S. charts in succession. The talented trio toured the world.

But backstage there were tensions. Long disenchanted by Ross's hijacking of her lead singer's role, Ballard became difficult and erratic. She was asked to leave. Cindy Birdsong took over. (Ballard died at the age of 32 from drug and alcohol abuse.)

The hits didn't stop, and the focus was now firmly on Ross. In 1967 the Supremes became Diana Ross and the Supremes.

DIANA GOES SOLO

"Someday We'll Be Together" was the twelfth number one for the trio. The Supremes carried on, but without Ross. Her very successful solo career was just beginning.

SOLO CAREER

When Diana Ross left the Supremes in 1970, Motown was determined that her new solo career thrive. Her first single, "Reach out and Touch," was written with an anti-drugs message.

Not content with her success as a singer, Ross was nominated for an Oscar for her acting debut in the film about blues singer Billie Holliday, *Lady Sings the Blues*. Diana Ross still tours the world, filling stadiums and concert halls with her loyal fans.

Ross sang Billie Holliday's songs in the film, Lady Sings the Blues.

The Supremes' act was choreographed.

The WHO

Musicians Pete Townshend, Roger Daltrey and John Entwistle met at school in West London. In 1960, with Doug Sandom, they formed the Detours. They discovered the rhythm and blues music that was crossing the Atlantic and inspiring so many UK bands. The Detours became the Who, but not for long. Their first manager, Peter Meaden, renamed them the High Numbers and negotiated a short-lived record contract with Fontana. Keith Moon replaced Doug Sandom. Manager Peter Meaden left. The band became the Who again, with new managers, Kit Lambert and Chris Stamp.

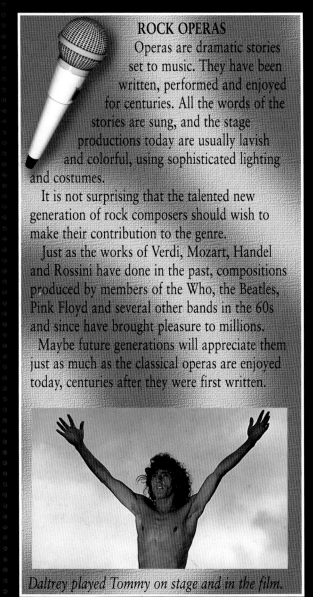

ROCK OPERAS

Operas are dramatic stories set to music. They have been written, performed and enjoyed for centuries. All the words of the stories are sung, and the stage productions today are usually lavish and colorful, using sophisticated lighting and costumes.

It is not surprising that the talented new generation of rock composers should wish to make their contribution to the genre.

Just as the works of Verdi, Mozart, Handel and Rossini have done in the past, compositions produced by members of the Who, the Beatles, Pink Floyd and several other bands in the 60s and since have brought pleasure to millions.

Maybe future generations will appreciate them just as much as the classical operas are enjoyed today, centuries after they were first written.

Daltrey played Tommy on stage and in the film.

MY GENERATION

By 1965 the Who were a big name around London's pubs and clubs. Playing in a low-ceilinged club, Townshend accidentally broke his guitar during an extravagant stage gesture. The crowd loved it, and guitar smashing stayed in the act.

The Who were mods in 1965.

But there was much more to the Who than destroying instruments. Townshend was a gifted songwriter. His songs "I Can't Explain" and "Anyway, Anyhow, Anywhere" (which featured feedback for the first time) gave the band two Top 10 singles. Their third single became an anthem for the 60s. "My Generation," with the words "I hope I die before I get old," was a comment on 60s pop culture of fast living, drug usage and consumerism. It was their biggest hit, reaching number two in the charts. Tours and TV appearances followed, and the Who lived up to their image of all-imbibing party animals. Townshend's "Substitute" was another witty song about life in the fast lane and was followed by "I'm A Boy" and "Happy Jack." All three made the UK Top 5, and "Happy Jack" charted in the U.S. too. In 1967 the Who began the first of many U.S. tours.

Repeated instrument smashing kept the Who in debt in their early years.

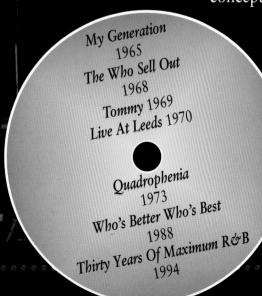

My Generation
1965
The Who Sell Out
1968
Tommy 1969
Live At Leeds 1970

Quadrophenia
1973
Who's Better Who's Best
1988
Thirty Years Of Maximum R&B
1994

TOMMY

In 1969 Townshend's rock opera *Tommy* was released. The powerful story of an abused deaf, dumb and blind pinball player thrust the band's career into overdrive and was later made into a film and a musical. Many hit singles and albums followed in the 70s, including another concept album, *Quadrophenia*.

Sadly, in 1978 drummer Keith Moon's reveling lifestyle finally killed him.

The Who continued to tour and record, and it was just before a tour was set to kick off that John Entwistle died of a heart attack in 2002.

GAZETTEER

There is no doubt that this decade produced some of the most successful and popular music of all time. Millions upon millions of records were sold all over the world. You have already read about some of the most famous 60s artists, but there were many more groups producing exciting and innovative music on both sides of the Atlantic.

The Hollies

MERSEY SOUND

After the Beatles' enormous early success, record producers realized that musical talent could be found outside London. They went to Manchester and Liverpool and signed up lots of local bands. Most of them were either talentless or, at best, one hit wonders, but there were some exceptions. Close harmony groups the Hollies and the Searchers became hit recording artists. Billy J. Kramer and the Dakotas and Gerry and the Pacemakers also had long and successful careers.

The Animals

RHYTHM AND BLUES ROOTS

The blues music that had inspired the Rolling Stones did the same for several other bands, which started out playing rhythm and blues. The Animals, the Yardbirds, the Pretty Things, Alan Price, Ten Years After, the Groundhogs and Manfred Mann all developed their own musical styles, but their blues roots were identical. The Yardbirds featured a guitarist who would became a household name — Eric Clapton.

PSYCHEDELIC UNDERGROUND MUSIC

Other bands played some weird but very creative music. Traffic, King Crimson, Procul Harum, Creation and the Move all caught the hippy mood of the late 60s and produced new electronic sounds (sometimes with mystical lyrics about goblins or space travel) influenced by the psychedelic underground movement that had its roots in San Francisco.

Manfred Mann

WOMEN ARTISTS

Fourteen-year old Millie reached number one with "My Boy Lollipop" and Twinkle, Sandie Shaw, Helen Shapiro and Cilla Black all had hits in the UK. In the U.S. Mary Wells, Martha and the Vandellas, The Ronettes, Little Eva, the Shangri-Las and Tina Turner did the same.

Dave Clark Five

Sandie Shaw

INSTRUMENTAL GROUPS

Instrumental groups became popular in the 60s. "Telstar" topped the U.S. charts, an unusual achievement for a UK band at the time. The Shadows were the most successful example in the UK, with 20 UK Top 10 hits during the decade. Every guitar band in the world played the Ventures' "Walk Don't Run." Johnny and the Hurricanes and the Champs introduced the saxophone (instead of the guitar) as the lead instrument in their bands with great success.

MOTOWN

The Detroit record company Motown produced some of the classic recordings of the decade. Smokey Robinson and the Miracles, the Temptations, Marvin Gaye, Otis Redding, Sam and Dave, the Four Tops, Percy Sledge and many other Motown artists thrilled fans with their soulful recordings and live performances.

The Doors

Marvin Gaye

OTHER 60s GREATS

The Byrds, the Doors and the Monkees were big successes in the UK and the U.S. The Monkees were four actors in a TV series about a fictitious band. They became popular and recorded several pop songs. In the UK quirky West Country band the Troggs, London's Dave Clarke Five, Johnny Kidd and the Pirates, Status Quo, Humble Pie and many other bands helped to make the 60s a very special decade indeed.

The Monkees

1970s Pop

CONTENTS

On these disks is a selection of the artists' recordings. Many of these albums are now available on CD and MP3. If they are not, many of the tracks from them can be found on compilations.

The Sex Pistols

These boxes give you extra information about the artists and their times.

Some contain anecdotes about the artists themselves or about the people who helped their careers or, occasionally, about those who exploited them.

Others provide historical facts about the music, lifestyles, fans and fashions of the day.

INTRODUCTION

The 1970s were turbulent. The Vietnam War raged, and there was political unrest all over the world. Margaret Thatcher became the first woman prime minister of Britain and U.S. President Richard Nixon, resigned in disgrace.

Believed by many to be the greatest guitarist ever, Eric Clapton plays on in 2000.

The Apollo flights to the moon ended and the supersonic Concorde service between London and New York began.

On the music scene, many different kinds of bands and musicians achieved success. Punk music exploded, contrasting with the sophisticated music of bands like the Eagles and Fleetwood Mac. Many of the superstars of the 70s began their careers earlier. Van Morrison, Eric Clapton, Fleetwood Mac and Rod Stewart all had their roots in the UK's "blues boom" that had erupted during the previous decade. David Bowie and the Sex Pistols could not have been more dissimilar, but they both presented a radical approach to their music, which was very different from the ethereal Procol Harum and the unashamedly commercial bands like the Bee Gees and ABBA.

The music industry lost some major artists during the 70s. Elvis Presley died in 1977, the same year as glam rock star Marc Bolan of T. Rex. Other deaths include those of Jimi Hendrix, Jim Morrison, Gene Vincent, Sid Vicious and Keith Moon. As with many of their predecessors, some of these untimely deaths were related to drug or alcohol abuse.

ABBA

The already successful and accomplished Swedish group unbelievably called Björn and Benny, Agnetha and Anni-Frid, decided that their name was too much of a mouthful. They decided to use an acronym. The first letters of their first names produced a much snappier title, ABBA. The four members were no newcomers to the pop scene when they joined forces in 1971. Agnetha Fältskog had had chart success in 1968, and Björn and Benny had worked together for some time on and off in various successful bands.

TRIBUTE BANDS

Imitation is the sincerest form of flattery, and there has been a development in the music industry over the last decade — tribute bands.

The Bootleg Beatles, the Strolling Bones, Fleetwood Back plus a dozen other bands perform their heroes' music – and make a good living doing so.

They generally do an excellent job and always demonstrate their knowledge of and affection for the classic bands they imitate. One of the most successful? Bjorn Again!

The ABBA lookalikes Bjorn Agam.

CAREER PLANS

Björn and Benny sometimes worked as session musicians and bumped into Agnetha and Anni. The four decided to combine their singing and writing talents. ABBA wanted to be successful internationally. With Stig Anderson, their manager and producer, a business plan was devised. First stop, the Eurovision Song Contest. Their second attempt won. "Waterloo" was a magnificently produced song. It made number one in six countries and was recorded in several languages to maximize sales.

Björn and Agnetha had three children together.

Benny and Anni got together in 1970 and divorced in 81.

HIT AFTER HIT AFTER HIT

Björn and Agnetha married, as did Benny and Anni. They toured extensively, used the media wisely and produced bouncy, commercial records. In the UK 15 singles made the Top Five, eight of them number ones. Their success was repeated all over the world. "Mamma Mia" was number one in Australia for ten weeks and stayed in the charts for two years. "Dancing Queen" topped the charts in the U.S., UK and eight other countries. Stig Anderson announced, "[W]e are the most successful band in the world, because we have sold more records than anybody else, between 75,000,000 and 100,000,000 — more than the Beatles or Elvis Presley." In 1982 ABBA were Sweden's biggest source of overseas earnings, beating Volvo and Ikea!

ABBA
1975
Greatest Hits
1976
The Album
1978

ABBA: The Collection : One
1987
ABBA: The Collection : Two
1988

ABBA SPLIT

The breakup of the couples' marriages led to ABBA's demise. All members were fabulously rich, and all four developed creative solo careers. Björn and Benny notably teamed up to produce the hit musical *Mamma Mia!*, which was turned into a movie starring Meryl Streep and Pierce Brosnan.

The BEE GEES

Widely recognized as one of Australia's best-known musical exports, the Gibb brothers were not actually born there. Barry Gibb was born in Douglas on the Isle of Man in 1946, and the twins, Robin and Maurice, were born in Manchester, England, in 1949. They all started performing at a very young age, making their first public appearance at the Gaumont Theatre in Manchester when the twins were just seven years old.

HEADING FOR THE BIG TIME

In 1958 the Gibb family emigrated to Australia. The brothers made a name for themselves as a harmony trio and had their own TV show. By 1962 they were signed to Australia's Festival record label. During the next four years the Bee Gees released 12 singles. Three of them topped the Australian charts. Their first album in 1965 was called, amazingly, *Barry Gibb and the Bee Gees Sing and Play Fourteen Barry Gibb Songs!*

The boys wanted to make it on the international music scene. In 1967, as their 13th single, "Spicks and Specks" hit the top of the Australian charts, the Gibb brothers were on an airplane bound for London, England. They had an appointment with Robert Stigwood, a director of Beatles' manager Brian Epstein's company. He loved what he heard and quickly secured the Bee Gees a recording contract with Polydor.

The young trio appeared on TV every week.

The Bee Gees formed their band soon after their arrival in the UK.

GETTING THE ACT TOGETHER

The brothers recruited drummer Colin Peterson and guitarist Vince Melouney, both Australians living in London. Their single "New York Mining Disaster, 1941" entered the Top 20 on both sides of the Atlantic. Their first album did even better, making the Top 10 in the UK and the U.S. Later, in 1967, "Massachusetts" gave the Bee Gees their first number one hit while they were still teenagers! But cracks appeared within the band. The twins disagreed about the group's direction, Melouney left and alcohol and drug abuse, together with a "rock star" lifestyle, took its toll. Robin left briefly; Peterson left for good.

SATURDAY NIGHT FEVER

By 1973 the Bee Gees were playing the UK cabaret circuit. Their career lurched up again in 1975 with their U.S. Top 10 hit "Nights On Broadway." In 1977 their album *Children Of The World* sold in truckloads, and their singles hit the 70s disco scene just right. Their greatest success was nigh. Robert Stigwood asked them to write songs for a film, *Saturday Night Fever*. The success of these songs was monumental. "How Deep Is Your Love" stayed at the top of the U.S. Billboard charts for 17 weeks. The next two singles "Stayin' Alive" and "Night Fever" also made number one. The album sold 30,000,000 copies and won five trophies at the 1978 Grammy Awards.

After the sudden death of Maurice in 2003, Barry and Robin decided to retire the group name and have pursued their own musical projects.

DISCO FEVER

Discomania gripped the UK and the U.S. during the 70s. Instead of hiring a band of musicians to play in a limited style, one DJ and a loud sound system could fill venues with customers who could dance to the latest records. DJs would program the music to create an atmosphere.

The phenomenon was captured in a classic movie starring John Travolta. *Saturday Night Fever* featured songs by the Bee Gees, Yvonne Elliman, KC and the Sunshine Band and more. It opened as a stage musical in London 20 years later, in 1998.

Saturday Night Fever captured the '70s disco mood.

First
1967
Odessa
1969
Best Of The Bee Gees
1969
Saturday Night Fever
1978
Bee Gees Greatest
1979
Staying Alive
1983

DAVID BOWIE

David Robert Jones was born on January 8, 1947, in South London. His first love was art, and he left Bromley Technical High School at 16 to be a commercial artist. But music came a close second. From the mid-1960s, he played in various mod bands and soon had to change his surname to Bowie — to avoid confusion with famous Monkees' star Davy Jones!

THE EARLY YEARS

After many early flops, Bowie made number five with his innovative single "Space Oddity" (1969). It told the story of Major Tom, an astronaut who does not want to return to Earth, and earned Bowie an award for "astounding originality" from the UK Songwriters' Guild.

CHANGES

Bowie was beginning to make waves. In 1971 he released *The Man Who Sold the World*, a heavy-guitar rock album, followed with *Hunky Dory*.

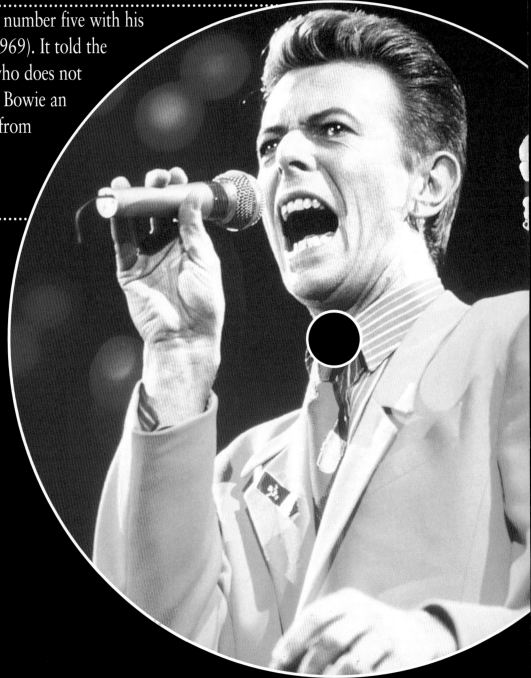

Young Bowie as a mod in the 60s.

BOWIE ON SCREEN

Bowie also achieved cult status as an actor. In his movie debut he played a TV-obsessed alien in the bizarre classic, *The Man Who Fell to Earth* (1976). A string of top parts followed. In *Merry Christmas Mr Lawrence* (1982), he gave an acclaimed performance as a British army officer in a Japanese prisoner-of-war camp. The following year he resurrected his early alter ego for *Ziggy Stardust — the Motion Picture* (83). *Absolute Beginners* and *Labyrinth* (both 86) were less successful, but in 88 Bowie was brilliant as Pontius Pilate in Martin Scorcese's controversial film, *The Last Temptation of Christ.*

Bowie in The Man Who Fell to Earth.

Hunky Dory contained the classics, "Changes," "Oh! You Pretty Things" and "Life On Mars." It seemed that Bowie had the talent to embrace any musical style with great success.

ALTERED STATES

Bowie's follow-up was the creation of one of his many misfit alter egos, Ziggy Stardust. As Ziggy, Bowie paraded his bisexuality — and taste for wearing dresses. *The Rise and Fall of Ziggy Stardust and the Spiders from Mars* brought him worldwide fame and is now a glitter-rock classic. The release of the cleverly titled *Aladdin Sane* brought another change of image. It gave him his long-awaited number one hit album, and one of its tracks, "Drive-In Saturday," made the UK Top Five. Bowie was unstoppable. His next two albums also topped the charts: *Pin Ups*, an album of cover versions, and *Diamond Dogs*, which featured the hit "Rebel, Rebel."

Bowie performs as his flamboyant creation Ziggy Stardust in the early 70s.

BEYOND THE 1970s

Bowie's success has not diminished. In the 1980s he enjoyed hit after hit, including "Let's Dance" and "This Is Not America." In 89 Bowie, ever restless, founded a new band, Tin Machine. The band did not do well, but Bowie was soon back in form. With the albums *Outside* (1995) and *Earthling* (97), he explored a more industrial sound, drawing on ambient, techno and jungle influences and proving that — after a quarter of a century — Bowie is still brilliant at reinventing himself.

In 1985 Bowie and Jagger previewed "Dancing in the Street" at Live Aid.

Hunky Dory
1971
The Rise and Fall of Ziggy Stardust and the Spiders from Mars 1972
Aladdin Sane
1973
Low
1977

Heroes 1977
Scary Monsters (And Super Creeps) 1980
Let's Dance 1983
Black Tie, White Noise 1993
Earthling 1997
Best of Bowie
2002

ERIC CLAPTON

Eric Clapp was born in 1945 in Ripley, England. He was brought up by his grandparents who encouraged his early interest in music. They bought him a guitar and the young Eric started his musical career as a busker, earning pennies on street corners.

Five Live Yardbirds
1964
Bluesbreakers
1966
Fresh Cream
1966
461 Ocean Boulevard 1974

Just One Night
1980
Timepieces: The Best of Eric Clapton
1982
The Cream of Eric Clapton
1989

HARD TIMES

Eric didn't stay on the street for long. In 1963, now called Clapton, he formed the Roosters with Tom McGuinness. But success eluded them.

Starving and broke, Clapton joined London's top rhythm and blues band, the Yardbirds, in 1964. Their first album, *The Five Live Yardbirds*, was frantic, fast and furious and perfectly captured the band's exciting but erratic stage show. Clapton was soon unhappy about the direction the Yardbirds took. Their chart

Clapton (center) felt the Yardbirds were not true to the "pure" blues he wanted to play.

single, "For Your Love," was the last straw. Clapton joined John Mayall's Bluesbreakers for half the salary and performed on the classic UK blues album of the same name. But he didn't stay long.

Every Cream album had sales of over $1 million.

CREAM

Clapton, bass player Jack Bruce and volatile drummer Ginger Baker formed arguably the first "supergroup" — Cream. They had a breathtakingly successful career from 1966 to 68.

After one album with ego-fuelled supergroup Blind Faith, Clapton craved a quieter life and joined Delaney and Bonnie. After one album with them Clapton recorded the first of his solo albums, *Eric Clapton*.

His wish to be "just the guitar player" stalled after he wrote and recorded the fabulous "Layla" with Derek and the Dominoes in 1970, which launched him again into the international spotlight.

BEATING DRUGS

But Clapton's drug addiction nearly killed him. He sold many of his beloved guitars as he spent thousands a week on his habit.

In 1973 Eric Clapton emerged from the wilderness. A concert in London, organized by his friend Pete Townshend of the Who, was a huge success. Although he was not entirely free from his demons — a period of alcoholism followed — Clapton made a steady climb back. Many more successful albums are testaments to his complete recovery and ever-increasing popularity. In 1992 *Unplugged*, one of his most successful albums, showed that he had not lost his touch.

Eric, as Derek, made one album with the Dominoes.

Clapton continues to pack venues around the world.

PATTIE BOYD

Beautiful women have always inspired writers, composers and painters to produce some of their best and most impassioned works. In 1965 the Beatles, then at the height of their fame, made their first film, *A Hard Day's Night*. A witty and entertaining production, it has a sequence on a train on which the Beatles are traveling to a concert. Fellow passengers included a group of schoolgirl fans. The actress portraying one of them became the inspiration for three beautiful love songs.

The Beatles' George Harrison composed "Something (In The Way She Moves)" and Eric Clapton wrote "Layla" and "Wonderful Tonight" for this attractive woman, Pattie Boyd.

George Harrison's wife Pattie, later married Clapton.

The EAGLES

Statistics don't reveal which records are played most often on radio stations all over the world year in, year out, but if they did, the Eagles' "Hotel California" would surely be close to the top of the list. Recorded in 1976, this beautiful song was a perfect example of band members drawing upon their country and folk music backgrounds and their strong feeling for rock music to create memorable compositions.

BACKING GROUP

The Eagles were formed in 1971 when founding members Glenn Frey and Don Henley worked together backing the acclaimed singer Linda Ronstadt.

Guitarist and singer Frey and drummer Henley soon got together with bass player Randy Meisner and guitarist Bernie Leadon. All had excellent musical pedigrees. David Geffen, the owner of Asylum Records, was impressed by their songwriting skills and offered them a contract.

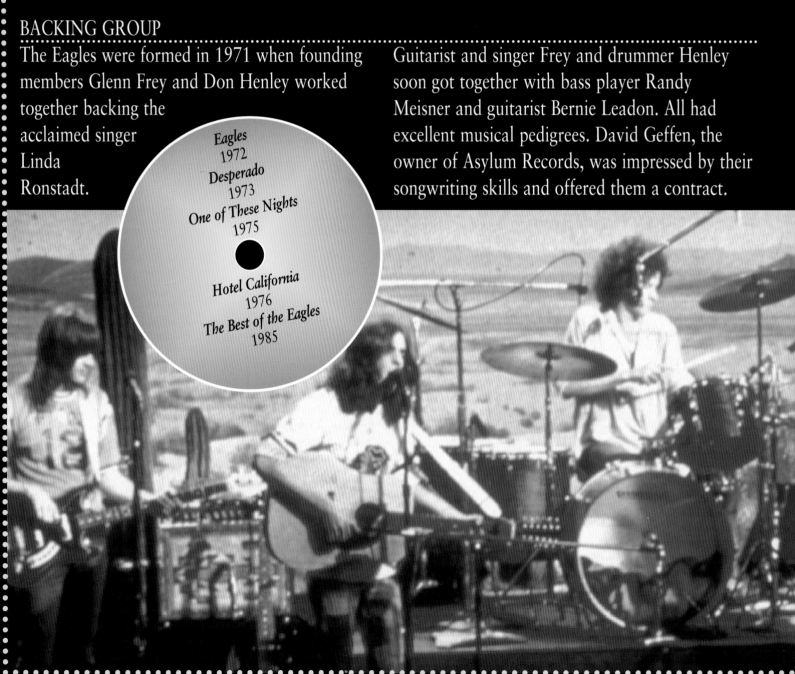

Eagles
1972
Desperado
1973
One of These Nights
1975

Hotel California
1976
The Best of the Eagles
1985

The Eagles play Wembley Stadium in London.

"Take It Easy" came out in June 1972. By the end of 72, the Eagles had their first two singles and their debut album in the Top 20 and 30 respectively. They parted from Ronstadt but remained close to her.

HOTEL CALIFORNIA

The Eagles recruited Don Felder on slide guitar. Frey said, "He just blew us all away. It was just about the best guitar work we had ever heard." Good sales of their album *On the Border* ensured sell-out concerts, and the classic "One of These Nights" gave them their first UK hit. "Lyin' Eyes" and "Take It to the Limit" reached the Top 5 in the U.S. and charted in the UK as well. Leaden left, so guitar player Joe Walsh joined. Walsh was a talented guitarist and songwriter. In 1976 the Eagles released "Hotel California," an album that for sheer, consistent quality surpassed everything else they had done. The album and memorable single of the same name went to the top of the charts. "New Kid in Town," another single from the album, had already made number one.

In 1979 Meisner left to go solo, and Timothy Schmit replaced him. Although some felt that the Eagles had passed their creative peak by the end of the decade, they had lost none of their commercial touch.

REUNION

Despite their success, band members eventually wanted to move on, and in 1982 members Henley, Frey and "new boy" Felder, all prolific writers, decided to break up. One of the all-time classic rock bands was no more. However, band members have gotten back together for reunions. The first happened in the 90s. The project? The Hell Freezes Over tour. The name came from the post-split avowal from Henley and Frey, "This band will only ever tour again when Hell freezes over…"

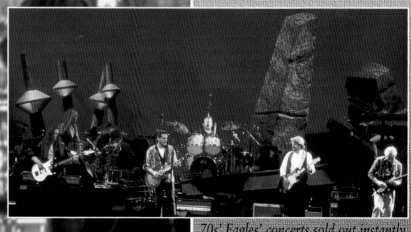

70s' Eagles' concerts sold out instantly.

FLEETWOOD MAC

Fleetwood Mac were formed in London in 1967 by guitarist Peter Greenbaum. Peter, shortening his name to Green, had just left John Mayall's Bluesbreakers. An enormously talented blues guitarist, Green decided to form his own outfit — originally called

Peter Green's Fleetwood Mac, but Green didn't like having his name in the band's title. Fleetwood Mac came from the surnames of the rhythm section, drummer Mick Fleetwood and bass player John McVie — but they hit a problem when John McVie wouldn't leave the Bluesbreakers!

McVIE MAKES UP HIS MIND

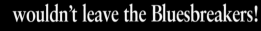

McVie received a secure income from Mayall. Why swap all that for the risks of joining a totally unknown group? Green hired Bob Brunning instead, fresh from his college band, Five's Company. Fleetwood Mac started rehearsing and recording, preparing for their debut concert at the Windsor Jazz and Blues Festival. They were joined there by second guitarist Jeremy Spencer, and the nervous band went down extremely well. Weeks later Brunning stepped aside when McVie decided to take the plunge. Fleetwood Mac were on their way. Their first album was released in 1967. It was a big success, and they toured incessantly in the UK and Europe. But Peter Green left! He was disillusioned with the whole music industry and wanted to give all of the Mac's earnings to charity.

Peter Green's
Fleetwood Mac:
Live at the Marquee
1967
Peter Green's Fleetwood Mac
1968
Then Play On
1969

Rumours
1977
Tusk
1979
The Dance
1997

46

At the Brit Awards.

Spencer and new guitarist Danny Kirwam also left. The band struggled to survive.

RESCUE

Fleetwood bumped into singer Stevie Nicks and guitarist Lindsey Buckingham. Fleetwood Mac had already recruited McVie's wife, Christine, and the five musicians found that their creative chemistry was magical. In 1976 they recorded *Rumours*, a collection of songs documenting the band's personal problems: in the same year the McVies split up, as did Buckingham and Nicks, and Fleetwood divorced his wife.

MAC SPLIT FOR A DECADE

Rumours was one of the most successful albums of all time, but the band disintegrated in the late 80s. In 1993 U.S. President Clinton asked them to perform at his inaugural party. Their "Don't Stop" single had been his campaign song. In 1997 they got together again, 31 years after their first appearance, and in 98 they received a special Brit Award for their lifelong contribution to popular music.

PETER GREEN

Mick Fleetwood and John McVie have consistently credited Peter Green for his vision and impressive writing skills. He wrote the band's early hits, "Albatross," "Oh Well," "Man of the World," "Black Magic Woman," "The Green Manalishi" and more.

By 1970 Green's personal life was disintegrating. Drug abuse and a long illness led to his complete withdrawal from the music business. Fleetwood kept in touch but could do nothing to help. But in the mid-90s Green began a miraculous recovery, performing with his own Splinter Group touring and apparently thoroughly enjoying the experience.

Green went back on the road in the 90s.

JETHRO TULL

The visual image that a band creates is an important factor in their success — or failure. How about trying to promote a band whose front man constantly twists one leg around the other and hops one-legged around the stage, dresses in a long, shabby coat and has uncombed frizzy hair flying madly around? Ian Anderson's choice of instrument was quite bizarre for the time too — the flute.

This Was
1968
Stand Up
1969
Aqualung
1971
Thick as a Brick
1972

A Passion Play
1973
Twenty Years of Jethro Tull
1988
The Very Best of Jethro Tull —
The Anniversary Collection
1993

THE MARQUEE

One of Jethro Tull's B sides was "One For John Gee," a character of the London music scene. The band's appearances at the Marquee were vital to their success. John Gee managed the club and was a benevolent tyrant — start your set two minutes late and his full wrath would descend. The Marquee saw the very first London performances of the Rolling Stones, the Who, Jimi Hendrix, the Yardbirds and many others. First located in Oxford Street, the Marquee moved to Wardour Street in the 60s and is now on Soho's Dean Street.

The Marquee in Soho's Wardour Street.

LEAVING HOME

Named after an 18th century agriculturalist, Jethro Tull were an innovative and unusual band. Leader Ian Anderson and bass player Glenn Cornick had worked together in a band. They joined forces with guitarist Mick Abrahams and his drummer, Clive Bunker, and moved to London. They started working on the busy clubs and pubs circuit there.

Anderson initially felt out of his depth: "I'd never been away from home before. It was just like the yokel hitting the city with all his belongings in a knotted handkerchief at the end of a stick."

UNDERGROUND ROCK

They soon secured a contract with Island Records and released the single "A Song For Jeffrey." It was a hit and so was their bluesy album *This Was*, which featured Anderson's Roland Kirk-inspired flute playing and helped establish underground rock as a musical force. Anderson's eccentric stage presence (he would often perform while lying down) made great entertainment, and Jethro Tull became a huge concert attraction, finding a following in the U.S. as "art-rock." In 1968 Abrahams left to form Blodwyn Pig and many changes followed. Cornick left in 1970 and Bunker in 71.

Anderson played guitar as well as the flute.

CONCEPT ALBUMS

In 1969 and 70 three Jethro Tull singles entered the UK Top 10, and in 71 the themed album *Aqualung*, accusing the church of damaging people's belief in God, was released. *Thick As A Brick* and *A Passion Play* followed. Each effectively contained only one piece of music. The press were critical, although both sold well. Anderson, upset, retired — but not for long.

FOLK ALBUMS

Toward the end of the 70s Jethro Tull's albums became more folkie. The band played through the 80s, making their 25th album, *Catfish Rising* in 1991. Alongside his country-squire lifestyle, managing a salmon farm on the Isle of Skye, Anderson still makes a big contribution to the music scene.

Abrahams still plays with Blodwyn

The MOODY BLUES

The Moody Blues began their career as a rhythm and blues band. However, the 70s brought a complete change of direction for the band, and their fortunes fluctuated dramatically until their temporary breakup in 1974. Denny Laine, Mike Pinder, Ray Thomas, Graham Edge and Clint Warwick formed the first version of the Moody Blues in Birmingham, England, in 1964.

AN R&B HIT

They moved to London. A residency at the Marquee club followed, and an appearance on the influential TV show *Ready, Steady, Go* led to a contract with the Decca record company. The Moody Blues' second single, with its descending piano introduction, was a hit in 1965. "Go Now" went to the top of the UK charts and made the U.S. Top 10. Their next three singles flopped, although they produced a debut album featuring some excellent original material and rhythm and blues covers. Exhausted and disillusioned, Laine and Warwick left the group.

John Lodge and Justin Hayward joined the band. Three flops later, the Moody Blues called a crisis conference. Their R&B phase had just ended.

The Magnificent Moodies
1965
Days of Future Passed
1967
On the Threshold of A Dream
1969

A Question of Balance
1970
Octave
1978
The Best of the Moody Blues
1984

Early days and a far cry from their supergroup gigs.

NIGHTS IN WHITE SATIN

Hayward wrote "Nights In White Satin." Quasi-classical and with obscure, poetic lyrics, the song was a million miles away from their previous material. It crashed into the UK Top 20, their first hit for three years. With the London Festival Orchestra they recorded the album, *Days Of Future Passed*. It was huge on both sides of the Atlantic.

Six great albums followed, all with a recurring theme. *On The Threshold Of A Dream* ("The Dream"), *A Question Of Balance* ("The Balance") and *Every Good Boy Deserves Favour* ("My Song") were dreams of a better world.

The Moody Blues toured using the revolutionary Mellotron, an organlike instrument that used tapes to reproduce orchestral sounds on stage. They founded their own record company in 1973 and that year, and again in 79, "Nights In White Satin" reentered the U.S. charts.

FOUR YEARS OFF

In 1974 the band members decided to pursue solo careers. They reunited in 1978 to record the excellent album *Octave*. By the end of the 70s they were unassailable. Although not all their albums released between 1974 and 93 were huge hits, their concerts have completely sold out at almost every venue they have played for the last two decades.

COLLEGE GIGS

British students in the 70s saw many bands just by wandering down to their college's halls. The college gig circuit drew impressive names.

Just imagine you are the student social secretary of a UK university, responsible for booking bands for college concerts. A van pulls up outside containing instruments, amplifiers and four musicians. One of them is Denny Laine. He offers to play a concert that evening for £200. You hesitate. Concerts should really have advance publicity. Who's in the band and what's its name? Paul McCartney and Wings. Missing life on the road after the Beatles broke up, McCartney took Wings all over the country in this way, thrilling countless lucky students.

Denny Laine (left) joined Paul and Linda McCartney in Wings.

VAN MORRISON

Part of the fun of being a teenager is irritating your parents by playing music very loudly in your bedroom. George Ivan, born in Belfast, Northern Ireland, found it difficult to rebel in this way because his parents were playing their music very loudly in the front room! Their impressively huge record collection, including blues, jazz and world music, made the Ivan household a very stimulating place to be.

PROFESSIONAL AT 15

The 12-year-old Ivan couldn't wait to make some music of his own, although the influences he gained through listening to his parents' music stayed with him. He started to learn the guitar and saxophone and joined a local group. By 15 Ivan had renamed himself Van Morrison, quit school and become a professional musician with the Monarchs. They played rhythm and blues and soul music and toured the UK and Europe. Quite a life for a teenager!

He released his first single before he left the Monarchs, "Boozoo Hully Gully."

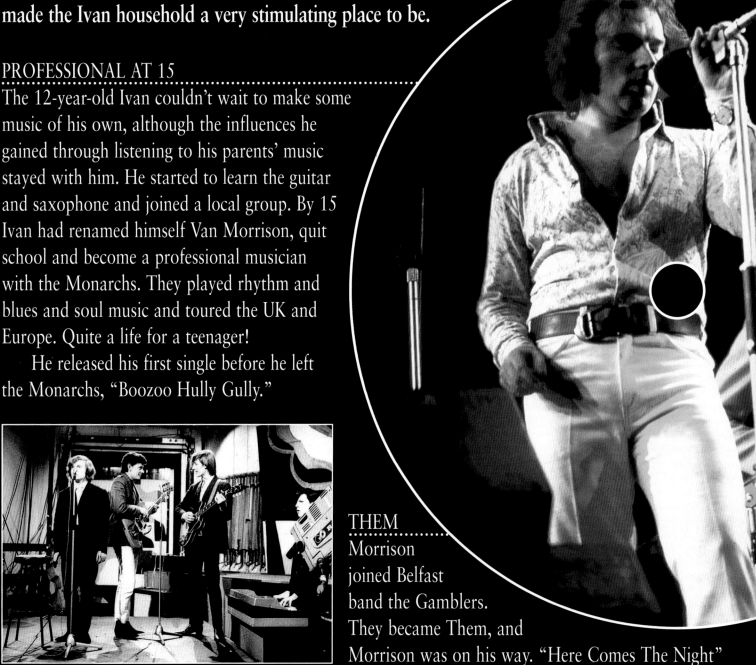

Them appeared on UK TV's Ready, Steady, Go! *in 1965.*

THEM

Morrison joined Belfast band the Gamblers. They became Them, and Morrison was on his way. "Here Comes The Night" and "Baby Please Don't Go" were both hits.

But probably their best known recording from this period (1965) is "Gloria."

Morrison is a master of the saxophone.

Astral Weeks
1968
Tupelo Honey
1971
The Best of Van Morrison
1990
The Best of Van Morrison: Vol. 2
1993
Too Long In Exile
1993

THEM HIT THE ROAD

Them toured Europe with some of Morrison's greatest heroes. Working with musicians such as Little Walter and Bo Diddley was an education for Van, still barely into his 20s. He toured the U.S.'s West Coast and worked with an unknown group who later recorded his "Gloria" with great success — the Doors. The classic Them lineup disbanded upon their return.

SOLO SUCCESS

After the success of his album *Moondance* in 1970, Morrison became a major concert attraction in the U.S. Although irritated by the 'star' element of the music business and moody and uncommunicative by nature, Morrison put his heart and soul into his committed performances. *Tupelo Honey* included love songs for his wife, and *It's Too Late To Stop Now* — a live album from a 1974 tour of the U.S. and Europe, brought Morrison to the height of his career. After his divorce in 1973 Morrison returned to Ireland for a while. The songs he wrote there appeared on the great *Veedon Fleece* album.

JOHN LEE HOOKER

In 1917 John Lee Hooker was born in Mississippi. Morrison had heard his wonderful blues music from a very early age, and his admiration of Hooker's work increased over the years. Morrison, himself a superstar into the 80s and 90s, never forgot his early touring experiences with Hooker and in 1993 invited him to duet on the album *Too Long In Exile*. Morrison had contributed to Hooker's hit album *Mr. Lucky*, released in 1991. It reached number three in the UK charts. Not at all bad for a 74-year-old!

STILL A STAR

Having released a steady stream of hit albums over 40 years, Van Morrison's career continues to thrive. He has a unique talent and a huge following.

Morrison and Hooker have mutual admiration of very long standing.

PROCOL HARUM

In 1959 five schoolboys formed a rhythm and blues band called the Paramounts and started playing versions of blues and soul music around the pubs and clubs of Southend on England's south coast. Gary Brooker was their singer.

ONE HIT WONDER

In 1962 the Paramounts left school and by 64 their single "Poison Ivy" was in the UK Top 40. But in 1966, many flops later, they disbanded. Brooker then teamed up with lyricist Keith Reid. They wrote many songs and advertised for musicians. They renamed themselves the Pinewoods, then Procol Harum (from Latin, meaning "far from these things").

A WHITER SHADE OF PALE

Reid and Brooker wrote a very unusual song. Based on the classical composer J.S. Bach's "Suite No. 3 in D Major," better known as "Air on a G String," the song had surreal lyrics and a cantatalike part for the organ. It sounded completely different from everything else in the pop charts at the time. The musicians persuaded influential producer Denny Cordell to record the song. He loved it and used his influence to get the popular pirate radio station Radio London to play it around the clock. "A Whiter Shade of Pale" went straight to number one in the UK charts and stayed there for six weeks. It entered the U.S. charts, peaking at number five. Ex-Paramounts guitarist Robin Trower returned to join Brooker in Procol Harum, with new drummer B.J. Wilson.

Procol Harum
1967
Shine on Brightly
1968
A Salty Dog
1969
Procul Harum in Concert with the
Edmonton Symphony Orchestra
1972
Grand Hotel 1973
The Collection
1986

In 1967 the new lineup had another Top 10 hit, "Homburg." They recorded their first album, *Procol Harum*, and soon became more successful in the U.S. than the UK. Their second album, *Shine On Brightly,* charted in the U.S. but not in the UK.

Classically influenced music with state-of-the-art lighting.

70s SUCCESS

The 70s brought Procol Harum yet more success. They played at the huge Atlanta and Isle of Wight pop festivals and in 1972 released their sixth album, recorded live in Canada with the Edmonton Symphony Orchestra. It sold a million copies, earning a gold record. The single, "Conquistador," entered the U.S. Top 20 in July of that year. With yet another lineup the band toured the world from 1973 to 77, to great acclaim.

They recorded four more albums, including the excellent *Grand Hotel*. But by June 1977 the band found themselves unable to compete with the burgeoning punk and new wave scenes and decided to call it a day. The members went their different (and extremely successful) ways. Procol Harum wasn't quite finished however. In 1991 they reformed with most of the original members and made the creditable but commercially unsuccessful album, *The Prodigal Stranger*.

70s FASHION FAILURES

While Procol Harum resembled medieval page-boys, their fans wore a mix of fashions that have earned the 70s the adjective "tasteless."

Knee-high boots with platform heels were worn with very long bell-bottoms. Hot pants were the new invention for girls. Long hair or afro perms were for everyone, with facial hair too for boys. T-shirts were tight and tie-dyed or plain. Later came the despised sweater vest, maybe even striped and worn over puffy-sleeved shirts! Overalls were fashion wear for young adults for the first time — but only briefly. Skirts could be knee-length, mid-calf or "maxi," a term coined as the opposite of the 60s mini.

Nostalgia, too, was rife with fashions taken from movies such as *The Godfather* and *The Great Gatsby*.

Tube tops and skin-tight lurex bell-bottoms were popular fashion items in 70s discos.

The SEX PISTOLS

The Sex Pistols were originally formed in 1975 by Steve Jones, Paul Cook and Glen Matlock. They were then known as the Swankers. Their manager, Malcolm McLaren, introduced them to John Lydon. Lydon changed his name to Johnny Rotten, and the Swankers became the Sex Pistols.

ANARCHISTS

The band projected an aggressive, confrontational image. Although not great musicians, they wrought an enormous influence on rock 'n' roll and the music industry. They railed against authority, flaunted their drug and alcohol abuse and made headlines. They persuaded the EMI record company to pay a £40,000 (around U.S. $70,000) advance and released a single, "Anarchy in the UK." They hijacked a TV talk show, arguing with presenter Bill Grundy and offending viewers with their obscene language. The record was banned. EMI promptly dropped the Sex Pistols, but the group kept their cash advance. The A&M company signed them up a month later, in March 1977.

Never Mind the Bollocks, Here's the Sex Pistols
1977
The Great Rock 'n' Roll Swindle
1979

The Best and the Rest of the Sex Pistols
1996

The archetypal punk wore a mohawk haircut, but any variety of spiky, colored hair sculpture would do.

VICIOUS JOINS

The band fired Matlock for being too "nice" and brought in a musician who better fitted the violent image they wanted to project — John Simon Ritchie, a drug addict and would-be bass player. Ritchie changed his name to Sid Vicious. His aggressive nature provoked countless fights on and off stage. When, tragically, he blinded a member of the audience at a Pistol's gig by hurling a glass into the crowd, A&M dropped the band, and they lost their £75,000 (about U.S. $130,000) advance. The Pistols had signed their contract outside Buckingham Palace just one week earlier.

VIRGIN DEAL

Virgin took them on next — this time for £15,000 (about U.S. $27,000). The single "God Save The Queen" ranted against the British monarchy. Banned, it went to number two in the UK charts. That same year their album, *Never Mind the Bollocks, Here's the Sex Pistols* made number one in the UK but barely cracked the U.S. Top 100.

THE END

After a shambolic U.S. tour, Rotten announced the breakup of the band. In October 1978 Vicious allegedly murdered his girlfriend in New York. By February 1979 he was dead himself, from a heroin overdose. The Sex Pistols were no more, but their influence survives.

PUNK

As a fashion movement, punk, with its safety pins, chains and spiky hairdos, had some followers and lots of press. As a music form it became a dominant force in rock culture. UK teenagers viewed punk as a brave new dawn, the overthrowing of authority, a celebration of anarchy.

In the U.S. punk's audience was small, perhaps because its ethos was too removed from the American Dream. New York's new wave scene, which included the New York Dolls and the Velvet Underground, came close but didn't quite match punk's popularity in the UK.

Punk guru Malcolm McLaren also briefly managed the New York Dolls.

ROD STEWART

For a while it looked as if Roderick David Stewart, born in 1945 in London, would appear in the UK's stadiums as a soccer hero. He signed as an apprentice for Brentford Football Club and longed to make a career in the sport he loved so passionately. But his equally fervent involvement with blues and soul music took precedence.

FIRST SUCCESSES

In the 60s, a "blues boom" was beginning to flourish in the UK. Blues bands packed the pubs and clubs with their fans. Rod Stewart's gravelly, soulful voice ensured him a place in the movement.

After stints as harmonica player and vocalist with three unsuccessful bands, Stewart was invited by the already successful Jeff Beck to join his new band. Beck had played in the Yardbirds with guitarist Jimmy Page (who later gained superstar status with the band Led Zeppelin) but wanted to create his own group. The Jeff Beck Group made two excellent albums, *Truth* and *Beck-Ola*, but when Beck hired two members of the U.S. band Vanilla Fudge, Stewart decided that he'd had enough.

An Old Raincoat
Won't Ever Let You Down
1970
Gasoline Alley
1970
Every Picture Tells a Story
1971

Atlantic Crossing 1975
A Night on the Town
1976
The Best of Rod Stewart
Vol. 1 & Vol. 2
1977

THE FACES

Life then got complicated. No sooner had he signed a contract as a solo artist in 1969 that Stewart joined yet another band, the Faces. Born out of the ashes of the brilliant Small Faces, they cheerfully undertook a chaotic life on the road. Stewart could out-party them all, but he amazingly found time to record both as a solo artist and as a "Face." His solo career brought him infinitely greater rewards.

Out came *An Old Raincoat Won't Ever Let You Down*. It wasn't a hit, but it certainly made people sit up and listen. In 1970 his second album, *Gasoline Alley*, scraped into the Top 50.

Stewart's stint with Jeff Beck was short.

GLAM ROCK

The 70s saw the emergence of "glam rock." Outrageous glitter and lurex-laden stage costumes, crazy haircuts and customized guitars enhanced the careers of many bands.

Ironically, many glam rock bands featured seasoned and accomplished performers who adopted their extravagant poses for entirely commercial reasons.

David Bowie was the master of glam, reinventing himself in the vanguard of each new fashion. Bands like Slade, the Sweet and T. Rex followed suit.

First a mod then a hippie, Marc Bolan of T. Rex became a glam rocker.

MAGGIE MAY

But in July 1971 his stunning version of the traditional song, "Maggie May," topped the singles charts. His third album, *Every Picture Tells A Story*, also reached number one on the album charts. Part of the charm of all three albums was their shambolic, under-rehearsed, we're-all-having-a-good-time feel. Stewart was still having fun on the road with the party-loving Faces and continued to record with them, although their albums were not as successful as his own. In August 1972 another solo "You Wear It Well" topped the UK chart and reached number 13 in the U.S.

Stewart embraced the glam rock look and has always taken good care of his image.

A SOLO CAREER

Stewart decided to concentrate on the solo side of things. He began to record more blatantly commercial songs, some of them unashamedly sexist.

The 20 studio albums he released from 1973 to 2006 all charted in the U.S. Top 20.

GAZETTEER

The visual image that bands choose to project has always been a very significant factor in their success or failure. In an ideal world, only the music would ever count, but impressionable young fans have always placed great importance on the way their heroes look, as well as sound. The Bay City Rollers were heavily dependent on their costumes of short, baggy plaid trousers and waist-length jackets, but they didn't have many imitators, except among their fans.

Slade

GLAM ROCK

The incredibly theatrical glam rock performers took image to the extreme, but while many, Queen, T. Rex and Elton John to name just a few, were producing excellent records, the quality of some "glam rock" music was a secondary consideration. Image was all!

The Clash

PUNK

However, the punk music explosion opened the door to many bands who chose to challenge the establishment rather than just pose. In the UK the Sex Pistols wanted to shock, as had the Prime Movers and the Stooges, both featuring Iggy Pop, and MC5 in the U.S., but other bands chose to be subversive and critical in a more subtle way.

NEW WAVE

The Stranglers, the Jam, the Clash, Elvis Costello and many other "new wave" bands brought sensitive musical skills to their political statements. Lou Reed kept the flag flying for U.S. new wave as did the interesting and provoking Blondie, Ultravox, the Ramones and Talking Heads.

The Stranglers

COUNTRY AND WESTERN

Dolly Parton also enjoyed huge commercial success during the 70s, spearheading a new generation of fine country and western performers who lovingly carried on the tradition established by their legendary predecessors, including Merle Travis, Hank Williams and many more. The new breed of country performers sold many millions of records all over the world.

Dolly Parton

TEENYBOPPER HEROES

While Bay City Roller-instigated "Rollermania" ran riot in the UK, in the U.S. the TV sitcom "The Partridge Family" took over where the Monkees had left off in the 60s. David Cassidy became the heartthrob of millions of teenage, and younger, girls and had many hits. The Osmonds too, first with Donny and later with "Little" Jimmy, kept a consistent presence in the charts through the early 70s.

The Bay City Rollers

But even more prolific than these were the Jackson 5, fronted by 11-year-old Michael, who were rarely out of the charts for the entire decade — and, in the case of Michael, long after.

POPULAR MUSIC MOVES EVER ONWARDS

All in all, the 70s turned out to be a rich and exciting time for the development of popular music. The 60s were indeed a hard act to follow, but the decade that followed produced a wide variety of influential performers.

Blondie

Lou Reed

1980s Pop

CONTENTS

On these disks is a selection of the artists' recordings. Many of these albums are now available on CD and MP3. If they are not, many of the tracks from them can be found on compilations.

Elton John

These boxes give you extra information about the artists and their times.

Some contain anecdotes about the artists themselves or about the people who helped their careers or, occasionally, about those who exploited them.

Others provide historical facts about the music, lifestyles, fans and fashions of the day.

INTRODUCTION

The 1980s were a turbulent time. High unemployment and worldwide political instability caused many problems.

The music business experienced changes too. Ex-Beatle John Lennon was murdered outside his New York apartment in 1980, and reggae's undisputed king, Bob Marley, succumbed to cancer in 81. Other sad losses included blues singer Muddy Waters, Bill Haley, Karen Carpenter, Beach Boy Dennis Wilson and Marvin Gaye.

The author Bob Brunning talks to Mark Knopfler at the famous 100 Club in London.

The baby boomers grew up but did not grow away from music: there was a wave of stadium rockers to suit this older audience. And Bob Geldof invented "charity rock" when he organized the biggest pop event in history — Live Aid.

Meanwhile, technology marched on. Synthesizers heralded the age of electronic music. State-of-the-art production could finally be appreciated with the advent of the CD. (Critics confidently predicted that the format would never be popular!) As the 80s drew to a close, revolutionary styles were emerging. Rap stripped down songs until they were punchy, spoken poems; techno stripped away all but the barest repetitive beats.

The fact that it is so difficult to pinpoint one particular sound for the decade only goes to show what a creative, exciting decade for pop it was.

DIRE STRAITS

Few guitarists can be identified after listening to just a few bars of their playing, but Mark Knopfler is one of them. His lyrical, blues-based style brought huge success for his band, Dire Straits. But this did not happen overnight. Knopfler discovered his love of music a little later than some performers.

A LATE START

Knopfler had already pursued careers as a journalist and a teacher when, aged 28, he left Newcastle and headed to London with his younger brother David. David's roommate, John Illsley, also took the plunge and joined Dire Straits alongside the experienced session drummer Pick Withers. The band couldn't have timed their entry into London's pub rock scene more badly. Punk reigned, and the delicate music of the Straits could hardly compete with all that fury and angst.

CD KINGS

Launched in the early 1980s, the compact disc (CD) promised — and delivered — top quality reproduction and it didn't scratch like an LP.

It appealed to yuppies (young urban professionals) with money to spend. At the same time the baby-boomers — who'd started buying pop music as teenagers in the 60s — had grown up. Suddenly there was a much bigger audience for AOR (adult-oriented rock). Dire Straits' easy rock was ideal for this new, mature market. *Brothers In Arms* was the first album to go platinum on CD alone.

NOT-SO-DIRE STRAITS

Knopfler returned to teaching, but did not give up on Dire Straits. In 1978 the band released the classic "Sultans of Swing." It was a worldwide hit. In June the band released their debut album, *Dire Straits* — which went gold! It made the UK and U.S. Top 10s, and so did their second album, *Communiqué*.

MAKING MOVES

David Knopfler left the band, wishing to pursue a solo career, and so the band's lineup changed.

Dire Straits
1978
Communiqué
1979
Making Movies
1980
Love over Gold
1982

Alchemy: Dire Straits Live
1984
Brothers in Arms
1985
Money for Nothing
1988

The next album, *Making Movies*, marked a shift in musical direction. The sound was jazzier, the production tighter and the style more lyrical; for example, "Romeo and Juliet" retold the classic tragedy in a modern setting.

Knopfler "scored" films including Cal *(above) in 1984.*

STRENGTH TO STRENGTH

The atmospheric album *Love over Gold* followed in 1982, and the Straits took to the road. The result was a fine live double album, *Alchemy*. Next came their biggest album success to date: *Brothers In Arms* sold nine million copies! Knopfler gave a working man's view of rock superstardom with the witty "Money for Nothing," and three other singles from the album were hits.

CLASS ACT

Knopfler pursued other projects in the late 1980s, but in 91 Dire Straits released a new album and went on tour. And as fans continue to lap up his superb guitar playing and songwriting, it is unlikely that we will see Mark Knopfler back in the front of the class!

In 1989 Mark Knopfler formed the fun country band the Notting Hillbillies. Their album, Missing... Presumed Having a Good Time reached number two in the UK charts.

EURYTHMICS

The career of Dave Stewart and Annie Lennox's successful band, Eurythmics, spans the decade. Their first hit came in 1979, and the two finally split up in 1990. Guitarist Stewart and singer Lennox met in London in 1976 and fell head over heels in love. (Dave's first words to her were "Will you marry me?"). Together with guitarist Pete Coombes, they formed a band called Catch, but they soon renamed themselves the Tourists.

STRICTLY FOR THE TOURISTS

Joined by bassist Eddy Chin and drummer Jim Toomey, the Tourists recorded their debut album in 1979. The same year they had minor hits with their single "The Loneliest Man In The World" and a second album, *Reality Effect*. And their next two singles both made the Top 10, and the best was yet to come. In late 1980 the Tourists disbanded, and Stewart and Lennox formed Eurythmics.

The Tourists were a hit in London's post-punk pubs and clubs.

Aware of the importance of image, Stewart chose his costumes with care.

SWEET DREAMS ARE MADE OF THIS...

By now, their romance was over, but the couple's working relationship was as strong as ever. Eurythmics' first five singles flopped, but in January 1983 they released "Sweet Dreams (Are Made of This)." The single topped the charts on both sides of the Atlantic, and the album of the same name — with its robotic, synthesiser sound — was a great success. In July the same year Eurythmics released the haunting "Who's That Girl?," a smash hit taken from their new chart-topping album, *Touch*. The hits kept coming: from the up-tempo, and very catchy, "Right By Your Side" to the maudlin "Here Comes The Rain Again" which finally took Eurythmics into the U.S. Top Five.

SHOWING OFF

People flocked to their concerts, thrilled by the startling special effects and the snappy image presented by Lennox. During the 1984 Grammy Awards ceremony Lennox flaunted her gender-bending image by performing in drag!

SOUL SEARCHING

More hits followed. Between May 1985 and June 1990, four of Eurythmics' albums and 13 of their singles entered the Top 40. The duo moved away from "synth-pop" toward rhythm and blues. For a track on their fourth album *Be Yourself Tonight*, they worked with the legendary singer Aretha Franklin on "Sisters Are Doin' It For Themselves." In 1988 Lennox contributed to soul giant Al Green's "Put A Little Love In Your Heart." At the end of the 80s the talented pair went their separate ways. Both went on to enjoy tremendous — and well-deserved — success in their solo careers.

Sweet Dreams (Are Made Of This)
1983
Touch
1983
Be Yourself Tonight
1985

Revenge
1986
Savage
1987
We Too Are One
1989
Greatest Hits
1991

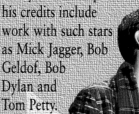

GOING SOLO

Annie Lennox and Dave Stewart wasted no time in establishing themselves as solo performers. Lennox released her sublime single "Why" in March 1992. In the same year her album *Diva* made the number one spot, and provided two more hit singles. In 1995 her covers album *Medusa* also topped the charts and led to a hit with her version of "A Whiter Shade of Pale."

Dave Stewart has written soundtracks and recorded several solo albums, including the excellent *Greetings From The Gutter*. He is also a very successful producer: his credits include work with such stars as Mick Jagger, Bob Geldof, Bob Dylan and Tom Petty.

MICHAEL JACKSON

Michael Joseph Jackson was born on the August 29, 1958, in Gary, Indiana. At an age when most youngsters would be nervously starting primary school, five-year-old Jackson joined four of his eight brothers and sisters on the road in the Jackson 5. Already a talented singer, dancer and immensely confident performer, his contribution to the group rapidly out-stripped the novelty value of his extreme youth.

AN EXTRAORDINARY CHILDHOOD

The Motown record company spotted the potential of the all-singing, all-dancing quintet and signed them — when Michael was just ten years old. The boys had four number ones in 1970 and their first two albums entered the Top 10. In 1972 Motown brought out Michael's first solo single "Got to Be There" and for almost a decade Michael juggled two careers: one as a successful solo singer, and the other as a member of the Jackson 5.

THE 1970s

In 1976 Michael appeared in his first movie, a musical called *The Wiz*.

Young Michael fronts the Jackson 5.

He worked on the soundtrack with producer Quincy Jones. In 1979 Jackson and Jones produced the soul album *Off The Wall*. It sold over seven million copies and stayed in the charts for five years. Jackson won a Grammy Award for the first single from the album, "Don't Stop 'Til You Get Enough," which was a number one in the U.S. and UK.

Forever, Michael
1975
Off the Wall
1979
Thriller
1982
Michael Jackson Anthology
1987
Bad
1987
Dangerous
1991
HIStory Past, Present & Future,
Book 1
1995

A Michael Jackson doll.

THRILLING SUCCESS

In 1982 Jackson released *Thriller*, which eventually became the best-selling album of all time. It sold 42 million copies, stayed at number one in the U.S. for 21 weeks and provided seven Top-10 singles. *Thriller* was nominated for a record-breaking 12 Grammys; at the event, Jackson and Jones won eight of the awards.

Topping *Thriller* would challenge any performer, and Jackson couldn't quite manage it. However, *Bad* sold three million copies in two months, and the first four singles lifted from it made number one. By anybody else's standards it was an enormous hit! By now the most famous man in the world, "Jacko" gave sell-out tours, dazzling audiences with his spectacular dancing prowess.

DARKER DAYS

Early on, Jackson had been portrayed in the media as an eccentric "Peter Pan" figure — the boy who refused to grow up. He had an amusement park built on his property and seemed more at home with children and animals than adults. As the decade drew to a close, his personal life attracted more attention: tabloids reported on his extensive plastic surgery and his ever-paler skin. In the 1990s unproven allegations of child abuse severely damaged Jackson's reputation, and his short-lived marriage to Lisa Marie Presley did little to remedy this. On June 25, 2009, Jackson died unexpectedly from cardiac arrest in Los Angeles. Still, nothing can detract from his phenomenal contribution to pop music.

MTV NATION

The first-ever television channel aimed solely at music-lovers was launched in the U.S. in 1981 and in Europe six years later. MTV broadcasted music videos around the clock, and before long the "promo" was crucial to a record's success. *Thriller* expertly made use of the new medium: every single from the album was promoted with a stunning video. The hype for MTV's unveiling of the *Thriller* video was enormous — and well deserved. More like a mini movie, it starred Michael Jackson in a frightening fantasy world against a backdrop of stunning effects.

Michael Jackson and ghouls pose for a promotional shot for the amazing Thriller *video.*

ELTON JOHN

Reginald Kenneth Dwight was born on March 25, 1947, in Pinner, Middlesex. At four he started piano lessons and this early promise certainly didn't fade. By the age of 11 Reginald was studying at London's prestigious Royal Academy of Music. However, Reg was getting turned on to the pop music of the day: rock 'n' roll and rhythm and blues. He abandoned the classics and hit the road with rhythm and blues band Bluesology in 1961.

A FAIRY TALE PARTNERSHIP

However, in 1966 singer Long John Baldry joined the band, pushing Dwight out. He responded to an ad placed by Liberty Records, who put him in touch with another aspiring writer. Neither knew it at the time, but the pair eventually became one of the most successful songwriting partnerships of all time.

Reg Dwight was now Elton John, and his new partner was 17-year-old Bernie Taupin. A pattern was quickly established: John wrote the music, Taupin the lyrics and they communicated by mail and phone. They wrote 20 songs together before they even met! It was a winning formula. In August 1970 "Your Song" entered the U.S. charts, albeit at a lowly 92. His first album, *Elton John*, featured his new band — Caleb Quaye (guitar), Dee Murray (bass) and Nigel Olsson (drums). It went to number four in the U.S. and entered the UK Top 10.

John, Olsson and Murray in 1970.

Elton John
1970
Tumbleweed Connection
1970
Honky Chateau
1972
Goodbye Yellow Brick Road
1973

Too Low for Zero
1983
Breaking Hearts
1984
Sleeping with the Past
1989

GLAMOROUS ROCKER

Elton John's mesmerizing, larger-than-life stage persona and Taupin's catchy lyrics ensured dozens of hits throughout the 1970s, such as "Rocket Man," "Daniel" and "Don't Go Breakin' My Heart" (with Kiki Dee).

THE MIDAS TOUCH

Toward the end of the 1970s John's career slowed down. He had serious problems with alcohol and drug abuse and briefly fell out with Taupin. But with the release of *Too Low for Zero* (83), the pair had another run of hits. The album went gold and featured several hit singles, including the defiant "I'm Still Standing," and melodic "I Guess That's Why They Call It the Blues."

John starred in the cult movie, Tommy released in 1975.

For the rest of the decade every album he released earned a gold record. By 1988 he had reached a turning point. He overcame his drug addiction at last. And a new, mature John announced that all future royalties from his singles would go toward AIDS research.

A MATCH MADE IN HEAVEN
While Elton worked on the tunes, ace lyricist Bernie Taupin wrote the words. Taupin respected Elton's skills and didn't begrudge him the limelight. Follow the notes below and see if you can identify this Taupin/John classic.

BURNING BRIGHT

For the funeral of Princess Diana in 1997, Elton John rearranged his haunting anthem "Candle in the Wind," as a tribute to her. His moving performance reduced millions of viewers to tears. In 1998 Reg Dwight became Sir Elton John — a just recognition for one of the most successful pop stars of all time.

Bernie Taupin made a rare public appearance at a book-signing session with Elton John.

MADONNA

Madonna Louise Veronica Ciccone was born in Rochester, Michigan, on August 16, 1959. One of seven children, she quickly learned to use her natural talents as a singer, dancer, actress, pianist and all-around show-off to get attention. Her ballet skills won her a scholarship to the University of Michigan, but she didn't stay long. Madonna was already beginning to demonstrate her restlessness and, more importantly, her ability to recognize — and seize — a good opportunity when she saw one.

BIG DEAL

After several false starts, Madonna finally signed with Sire Records in 1982. Sire, a subsidiary of entertainment giants Warner Brothers, had faith in Madonna and were prepared to spend money promoting her — it paid off! The singer achieved a few minor club hits before her debut album, *Madonna*, hit the U.S. and UK Top 10s in 1983. Many of the songs were written in collaboration with her ex-boyfriend Steve Bray, and they were all slickly produced. Her pop hit "Holiday," made the Top 40, but with the catchy "Lucky Star," Madonna scaled to number four in the charts.

TEEN IDOL

Madonna cultivated and reveled in her extravagant image and, of course, showed off her real talent as both a singer and dancer.

In July 1985 Madonna performed at Live Aid.

ACTING AMBITION

Madonna was already a pop success when she starred with Rosanna Arquette in the box office blockbuster, *Desperately Seeking Susan* (85). But she floundered with her next two films — *Shanghai Surprise* (86), alongside her (now ex-) husband Sean Penn, and *Who's That Girl* (87). She received good reviews for her work opposite Warren Beatty in her next film, *Dick Tracy* (90) about the comic strip sleuth. *A League Of Their Own* (92) was nothing special — a run-of-the-mill baseball film. But at last, in 1996, Madonna secured a part she'd been after for eight years. It was worth the wait. She won a Golden Globe for her mature performance in the film musical *Evita*, as Argentinian first lady, Eva Perón. Madonna the actress had finally made it!

Madonna's "Evita" won the Golden Globe for Best Actress.

Madonna 1983
Like a Virgin 1984
True Blue 1986
Like a Prayer 1989
I'm Breathless 1990

The Immaculate Collection 1990
Best Of The Rest Volume II 1993
Ray of Light 1998
Confessions on a Dance Floor 2005

Her next album, *Like a Virgin*, was a number one in the UK and U.S. Supported by the first of many raunchy videos, it was followed by no less than 10 more hits. She had universal appeal but was especially popular in the teen market: young boys swooned over her up-front sexiness, while girls admired her raw ambition — and her wild, eccentric taste in clothes!

MATERIAL GIRL

Ten hits followed. Naked ambition was the theme for "Material Girl," in which she re-invented herself as a Marilyn Monroe-style femme fatale. "Crazy For You" proved she was just as at home with soulful ballads and "Vogue" cashed in on the very latest — and very short-lived — spiky dance craze the vogue.

IN THE PUBLIC EYE

Madonna had achieved her ambition of becoming an international superstar, as an actress as well as a singer, but with this came tabloid attention. Her tempestous relationships with a string of larger-than-life partners kept the press busy. So did the publication of her controversial photo album, *Sex*, which featured erotic photos of Madonna — and friends. The first print run sold out within days, and the coffee-table book reprinted several times.

TODAY

Today Madonna has left her raunchy image behind but shows no signs of slowing down.

Madonna and daughter Lourdes Maria Ciccone Leon, who was born in 1996.

The POLICE

In the northern English town of Newcastle, Gordon Sumner, a teacher, was enjoying working with his jazz group, Last Exit. He was dismissive of rock and pop music, but two musicians who attended one of his gigs had other ideas. Stewart Copeland and Henry Padovani wanted to form a rock band. The pair persuaded Sumner, nicknamed "Sting," to join them, and the Police were born. It was 1977.

AWAITING FAME

They immediately adopted their characteristic spare, slightly punky and definitely reggae-based style. Copeland made a feature of his unusual drum style (his kit was set up the wrong way around). On the brink of fame, the Police were hard up and agreed to appear on a chewing gum ad. They happily dyed their hair blond for the ad — and kept the look for a while.

RECORDING SUCCESS

In April 1978 the Police made the first of many brilliant records. "Roxanne" was not an instant hit, but later, in 78, they released "Can't Stand Losing You." Padovani left, unwilling to play second fiddle to Sting and in came Andy Summers.

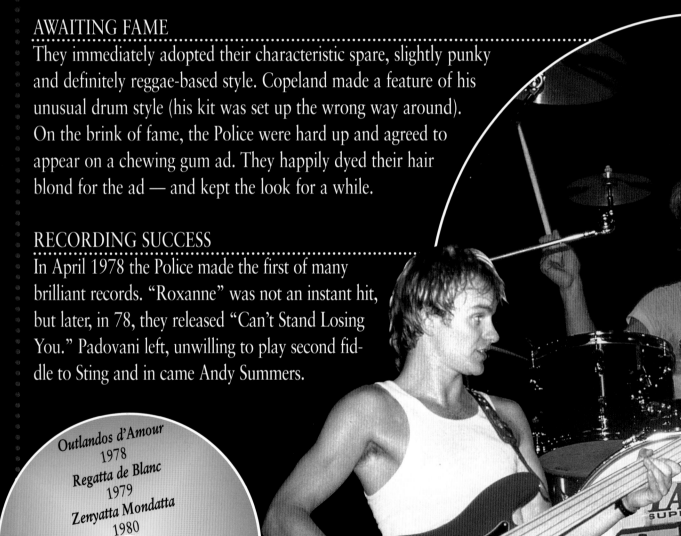

Outlandos d'Amour
1978
Regatta de Blanc
1979
Zenyatta Mondatta
1980

Synchronicity
1983
Every Breath You Take: The Singles
1986

Gordon Sumner (Sting)

Stewart Copeland

The first album, *Outlandos d'Amour* was released in late 1978 and contained a challenging collection of songs. "Roxanne," their song about a young man's love for a prostitute, had reggae-styled verses and a rocking harmony chorus. It was re-released in 79 and finally made it into the British charts, despite a BBC ban in the UK.

MAGIC!

In the 1980s the Police made it big, starting with their claustrophobic single "Don't Stand So Close to Me." Perfect, catchy pop seemed to come naturally to the Police. "Every Little Thing She Does Is Magic" taken from the album *Ghost in the Machine* was another sing-along tune. Sting's voice always seemed strained with emotion, but never more so than on the creepy classic, "Every Breath You Take." The single appeared on *Synchronicity*, the melancholic but humorous album that marked the peak of their career. The Police have not recorded any new material together since.

The band reunited in 2007 to markup the 30th anniversary of the release of Synchronicity and toured into 2008.

SLEEPING PARTNERS

Oddly, although they ceased recording in the mid-80s, the Police never officially broke up.

Sting, Summers and Copeland all enjoyed successful solo careers. *Dream of the Blue Turtles* (85) was Sting's first solo album and illustrated his strong jazz influences. He has also performed some accomplished acting roles in movies such as *Quadrophenia*, *Radio On*, *Brimstone and Treacle* and *Dune*.

ndy Summers

SAVE THE RAINFORESTS

Environmental issues came to the fore during the 80s. In particular, there was concern that large areas of tropical rainforest were being cleared for timber at the expense of countless species of plants and animals. The forests were also home to tribal Indians who had lived there for centuries.

Sting had taken part in Amnesty International's Human Rights Now! tour, which took him all over the world. What he saw in South America led him to campaign about the aboriginals in the Brazilian rainforest whose homelands were being sold off to loggers by the Brazilian government.

With Chief Raoni, Sting pleads for rainforest conservation.

PRINCE

Prince Rogers Nelson was born in Minneapolis on June 7, 1958. At the age of 10 he was taken to see the legendary soul performer, James Brown. Prince was inspired by the experience. Already an accomplished musician, he began furiously writing songs and developing his technical expertise on bass, saxophone, guitar and drums.

GETTING STARTED

By the time he was 16 Prince was leading his third band, Flyte Time. Producer Chris Moon took a gamble and allowed Prince free use of his studio during "dead" time. The young musician produced a stunning demo tape and was snapped up by Warner Brothers to produce and record three albums. Prince was just 19. For his debut album he insisted on doing everything himself. He racked up huge studio bills and went six times over budget. Sales of his debut were modest, but Warner kept faith. Prince put a band together for the next album, finished it in just six weeks and hit the jackpot! *Prince* went platinum, and one of its tracks, "I Feel For You" gave Chaka Khan a number one in 1984.

Prince's trademark was suggestive performances with his beloved guitar.

WHAT'S IN A NAME?
In 1993 Prince changed his name to the symbol that had first appeared a year earlier on the *Love Symbol Album*. He insisted that all references to him should only display what unkindly became known as the "squiggle." Later, he insisted on being referred to as the "Artist Formerly Known As Prince." In 95, during his visit to the UK to receive a Brit Award, he refused to speak to the press and appeared at the ceremony with "SLAVE" written across his face to draw attention to his bitter battle with Warner Brothers over their refusal to release *Gold Experience*.

ROYAL PERFORMER

By the 80s Prince was a superstar. He toured the world with his extravagant show, featuring exotic dancers and, of course, his own larger-than-life self.

Prince in concert in March 1995.

His third album, *Dirty Mind*, was another solo effort. As its title suggests, it was sexually explicit — but there was more to it than just shock value. Critics agreed that it was a musical masterpiece. Two more albums quickly followed. *Controversy* continued the funk style and sex content of its predecessor; *1999* revealed a new synthesiser-based sound.

MIXMASTER MUSICIAN

Prince's next project showed once and for all his ability to fuse different styles and come up with something refreshingly original. *Purple Rain* was the soundtrack album to his semi-autobiographical movie. Its three singles, "When Doves Cry," "Let's Go Crazy" and "Purple Rain," sold millions and the album itself earned Prince four Grammy Awards and an Oscar. In 1989 Prince gained his third U.S. number one with his soundtrack to the hit movie *Batman*.

Leather-clad Prince stars in the award-winning film, Purple Rain.

TOWARD 1999

As the 1990s dawned, Prince's song *Nothing Compares 2 U* topped the UK and U.S. charts, performed by Irish singer Sinead O'Connor. In 1991 Prince assembled a brand new band, the New Power Generation. Their first album, *Diamonds and Pearls*, skillfully combined hip-hop and soul. Their second album together, *Love Symbol Album*, was a return to Prince's early form. Its raunchy single, "Sexy MF," was banned from UK radio because of its suggestive lyrics! Prince kept up his reputation as one of the most creative and controversial performers of recent years.

Prince
1979
Dirty Mind
1980
1999
1983
Purple Rain
1984

Sign O' the Times
1987
Love Symbol Album
1992
The Hits: Volume I & II
1993

QUEEN

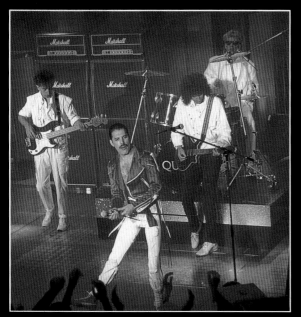

In 1959 Frederick Bulsara, aged 13, moved to London from his birthplace in Zanzibar. In 1973 Bulsara put out his first single, "I Can Hear Music," calling himself Larry Lurex. But by then he was already Queen's front man under a different stage name — Freddie Mercury. *That* was the name that would make him famous.

SMILE, PLEASE!

In 1971 Mecury had started work with guitarist Brian May and drummer Roger Taylor in a band called Smile. They were soon joined by bassist John Deacon, and Queen were born. Their first single, "Keep Yourself Alive," was released in July 1973, followed by a superb album debut, *Queen*. There was no time for playing around as Larry Lurex!

Queen
1973
Queen II
1974
A Night At The Opera
1975
Jazz
1978

The Game
1980
Hot Space
1982
A Kind Of Magic
1986

The band toured the UK and U.S. with huge success in 1974. Their second album, *Queen II* made the UK and U.S. charts. Mercury's increasingly over-the-top leadership style and camp, glam-rock image were cheerfully indulged by the rest of the band. Queen remained tight-knit during their 18-year career — a rare feat in the ego-driven music business.

WE ARE THE CHAMPIONS

In 1975 Queen released "Bohemian Rhapsody." The single stayed at number one in the UK for nine weeks even though (or perhaps because) it broke all the rules of what a pop song was supposed to be. At six minutes long, it was twice the usual length for a

The king of camp: Mercury gave dazzling performances.

single. Its style was mock-opera, and it was promoted by one of the first-ever music videos. Queen became international stars with a string of hits. Everyone knew at least some of the words to "Killer Queen" or "Bicycle Race."

STADIUM ROCK

In 1980 Queen achieved their first U.S. number one single with the infectious "Crazy Little Thing Called Love" and punchy "Another One Bites the Dust," both taken from their number one album, *The Game*. They became used to performing to massive audiences.

Of all the star-studded acts that took part in Live Aid, Queen slickly stole the show. Their aptly named double album *Live Magic* (86) recorded Queen in their element — playing to massive crowds.

AIDS PANIC

One of the tragedies of the decade was the discovery of a "new" disease, AIDS (aquired immune deficiency syndrome). The disease was not a killer in itself, but it destroyed the immune system, making its carrier unable to fight off even a simple cold. At first no one knew how it was transmitted, but it seemed to affect only homosexuals, and the tabloids spread panic with stories of the "gay plague." In fact, the disease could affect anyone who had come into contact with HIV (human immuno-deficiency virus), which was transmitted through sexual contact or through contact with infected blood.

But the plague mentality of the early days lived on. Gay men and drug users who shared needles had been at highest risk. Admitting that you had AIDS often revealed aspects of your lifestyle that had previously been private. Many sufferers, like Freddie Mercury, chose to keep their illness secret.

THE FINAL CURTAIN

By the start of the 1990s, Queen toured less and less. The press speculated on Mercury's health, but it was not until two days before his death that he announced he had AIDS. He became a victim of the ignorance of the risks of his decadent lifestyle. Mercury died on November 24, 1991. May, Taylor and Deacon held a memorial concert for him the next spring. Watched by over a billion people across the world, guest artists such as Elton John, George Michael, David Bowie and Annie Lennox paid tribute to one of rock's glitziest, best-loved superstars.

BRUCE SPRINGSTEEN

In 1974, the influential *Rolling Stone* magazine critic Jon Landau bravely pronounced: "I've seen the future of rock 'n' roll — and its name is Bruce Springsteen!" Well, it was quite a prediction to live up to.

HUMBLE BEGINNINGS

Bruce Springsteen was born in Freehold, New Jersey on September 23, 1949. His father was variously a bus driver and factory laborer, and Springsteen experienced first hand the social injustices that so many "blue collar" Americans were experiencing. Throughout his entire career, he has never forgotten his working-class roots.

Springsteen got his first guitar when he was nine years old. By the time he left school, he had already written dozens of songs. In the mid- to late-60s he played in several local rock bands.

GOODBYE NEW JERSEY

Springsteen moved to Greenwich Village and in September 1971 formed the Bruce Springsteen Band. Musicians came and went, but significant players were saxophonist Clarence Clemons and keyboard player David Sancious. In May 1972 Springsteen signed a deal with CBS to record 10 albums over the next five years. The record label hoped they signed the new Bob Dylan. Like Dylan's, Springsteen's songs used powerful, poetic lyrics to address complex issues. The first album was called *Greetings from Asbury Park, New Jersey*.

Springsteen wearing a rocker's bandanna.

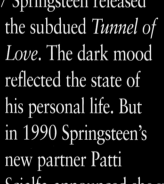

Born to Run
1975
The River
1980
Nebraska
1982
Born In The USA
1984

Live 1975–1985
1986
Tunnel of Love
1987
Human Touch
1992

It did not sell well. Neither did its follow-up, *The Wild, the Innocent and the E Street Shuffle*. Nevertheless, Springsteen's reputation as a serious performer was growing. His next album, the explosive *Born to Run*, brought superstardom and a place in the U.S. Top five. Springsteen even appeared on the covers of *Time* and *Newsweek*.

BORN TO ROCK

The beginning of the 1980s saw the release of yet another masterpiece, *The River*. Three tracks from the album were hit singles. In 1982, Springsteen bravely recorded *Nebraska*, a dark, moody and completely solo acoustic set.

HIT MAN

Two years later came his most accomplished album, *Born In the USA*. The songs captured the angry mood of the poor and disadvantaged and turned it into belting rock. *Born* spent two years on the U.S. and UK charts and gave him seven hit singles.

BRUCE THE BRAVE
Springsteen doesn't just write about social injustice. He raises funds for good causes in the way he knows best. He donated a live recording of "Trapped" to the *USA for Africa* album. He has also helped out Artists United Against Apartheid, the Harry Chapin Memorial Fund and the Human Rights Now Amnesty Tour. In 1990 he played a concert for Sting's Rainforest Conservation charity and also performed at a protest concert against alleged U.S. government arms deals. A man true to his convictions!

Springsteen teamed up with singer-songwriter Paul Simon for the Harry Chapin Memorial Concert in aid of homeless kids.

A FRESH START

In October 1987 Springsteen released the subdued *Tunnel of Love*. The dark mood reflected the state of his personal life. But in 1990 Springsteen's new partner Patti

"I've seen the future of rock 'n' roll..."

Scialfa announced she was pregnant. It was a bright start to the decade, during which Springsteen released three albums and won an Oscar for his contribution to the *Philadelphia* soundtrack. Springsteen isn't showing any signs of slowing down in the 2000s, with the number-one releases *The Rising* (2002), *Devils & Dust* (2005), *Magic* (2007) and *Working on a Dream* (2009).

TINA TURNER

Tina Turner's long career as a powerful singer has had two distinct and quite different phases. Annie Mae Bullock was born on the November 26, 1939, in Brownsville, Tennessee. As a teenager, her soulful voice was soon earning her a living in the smoky clubs around Saint Louis.

DOUBLE ACT

Tina was discovered by the established band leader Ike Turner. The pair married in 1958 and toured the U.S. with their successful rhythm-and-blues act. With the gospel-inspired soul classic "River Deep, Mountain High" (66), they broke into the mainstream — in Europe, at least. With "Proud Mary" (71) and "Nutbush City Limits" (73), they became stars in the U.S. too.

Tina was the star of the show, and her possessive husband found this hard to handle. In 1975 Tina, no longer in awe of Ike's bullying both on- and off-stage, walked out of the stormy marriage. She was free at last. She gave a sizzling performance as the Acid Queen in the Who's film musical *Tommy*. But then came a lean period — until the 1980s.

Ike and Tina's duo lasted for 17 years.

A FRESH START

Tina Turner had always had a big UK following. UK synth-pop band Heaven 17 invited her to work with them in 1983, and she eagerly agreed. This led to a new contract with Capitol Records. Tina was 45 years old. Out came a husky cover of an Al Green song.

"Let's Stay Together" made the Top 20 on both sides of the Atlantic. In 1984 Tina recorded her comeback album *Private Dancer*. Its tormented title track (about a lonely stripper) was written by Mark Knopfler; the album also featured the number one single, "What's Love Got To Do With It." Tina especially appealed to 40-somethings who had heard her singing the first time around. They were delighted to discover she was still just as sexy and energetic 20 years on.

Turner wowed film-goers with her role in Mad Max.

SHOWSTOPPER

In 1984 Tina astutely accepted a part in the sci-fi adventure movie *Mad Max: Beyond the Thunderdome*. The theme song, "We Don't Need Another Hero," was delivered with her trademark gutsy passion and gave her another massive hit.

Tina concentrated on projecting her stage persona as a wild, larger-than-life soul and rock performer. Over 180,000 went to her show in Rio de Janeiro, and she performed to millions at Live Aid.

GLAMOROUS GRANNY

In 1993 Tina's autobiography was filmed as *What's Love Got To Do With It?* Soon after Tina decided to spend more time with her family (which includes her grandchildren!) and to develop her interest in Buddhism.

However, the superstar couldn't resist doing the title song for a Bond film, *Golden Eye*, in 1995, and the following year she was back in the studio to record *Wildest Dreams* with producer Trevor Horn.

Acid Queen
1975
Private Dancer
1984
Break Every Rule
1986

Proud Mary & Other Hits (with Ike Turner)
1988
Foreign Affair
1989
Simply the Best
1991

CHARITY ROCK

In 1984 the world was shocked by footage of the Ethiopian famine. Ex-Boomtown Rat Bob Geldof decided to do something about it. Together with Midge Ure, he wrote the charity single "Do They Know It's Christmas?."

The following summer Live Aid, performed live from London and Philadelphia, raised more for the cause. The galaxy of stars included Tina Turner, who sang "Honky Tonk Woman" with Mick Jagger.

Broadcast live around the world, the concert raised over £50 million (U.S. $64 million).

U2

Musicians Paul Hewson, David Evans, Adam Clayton and Larry Mullen, Jr., started playing covers in Dublin's pubs and youth clubs in 1977. Known as Feedback (and later, Hype), they played Beach Boys', Stones' and Shadows' songs for a pittance, until their above-average musical prowess won them a talent contest staged in Limerick in 1978. Hewson became Bono, Evans renamed himself the Edge — and, most importantly, Hype became U2.

THE EARLY YEARS

Astute local manager Paul McGuiness spotted their potential and secured a recording contract with CBS. Their first two releases topped the Irish charts, and U2 were keen to repeat their success outside their native land. They started their first album with producer Steve Lillywhite. *Boy* (1980) dealt sensitively with the pangs and problems of adolescence and was warmly praised by the critics.

U2 were gaining a well-deserved reputation as a performing band, thanks to Bono's raw singing power and the rock-solid backing of his musical colleagues.

They toured the U.S. in 1981, and then released their second album, *October*. They were at last finding their true voice. This moving set was followed by a single called, "New Year's Day." Written in support of the Polish

Frontman Bono delivers another belter.

86

Solidarity movement, it entered the Top 10 in January 1983. A month later their new album, *War*, topped the UK charts. Fiercely political in content, *War* opened with the blistering "Sunday, Bloody Sunday." The song referred to January 72, when the British Army opened fire on Catholic protestors and killed 14 people.

October
1981
War
1983
The Unforgettable Fire
1984

The Joshua Tree
1987
Rattle & Hum
1988
Achtung Baby
1991

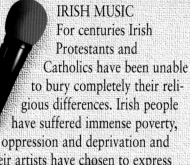

IRISH MUSIC
For centuries Irish Protestants and Catholics have been unable to bury completely their religious differences. Irish people have suffered immense poverty, oppression and deprivation and their artists have chosen to express their anguish in the way they know best.

U2's Irish background was the perfect education for producing music with a message.

Traditional Gaelic music ranges from swirling poetic ballads to furious jigs and reels played on a variety of acoustic instruments — such as guitars, banjos, mandolins, fiddles, whistles — to appreciative audiences in pubs and clubs.

Music-making is informal at a "ceili."

MUSIC WITH A MESSAGE

U2's next release, the EP *Under A Blood Red Sky* (1983), documented their impressive stage show. But their political conscience was not neglected. *The Unforgettable Fire* included their tribute to the black civil rights leader Martin Luther King, Jr., "Pride (In the Name of Love)." Next came the outstanding *The Joshua Tree*, another chart-topping hit.

WE ARE THE PASSENGERS

After a couple of quiet years, U2 returned in 1991 with a new sound. Their inspired album *Achtung Baby*, produced by Brian Eno, drew heavily on dance music and techno. Hailed as their best album yet, it went straight to number one!

In 1995 they collaborated on Eno's *Passengers* project, along with opera star Luciano Pavarotti. Another good cause — this time for the children of Bosnia.

U2 maintain their reputation as one of the world's most exciting bands. But quite clearly, their huge success has not gone to their heads.

U2 in their video, Rattle & Hum.

WHAM!

When Yorgos Kyriako Panayiotou befriended schoolmate Andrew Ridgeley at Bushey Meads Comprehensive school in the mid-70s, the pair quickly discovered their mutual interest in soul, reggae, dance and ska music. They decided that music would be their passport to fame. Yorgos rechristened himself George Michael, and he and Ridgeley formed a ska band, the Executive.

WHAM!
Fantastic
1983
Make It Big
1984

GEORGE MICHAEL
Faith
1987
Listen Without Prejudice Volume One
1990

WHAM! BAM!

In 1982 they formed their own duo, Wham!, and spent hours composing and recording Michael's songs then sending demos of their work to every record company they could think of. Their persistence paid off. Small local record company Innervision gave them an advance of £500 (around U.S. $870) and the freedom to write, record and produce their first single. Out came *Wham! Rap (Enjoy What You Do)* with the boys backed by singers Amanda Washbourn and Shirlie Holliman. The record attracted little attention. However, their second single for Innervision brought them overnight success. "Young Guns (Go for It)" went to number three in the UK charts and projected an image of leather-clad rebels. Less than a year later, Wham!'s third single, "Bad Boys" was equally successful. Their first album, *Fantastic*, was a fantastic success and went straight to number one! The pair had hordes of teenage fans, thanks to the macho image portrayed in their stylish videos and slick stage show.

Wham! make their debut with Wham! Rap (Enjoy What You Do).

AMERICAN DREAM

"Club Tropicana" and "Club Fantastic Megamix" provided Wham! with two more Top 10 hits, but the boys were eager to make it big in the U.S., where the real money was to be made. Record giant Columbia had noticed Michael's songwriting skills and the band's punchy videos.

Wham! hit the number one spot with "Wake Me Up Before You Go-Go" in May 1984. Their next single, "Careless Whisper," was a much slower ballad — but nevertheless a hit.

That same year "Freedom" and their aptly titled album *Make It Big*, hit the jackpot again. Suddenly Wham! were one of the hottest acts in the world.

The handsome stars were idolized by their teenage fans.

Wham!'s Christmas single that year, titled "Last Christmas," was only prevented from making the number one spot by the charity number from Band Aid (to which they had contributed). Nevertheless "Last Christmas" sold more copies in the UK than any other Wham! or George Michael single before or since.

THE END

March 1986 saw a significant release: "A Different Corner" that was credited to Michael alone. The pair went their separate ways. George Michael's first official solo album, *Faith* proved he could repeat Wham!'s success on his own. In 1990 he appealed to his audience to *Listen Without Prejudice*. They did, and provided him with his fifth number one album!

GOODBYE BOYS!

Nobody could deny that in terms of creativity, George Michael was the driving force of Wham! He wrote the songs and played most of the instruments on the recordings. Certainly, Andrew Ridgeley's post-Wham! career has been less than startling. His 1990 album *Son of Albert* didn't even make the U.S. Top 100.

However, at least the boys went out with a bang. Their final concert in London's Wembley Stadium was attended by over 80,000 fans!

Wham! sing farewell to their fans on stage at Wembley, July 1986.

GAZETTEER

The 1980s was a rich decade for music, and the previous pages have included only a few of its stars. The audience for pop was bigger than ever, and new styles sprang up to suit every taste.

INXS

BIG SOUNDS

Australian band INXS filled stadiums around the world and moved smoothly between rock 'n' roll, pop and dancey beats. The decade also saw old-timers Status Quo still going strong, although they had to wait until the 90s for the second number one of their long career with their football anthem "Come On You Reds."

GOING SOLO

There were lots of talented solo stars to enjoy. Kate Bush dazzled with songs such as "Running Up That Hill." She also worked with Peter Gabriel, who had left Genesis in 1975. Gabriel had hits in the 80s with "Sledgehammer" and "Big Time." His replacement as Genesis's front man, Phil Collins, also launched a solo career. He won a Grammy for his album *No Jacket Required* (85). Nigerian singer Sade cornered the pop-meets-jazz market with her stunning debut *Diamond Life* in 84 — another Grammy-winner. And Jamaican diva Grace Jones had a hit with the extraordinary "Slave to the Rhythm" in 85.

Phil Collins

MUSIC MACHINES

Grace Jones

Computers began to play an important role. Spandau Ballet, Human League, Simple Minds, Depeche Mode and Tears for Fears were just some of the bands that moved away from traditional instruments. They experimented with synthesizers, drum machines and new recording techniques to produce highly original "synth pop." Producer Trevor Horn took electronica a step further with his outfit the Art of Noise. No "band" featured on the video of their hit "Close (To the Edit)," which was made up of samples of other tracks chopped up and stitched back together.

IN THE MIX

Samplers and drum machines were central in creating a new musical form — house music. Named after the acid house parties where it was played, this music featured unfeasibly fast beats and squelchy electronic sounds.

Spandau Ballet

Human League

IT'S A RAP!

Rap and hip-hop were born. Taking inspiration from the fast-talking reggae "toasters," rappers spoke their fiercely political lyrics. Rap expressed the "gangsta" culture of young African-Americans. Pioneers of the sound included Run DMC (the first rap stars to appear on MTV), Grandmaster Flash and Ice-T.

Run DMC

PUBLICITY MACHINE

Performers such as the Smiths, Style Council and Billy Bragg all used their music to publicly express their strong political beliefs. And, of course, popular music wouldn't be complete without its show-offs. Frankie Goes to Hollywood were hugely hyped. Their controversial debut single "Relax" was banned by the BBC. Culture Club first topped the charts with "Do You Really Want To Hurt Me," sung by glamorous Boy George whose gender-bending image attracted lots of press attention!

Frankie Goes To Hollywood

Culture Club

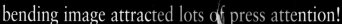

1990s Pop

CONTENTS

On these disks is a selection of the artist's recordings. Many of these albums are available on CD and MP3. If they are not, many of the tracks from them can be found on compilations.

These boxes give you extra information about the artists and their times.

Some contain anecdotes about the artists themselves or about the people who helped their careers or, occasionally, about those who exploited them.

Others provide historical facts about the music, lifestyle, fans, fads and fashions of the day.

The MTV awards are a popular fixture on the music calendar each year.

INTRODUCTION

Pop music had been around for a long time by the 1990s. It was becoming increasingly difficult for musicians to come up with any new ideas, and much of the music of that decade owed a huge debt to the fashions of the past. There were the boy bands who revived a trend that had been out of fashion since the 70s, and Madonna was a vast influence on the female singers and girl groups of the 90s. If the 1980s had been dominated by synthesizers and drum machines, the 90s saw the return of guitar bands.

The Icelandic singer Björk took the charts by storm with her 1993 album Debut, *with its blend of dance music and strident vocals. Her other albums included* Post *and* Telegram. *The picture above shows how she appeared on her 1997 album* Homogenic.

But there was some great original music too. Artists such as Björk used modern recording technology to create new sounds and explore new musical territory. And 80s favorites, such as Sting, George Michael, U2 and R.E.M., filled stadiums with their brand of rock that was bold and experimental but easy on the ear.

The future of songwriting was in good hands too. Even the boy bands and girl groups, who were condemned as lightweight and manufactured, came up with songs that will still be sung long into the future. And 90s teen idols like Justin Timberlake have matured into sophisticated entertainers, reaching new heights in the 21st century.

ALL SAINTS

In the early 1960s the Beatles were popular with the entire family. The Rolling Stones were the exact opposite — the bad boys of pop. Thirty years later, All Saints were promoted as the harder, grittier version of the Spice Girls.

A BAND TO BE TAKEN SERIOUSLY

There were marked similarities between the two girl groups. All Saints were two brunettes, one blonde and an Afro-Caribbean, and they were all singers (not instrumentalists). Only a red-headed singer was missing. But they made much of their original songwriting skills, and they were a street band, composed of four musicians, not products of stage school and the modeling circuit. Shaznay Lewis and Melanie Blatt began recording together in a studio in All Saints Road, London, in 1993.

All Saints
1997

Saints And Sinners
2000

All Saints were overwhelmed by their Brit Award success in 1997.

A LONG WAY TO THE TOP

Their first single in 1995 was a failure, and they were promptly dumped by their record label. Uncowed, they recruited Canadian sisters Nicole and Natalie Appleton to make All Saints a quartet. Their manager, John Benson, secured them a new deal and enlisted the help of top producers Nellee Hooper and Cameron McVey. "I Know Where It's At" hit number four in the UK charts and launched the group throughout Europe and Asia.

A STRING OF HITS

All Saints' next single, penned by Shaznay, was a monster hit in Europe. The tale of a doomed love affair, "Never Ever" won them a Brit Award and much respect from fans and critics alike. Two more chart toppers followed in 1998. Their single "Pure Shores" was the biggest UK hit of 2000, but all was not well with All Saints.

Shaznay Lewis was the chief songwriter for All Saints.

FROZEN OUT

Their 2001 European tour was canceled, and the band was officially put on ice, owing to business disagreements. But Melanie Blatt has not ruled out a future reunion for All Saints — but rumors of new recordings have not yielded any releases.

HONEST

While Shaznay Lewis was in the studio, writing material for All Saints, the other three group members starred in a wacky crime comedy film, called *Honest*. The movie was the first by director David A. Stewart, better known as half of the 80s duo the Eurythmics. The movie wasn't the box-office smash they had hoped for, and its relative failure might have hastened All Saints' split.

Honest was premiered at the 2000 Cannes film festival.

BLUR

The career of the "Britpop" band Blur nearly stalled before the 90s were truly underway. It took them five years of hard work before they hit the top of the UK charts.

Leisure
1991
Modern Life Is Rubbish
1993
Parklife
1994
The Great Escape
1995

Blur
1997
13
1999
Think Tank
2003

EARLY STRUGGLE

Damon Albarn, Graham Coxon and Alex James formed Seymour in London in 1989, with drummer Dave Rowntree joining the lineup soon after. They signed with the Food label, who suggested they change their name and released their first album *Leisure*. Many critics thought the band sounded too old-fashioned, and Blur struggled to adopt a harder sound. Their second album, *Modern Life Is Rubbish*, was initially rejected by Food, so it was back to the studio again. Food was eventually satisfied, but Blur's American label was not. The band was exhausted when the record was eventually released, but they learned from their mistakes and returned in 1994 with one of the biggest British albums of the 90s.

Blur celebrate their success at the 1995 Brit Awards.

BLUR vs. OASIS

The album was *Parklife*, which entered the UK chart at number one, and catapulted the band to stardom. It gave them the hit singles "Girls And Boys" and "To The End," and paved the way for a new movement of guitar bands, labeled Britpop. The media were determined to fuel a rivalry between Blur and the northern act Oasis, and Blur eagerly rose to the bait, releasing the single "Country House" on the same day as Oasis's "Roll With It" in a battle for the number one slot in the British charts. Blur won that battle, but Oasis would win the war. Blur's next album, *The Great Escape*, failed to match the impact of Oasis's *(What's the Story) Morning Glory* on either side of the Atlantic.

ELASTICA

Elastica was one of the leading Britpop bands to emerge in the early 1990s. Lead-singer Justine Frischmann was romantically linked with Blur's Damon Albarn, as both bands were high in the charts. Elastica's self-titled album was said to be the fastest-selling debut in chart history, but they failed to build on this success. The second album, *The Menace*, only appeared in 2000, six years after its predecessor.

Justine Frischmann (second from right) was in the London Suede at the start of her career.

TIME OFF

Blur almost split in 1996 but decided instead to take a year off to recuperate. They returned with their fifth album, which gave them their most successful single to date, "Song 2." They even enjoyed some long-awaited success in the U.S., before Damon Albarn took a break from Blur to play with the "virtual hip-hop" act Gorillaz.

Damon Albarn is an accomplished songwriter.

BOYZONE

The phenomenon of the boy band was not new to the 90s. The 1970s had seen some enormously popular boy bands, such as the Jackson 5 and the Osmonds, but this style of singing and dancing group had gone out of fashion in the 80s. But the huge success of Britain's Take That opened the floodgates for dozens of boy bands. Ireland gave the world Boyzone.

AUDITION TIME

Like so many other acts of the 90s, the idea of Boyzone was conceived by an ambitious manager, in this case Louis Walsh, who advertised for five male singers and dancers (just like Take That). Three hundred hopefuls were boiled down to five lucky winners — lead singer Ronan Keating, plus Mikey Graham, Stephen Gately, Shane Lynch and Keith Duffy. Their first singles were cover versions of popular 1970s hits.

Boyzone covered "Father and Son" by Cat Stevens.

Said and Done
1995
A Different Beat
1996

Where We Belong
1998
By Request
1999
Back Again No Matter What
2008

ORIGINAL MATERIAL

Boyzone's renditions of the Detroit Spinners' "Working My Way Back to You" and the Osmonds' "Love Me for a Reason" both made the Irish top three, and the Bee Gees' "Words" hit UK number one. But Boyzone wisely realized that they needed original material if they were going to last. They hired Take That songwriter Ray Hedges, and Boyzone's first original single "Key to My Life" topped the UK chart, as did their debut album *Said and Done*.

Keating hit number one in the UK with "Life Is a Rollercoaster."

WESTLIFE

Ronan Keating proved himself to be a clever businessman when he was introduced to fellow Dubliners Westlife. He offered to become the group's co-manager, despite their obvious threat to Boyzone's popularity. Westlife's first single, "Flying Without Wings" entered the chart at number one in 1999, and they repeated this success with "Seasons in the Sun," "Swear It Again" and their self-titled first album, *Westlife*.

Boyzone's manager Louis Walsh introduced Westlife to Ronan Keating.

TIME TO GROW UP

The members of Boyzone are proud of the hard work they put into their music. They became the first act in chart history to hit the top three with their first 14 singles. As they grew up they managed that most difficult feat for a boy band — they began to be taken seriously by their musical peers. As the new millennium dawned, the group members developed solo careers, and Ronan Keating hit number one with "When You Say Nothing At All."

Boyzone's stage show was expertly choreographed.

EAST 17

All Saints weren't the only 90s group to name themselves after an area of London. One of the biggest UK boy bands came from Walthamstow — its postcode is East 17.

Walthamstow
1993
Steam
1995

Around The World: The Journey So Far
1996
East 17: The Platinum Collection
2006

A CHANGE OF STYLE

Tony Mortimer, Brian Harvey, Terry Coldwell and John Hendy hooked up with the aim of emulating the best American rap and hip-hop acts of the day. But East London isn't downtown LA, and it was only when they changed their sound, to appeal to the teen-market, that success came their way. Their good looks helped, and East 17 was signed by Tom Watkins, who had launched Bros and the Pet Shop Boys in the 80s.

OVERSEAS SUCCESS

In 1992 East 17's first single, "House of Love" shot into the UK top 10, and the band found themselves darlings of the tabloid press. A critical panning didn't stop their debut album, *Walthamstow* from racing up the charts, as new fans in Australia and East Asia discovered the band.

IN CONCERT

East 17 struggled to gain respect among the music press as they played to arenas packed with swooning teenage girls accompanied by their grumpy boyfriends. They achieved the coveted Christmas number one slot in the UK with "Stay Another Day" in 1994, even playing their own instruments!

SONG AND DANCE

Boy and girl bands depend heavily on choreography (dance arrangements) in their stage shows. Music critics tend to dismiss these bands as lightweight and manufactured, but you don't look that good without a lot of skill and practice. The soul acts of the 1960s and 70s were among the first to accompany their songs with complex dance routines. Boyzone were very influenced by the Jackson 5, while East 17 paid tribute to American street acts, both in their dance and clothing. And if you think it looks easy, just try singing and dancing at the same time without losing your breath!

N'Sync working the crowd.

East 17 were proud of their East London roots.

WHOOPS!

But East 17 was not destined to stay in the public eye for much longer. Brian Harvey foolishly endorsed the use of the illegal drug ecstasy in an interview and was thrown out of the band. Some fans hoped East 17 could survive without him, but the damage was done, and guitar bands now reigned supreme in the charts.

East 17's fans copied their way of dressing.

HANSON

When no fewer than five record labels turn you down in succession, surely it's time to give up your ambition to be the next pop sensation. Not for brothers Isaac, Taylor and Zac Hanson — showing indomitable spirit, the trio from Tulsa, Oklahoma, simply would not give up.

GOING IT ALONE

The singing brothers muscled in on music lawyer Christopher Sabec and sang for him. He agreed to manage them and touted tapes of the group around several record companies. As no one was willing to sign Hanson, they decided to record an independent album, *Boomerang*. The single "MMMBop" won them a contract with Mercury Records.

Middle of Nowhere
1997
Snowed In
1997
3 Car Garage
1998
Live from Albertane
1998
This Time Around
2000
Underneath
2004
The Walk
2007

Hanson first performed at school.

POWERFUL BACKING

Mercury put their full weight behind Hanson, and in 1997 the group happily watched the album *Middle Of Nowhere* and "MMMBop" storm up the charts. The three Hanson boys were suddenly the biggest teen sensation in the U.S.

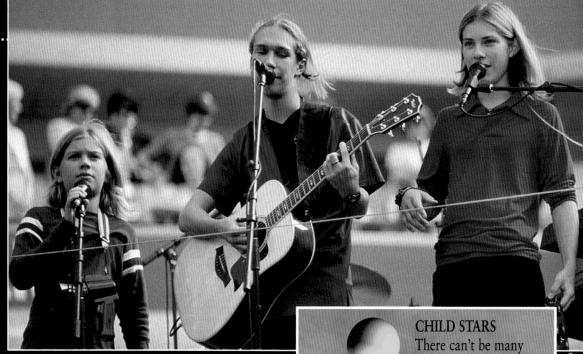

Middle of Nowhere was one of the biggest-selling albums of 1997.

COOL YULE

The boys quickly recorded a new album for the lucrative Christmas market, *Snowed In*, and cleverly re-released their earlier independent recordings. They also captured the excitement and intensity of their live performances with a recording from one of their concerts, *Live from Albertane*.

BOYS TO MEN

Hanson realized the need to reach out beyond the teenage audience and wisely took time off to produce a more mature record. After a long break they emerged with *This Time Around* in 2000, which raised its hat to the heavy sounds that dominated the charts. The album did not match the commercial success of their previous releases, and in 2003 Hanson left Mercury, by then owned by Island Def Jam Records.

Isaac was 16, Taylor 13 and Zac only 11 at the time of their debut album.

CHILD STARS

There can't be many children who haven't dreamed of being a star. But fame can be short-lived. Frankie Lymon was only 13 when he hit the top of the chart with his band the Teenagers in 1956. But at 14 Frankie's voice had broken, and his fame was slipping away. His solo career without the Teenagers stalled, and Frankie lapsed into heroin addiction. He was found dead in 1968, aged just 25.

Frankie Lymon and the Teenagers' biggest hit was "Why Do Fools Fall In Love."

OASIS

You can choose your friends, but you can't choose your family, as the saying goes. When Liam Gallagher invited his brother Noel to join his band, could he have known that this was the start of one of the most bitter, turbulent but inspired relationships in pop history? Some would say that this tension was the secret of Oasis's success.

TAKING THE REINS

Liam Gallagher formed Oasis in Manchester with Paul "Bonehead" Arthurs, Paul McGuigan and Tony McCarroll, but the band was going nowhere fast. Brother Noel had already experienced life on the road, as a guitar technician for the Inspiral Carpets, when Liam offered him a place in the band. Noel agreed to join on one condition — he insisted on full creative control, including writing all their songs. After a year of intensive rehearsal, Oasis was signed by Alan McGee, the head of Creation Records.

SIBLING RIVALRY

Their first album, *Definitely Maybe*, released in 1994, sold well in the UK, supported by

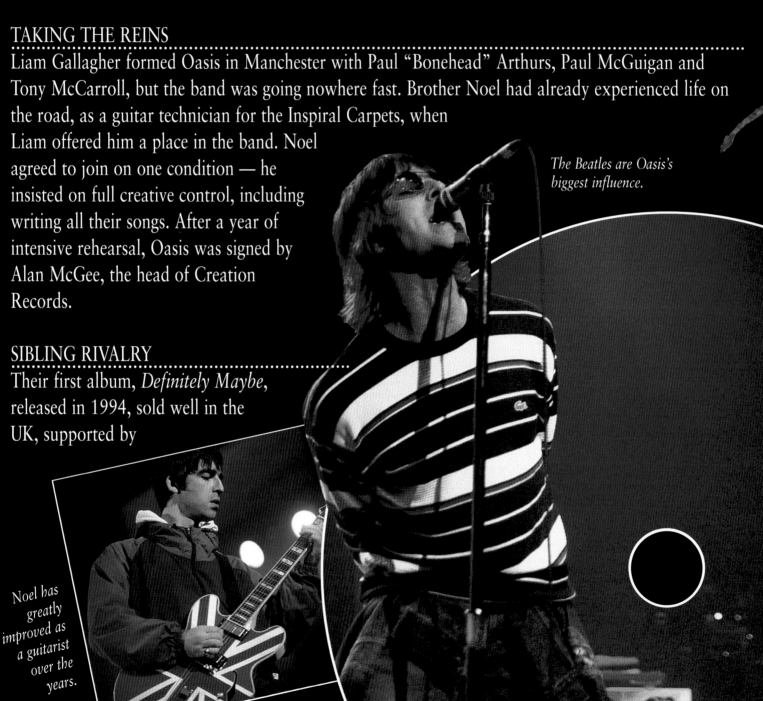

The Beatles are Oasis's biggest influence.

Noel has greatly improved as a guitarist over the years.

Definitely Maybe
1994
(What's The Story) Morning Glory
1995
Be Here Now
1997
Standing On The Shoulder Of Giants
2000

Heathen Chemistry
2002
Don't Believe the Truth
2005
Dig Out Your Soul
2008

TROUBLE AND STRIFE

Noel Gallagher has blamed many of Oasis's troubles on the women around the band. Noel dedicated the love song "Wonderwall" to his wife Meg Matthews, and Liam had a passionate but stormy marriage to Patsy Kensit. But neither brother got on with the other's wife, and both marriages ended in divorce. Noel has settled into a quiet life in the country and Liam has started a family with Nicole Appleton of All Saints. Oasis has never been so happy.

Noel with Meg (left) and Liam with Patsy (right).

the singles "Supersonic" and "Live Forever." The band was one of the only new British acts to find fame in America during the 90s, but trouble was brewing. Noel and Liam refused to conduct joint interviews because they always ended up quarreling, and a counterfeit recording of the brothers fighting sold thousands of copies.

SPOILING IT ALL

(What's the Story) Morning Glory was Oasis's finest hour. Released in 1995, it quickly became the second-biggest British album in history. Noel was hailed as the major songwriter of the day, and the band embarked on an important U.S. tour, but fighting got in the way again. Oasis lost a lot of respect — and many American fans — when the tour was abandoned, and a split seemed certain. The band retreated to lick their wounds and took several months to record the follow-up, *Be Here Now*. The album sold well, but many people felt that it was self-indulgent and over the top, and yet another tour collapsed, partly because of Liam's heavy drinking.

MATURING AT LAST

To the surprise of many, Oasis seemed to grow up in the new millennium. The Gallaghers made peace, and managed to complete a U.S. tour in 2001. They also played some triumphant shows at home to celebrate the 10th anniversary of the band (even though Noel and Liam are now the only original members). Despite a number of lineup changes, the band continues to record and tour, releasing *Don't Believe the Truth* in 2005 and *Dig Out Your Soul* in 2008.

PULP

There cannot be another band in chart history that has taken so long to reach the top. For the first 12 years of their existence, Pulp remained in almost total obscurity, until the music press picked up on an independent single and the band was hailed an overnight success. It must have been satisfying for Jarvis Cocker, the only band member to hang on since Pulp's first gig in 1978.

FALSE START

Cocker founded Arabicus Pulp at school, and after a handful of shows he shortened the band's name and arranged a recording session. The results impressed BBC Radio 1 DJ John Peel, and he invited Pulp to perform on his show. Instead of the session leading to a record deal and instant stardom, Pulp's appearance led nowhere. The entire band abandoned Cocker in 1982.

Different Class entered the UK chart at number one.

FALL FROM GRACE

Cocker formed a new Pulp at university and, at last, he landed a record deal in 1984. But the album, *It*, wasn't a success, and the band was rearranged once more. Cocker was badly injured in 1985, when he fell from a balcony, while trying to impress a girl, and Pulp floundered once more.

Pulp were influenced by David Bowie and Roxy Music.

THE FESTIVAL SCENE

Pulp sealed its success at the 1995 Glastonbury rock festival in Southwest England. The band accepted a headlining slot when the Stone Roses were forced to pull out at the last minute. Pulp was enthusiastically greeted by the crowd, and Cocker turned out an amazing performance. Glastonbury has been taking place most summers since the 1970s and attracts huge numbers of fans, who come from all over the world to see new and established acts.

Glastonbury is famous for its happy atmosphere.

Separations
1992
His 'n' Hers
1994

Different Class
1995
This Is Hardcore
1998
We Love Life
2001

FAME AT LAST

Cocker found a soulmate in Russell Senior, and the two of them developed the band while Cocker studied filmmaking. An album recorded in 1989, *Separations*, was finally released three years later, and the press picked up on the single "My Legendary Girlfriend." A major record deal followed with Island, and Pulp started to sell serious amounts of records in the UK. The hits kept on coming throughout the late '90s — the singles "Babies" and "Common People" and the albums *His 'n' Hers*, *Different Class* and *This Is Hardcore*. The gangly Cocker suddenly found himself an unlikely pinup and a popular contributor to British TV talk shows and game shows. But Cocker is also a serious and thoughtful songwriter, and one of the true originals to emerge from the 90s Britpop scene. It was worth the wait!

R.E.M.

Warner Brothers had high hopes for R.E.M. at the beginning of the 1990s. Bill Berry, Peter Buck, Mike Mills and Michael Stipe had been playing together for a decade to steadily larger audiences, and their album, *Green*, had sold well. Most bands would have hit the road, but not R.E.M.

Murmur 1983
Reckoning 1984
Fables of the Reconstruction 1985
Life's Rich Pageant 1986
Document 1987
Green 1988
Out of Time 1991

Automatic for the People 1992
Monster 1994
New Adventures in Hi-Fi 1996
Up 1998
Reveal 2001
Around the Sun 2004
Accelerate 2008

OUT OF BREATH

After releasing five independent albums, R.E.M. signed to Warner Brothers in 1988 for a reputed seven-figure sum. But eight years of non-stop touring had left the band exhausted, and R.E.M. firmly refused to go on the road to promote its 1991 album, *Out of Time*. Despite this, the album entered the UK and U.S. charts at number one, and the singles "Radio Song," "Shiny, Happy People" and "Losing My Religion" became anthems for the new decade. Michael Stipe's pure vocals and Peter Buck's jangly guitar and mandolin dominated the album, which included fine songwriting contributions from the whole band.

CAREER HIGH

Many critics regard *Automatic for the People* as R.E.M.'s greatest album, and it was another huge hit, although the band still refused to go on tour. The singles "Drive" and "Man On The Moon" cemented R.E.M.'s reputation as the most radio-friendly band of the decade, but they changed their sound radically for the next album, *Monster*.

R.E.M. formed in the college town of Athens, Georgia.

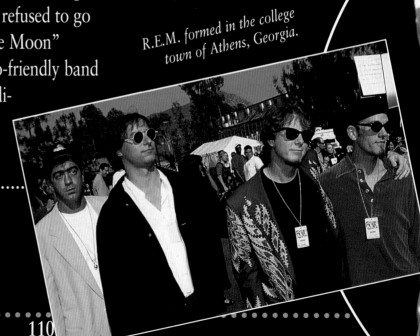

ONE THING AFTER ANOTHER

The album was heavier and louder than anything R.E.M. had produced before, but it won over new fans, who had dismissed the band as too commercial.

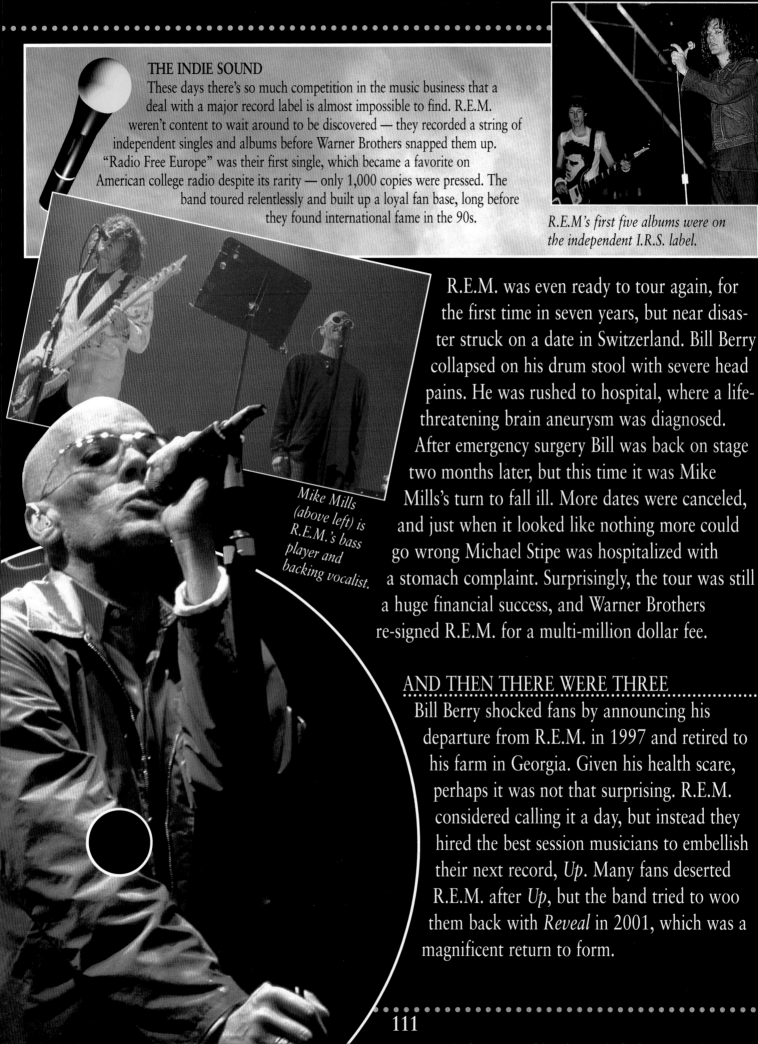

THE INDIE SOUND
These days there's so much competition in the music business that a deal with a major record label is almost impossible to find. R.E.M. weren't content to wait around to be discovered — they recorded a string of independent singles and albums before Warner Brothers snapped them up. "Radio Free Europe" was their first single, which became a favorite on American college radio despite its rarity — only 1,000 copies were pressed. The band toured relentlessly and built up a loyal fan base, long before they found international fame in the 90s.

R.E.M's first five albums were on the independent I.R.S. label.

Mike Mills (above left) is R.E.M.'s bass player and backing vocalist.

R.E.M. was even ready to tour again, for the first time in seven years, but near disaster struck on a date in Switzerland. Bill Berry collapsed on his drum stool with severe head pains. He was rushed to hospital, where a life-threatening brain aneurysm was diagnosed. After emergency surgery Bill was back on stage two months later, but this time it was Mike Mills's turn to fall ill. More dates were canceled, and just when it looked like nothing more could go wrong Michael Stipe was hospitalized with a stomach complaint. Surprisingly, the tour was still a huge financial success, and Warner Brothers re-signed R.E.M. for a multi-million dollar fee.

AND THEN THERE WERE THREE
Bill Berry shocked fans by announcing his departure from R.E.M. in 1997 and retired to his farm in Georgia. Given his health scare, perhaps it was not that surprising. R.E.M. considered calling it a day, but instead they hired the best session musicians to embellish their next record, *Up*. Many fans deserted R.E.M. after *Up*, but the band tried to woo them back with *Reveal* in 2001, which was a magnificent return to form.

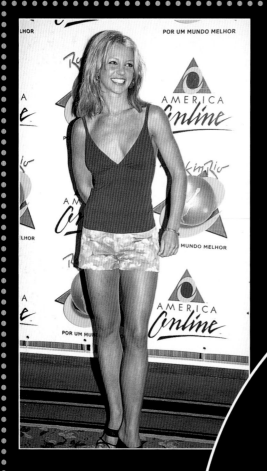

BRITNEY SPEARS

If you fed into a computer the ingredients needed to produce a 90s female pop star, the chances are it would come up with somebody remarkably similar to Britney Spears, a symbol of clean-cut youth.

EARLY AMBITION

Spears had it all. A Californian tan, perfect gleaming teeth, a wide smile, a well-honed figure and a great voice to put her right at the top of the pile. She was born in Kentwood, Louisiana, in 1981, and from a very early age she loved to dance and sang with her local church choir. Ambitious from the start, Spears auditioned for the TV show *The Mickey Mouse Club* when she was just eight years old. The producers were impressed and helped her to gain a place at a school for the performing arts.

DISNEY DIVA

The Mickey Mouse Club was ready for Spears by the time she was 11, and she appeared on the show for two seasons and featured in a number of TV commercials. But singing was her first love, and in 1999 Jive Records released her first album, *Baby One More Time*.

Spears uses a headset microphone to free up her hands.

Spears has co-written a novel with her mother Lynne.

Baby One More Time
1999
Oops!...I Did It Again
2000
Britney
2001
In the Zone
2003

Greatest Hits: My Prerogative
2004
Blackout
2000
Circus
2008

MUSIC TELEVISION

MTV was founded in 1981 as a channel for music videos. Today it's almost unheard of for a new song not to be accompanied by an expensive video, but back then videos were quite a novelty. Record companies realize that, however catchy a song might be, it will get nowhere without heavy video airplay on MTV and other channels, such as VH1.

Britney Spears has won several MTV awards.

BRITNEY DOES IT AGAIN

Britney was just 18 when the album entered the U.S. chart at number one. It produced a string of radio-friendly hits and became the best-selling album ever by a teenage girl. Spears's huge success paved the way for dozens of imitators, notably Christina Aguilera. She returned with a more mature, raunchy image for her 2000 album *Oops!...I Did it Again*. Spears's clean-cut image has taken a number of hits in recent years, most notably during the breakdown of her marriage to Kevin Federline and the subsequent custody battle for their two sons, Sean and Jayden. However, she rebounded with her sixth album, *Circus*, and earned some big wins at the 2008 MTV Video Music Awards, including Video of the Year for "Piece of Me."

SPICE GIRLS

Record companies and managers have been manufacturing pop groups for decades, but the idea of the Spice Girls was pure genius. Take five young women, each of them flamboyant and attractive in different ways, add some catchy pop songs and a large dose of attitude, and you have a hit-making formula. But despite appearances, the Spice Girls were no overnight success.

GETTING WHAT THEY REALLY, REALLY WANTED

Victoria Adams, Melanie Brown, Emma Bunton, Melanie Chisholm and Geri Halliwell were all active on the British modeling and theatrical circuit when they answered an advertisement for "five lively girls" to form a new singing group in 1993. The manager who chose the lucky five was soon ditched, after the girls decided they would rather run their own careers, and for the next two years they struggled to secure a record contract. Most labels insisted that one of them should stand out as the group's leader, but the girls rejected the idea. Eventually signed to Virgin, and teamed with new manager Simon Fuller and songwriter Elliot Kennedy, they released their first single, "Wannabe," in 1996. It entered the UK chart at number one — a first for a girl group.

Spice
1996

Spiceworld
1997
Forever
2000

The Spice Girls quickly became multimillionaires.

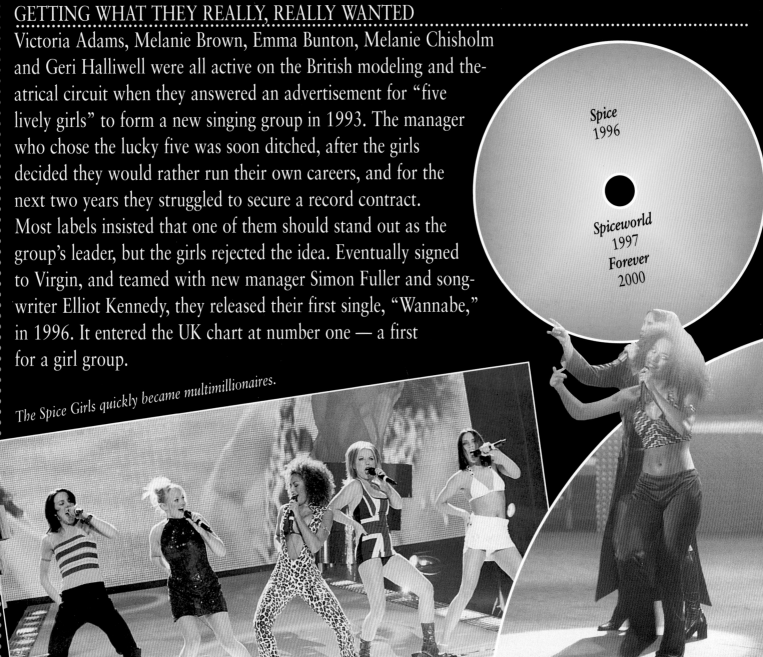

STANDING OUT

The girls each adopted a memorable identity. Victoria was Posh Spice, Emma was Baby, Mel B. was Scary, Mel C. was Sporty and Geri was Ginger Spice. The group immediately captured the imagination of the public and press alike, and they were rarely out of the charts in Britain, the U.S. and all over the world.

The Spice Girls were a major live attraction.

FIVE BECOME FOUR

The hit movie *Spiceworld* capitalized on their success, but rifts were beginning to emerge. Simon Fuller was the first to go, and, in May 1998 Geri left the group to pursue a successful solo career. The remaining four girls surprised many by opting to continue and completed a successful world tour. Mel B. started a family, as did Victoria, who married David Beckham, and all four girls launched solo careers — critics dubbed Mel C. "Talented Spice" after the release of her acclaimed album *Northern Star*. In 2001 the group announced they would go on hiatus, although they stressed they were not officially splitting up, which was indeed the case. All five members teamed up in 2007 for a very successful world tour.

GIRL POWER

The Spice Girls were as much about rebellion and attitude as music, and they were experts at filling up newspaper columns. They coined the expression "girl power," and promoted themselves as strong, independent women. The craze for girl power spread to playgrounds all over the world, where young girls were now more likely to be seen practicing martial arts than skipping rope. The group even announced that ex-Prime Minister Margaret Thatcher was the original Spice Girl, even though she was born way back in 1925!

The Spice Girls in 1997.

SUEDE

Better known outside the U.S. simply as Suede, the London Suede were forced to adopt a new name for their U.S. releases when a lounge singer who had trademarked the name Suede threatened to sue. The bands lead singer, Brett Anderson, made no secret of his resentment at having to make the change.

GUITARIST WANTED

Anderson and bass guitarist Mat Osmon formed Geoff in 1985, and though the band soon fell apart, the pair remained friends and dreamed of fronting a serious group one day. At university in London four years later, they advertised in the rock magazine *NME* for a guitarist. Bernard Butler responded, and the three started writing and recording. An early demo tape, "Specially Suede" won the band a contest on BBC local radio, and an independent record contract with RML.

Suede
1993
Dog Man Star
1994

Coming Up
1996
Head Music
1999

Coming Up gave Suede five UK top 10 singles.

SETTLING DOWN

Anderson's girlfriend Justine Frischmann joined Suede as second guitarist, and Mike Joyce, formerly of the Smiths, filled the drum stool. Unfortunately the band fell out with RML, and after another year of simply rehearsing, Joyce was replaced by Simon Gilbert and Frischmann left to form Elastica. The new four-piece Suede gained a strong reputation and was hailed by *Melody Maker* magazine as the best new band in Britain — even though they hadn't released a record.

TROUBLE AHEAD

A contract with Nude Records finally gave Suede the chance to record some singles and an album. A UK tour was a great success, and *Suede* became the fastest-selling debut album of early 90s Britain. The lucrative American market beckoned.

LOST OPPORTUNITY

Sadly, Butler's father died as the band was trying to crack the U.S., forcing the cancellation of their second tour.

Back in the studio, Butler and Anderson frequently quarreled, and Butler left the band near the end of the sessions for *Dog Man Star*.

Brett Anderson is a provocative and suggestive performer.

THE SMITHS

Suede took their name from a song by Morrissey called "Suedehead." Morrissey was the singer of the 80s band Smiths, who were a huge influence on a generation of British 90s bands. Guitarist Johnny Marr was also a favorite of many aspiring players. The Smiths disbanded in 1987 after a string of hit albums, including *The Queen Is Dead*, *Hatful of Hollow* and *Meat Is Murder*.

The Smiths are much missed.

The band nonetheless achieved great success at home, pioneering the Britpop sound and rejecting the dance-pop music that had dominated the British charts in the 80s.

INSTANT FAME

Butler was replaced by 17-year-old Richard Oakes, who found himself in the unusual position of having to perform the new album on stage even though he had not appeared on it. The band added a keyboard-player and built up a loyal fan base in the UK through the rest of the 90s, but stateside success still eluded them. Without those early squabbles and problems on tour, who knows how huge Suede could have been?

117

TAKE THAT

Many groups have rashly claimed to be "the biggest band since the Beatles," but Take That could certainly make a strong case for the description. As far as sales of singles are concerned, it's probably true that Take That sold more than any English act since the 60s. The group fired up hysteria among their teenage fans that is rarely seen — and made some great music too.

FIVE WHOLESOME BOYS

Take That was conceived as the British answer to New Kids on the Block, who had taken the charts by storm in the late 80s. Manager Nigel Martin Smith approached Gary Barlow, Mark Owen and Robbie Williams, who sang together in the Cutest Rush, and teamed them with break-dancers Howard Donald and Jason Orange to form Take That in 1990. An independent single "Do What U Like," accompanied by a raunchy video launched the group in 1991.

SOLO SUCCESS

No one pinned much hope on Robbie Williams's chances of success after he left Take That. His weight ballooned, and he has talked openly about his problems with drugs and alcohol at the time. But Williams made an astonishing comeback in the late 90s. He captured the hearts of the British people and sold millions of copies of his singles "Angels," "Millennium" and "Rock DJ," and his albums *The Ego Has Landed* and *Sing When You're Winning*.

Robbie Williams is one of the most talented singers in Britain, but he has yet to make it in America.

BACK FOR GOOD

Take That's early singles were mostly cover versions, but the need for new material prompted Gary Barlow to start writing himself. "Back for Good" was a sensitive ballad, which won acclaim from fans and critics.

Take That and Party
1992
Everything Changes
1993

Nobody Else
1995
Greatest Hits
1996

REBEL

Barlow's songwriting skills set him apart from the rest of the band, and rumors of a split started to take hold. Williams, long held to be the "bad boy" of the band, was noticeably quiet on their third album and departed in 1995. He threw himself into a life of partying and heavy drinking, and he was widely dismissed as a has-been by critics. He would prove them wrong.

GONE FOR GOOD

Ironically, the band was unraveling just as "Back For Good" was giving them long-awaited American success. Take That disbanded in February 1996. However, Barlow's solo career never really took off, and the band, minus Robbie Williams, reunited with a new album and tour in 2006. They released another new album in 2008.

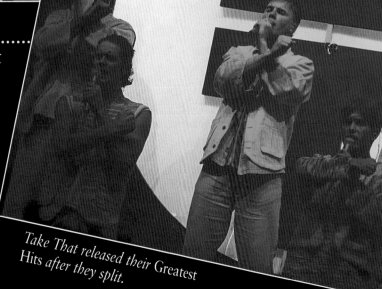

Take That released their Greatest Hits after they split.

GAZETTEER

At the start of the 1990s there was a lot of pessimism about the future of pop music. The newspapers were full of stories about how youngsters no longer listened to records, preferring computer games instead. But good music never goes out of fashion, and the following acts helped to keep it alive.

Supergrass formed in Oxford, England.

Sharleen Spiteri of Texas was once a hairdresser.

TALENTED TRIO

Supergrass were the sound of the summer of 95 in the UK, with their top three hit "Alright." This pop song never hinted at the group's heavy sound on the albums *I Should Coco* and *In It for the Money*.

The Scottish band Texas was in the doldrums for years after their 1989 hit "I Don't Want a Lover," but singer Sharleen Spiteri was determined to return to the top. She enjoyed a remarkable comeback with *White on Blonde* in 1997, and Texas became one of Britain's top bands. Echobelly was formed in 1992. The band was touted as another Oasis after their debut album in 1994, but legal problems stalled their career in 1997, and everything went quiet.

Christina Aguilera performed for President Clinton.

Echobelly were part of the Britpop scene.

BOY BANDS

Two American boy bands battled for chart supremacy during the 90s: the Backstreet Boys and N'Sync. The Backstreet Boys' first album sold 13 million copies, and their second sold more than a million in in its first week.

The London Suede supported Dolores O'Riordan (right) and the Cranberries on a U.S. tour.

Backstreet Boys were named best newcomers of 1995.

GIRL POWER

Salt 'n' Pepa were the biggest female hip-hop group of the decade. They hit number one in 1994 with their third album *Very Necessary*. Dolores O'Riordan fronted the Cranberries from Ireland, who became one of the most popular acts in the U.S. after they released "Linger," taken from their first album in 1993. B*Witched, also from Ireland, were the youngest girl group to hit number one. And Christina Aguilera challenged Britney Spears for the title of top teen pop diva.

Salt 'n' Pepa won numerous awards.

*B*Witched were Ireland's biggest girl group.*

Blues

CONTENTS

On these disks is a selection of the artist's recordings. Many of these albums are now available on CD and MP3. If they are not, many of the tracks from them can be found on compilations.

These boxes give you extra information about the artists and their times.

Some contain anecdotes about the artists themselves or about the people who helped their careers or, occasionally, about those who exploited them.

Others provide historical facts about the music, lifestyle, fans, fads and fashions of the day.

Blues star Bo Diddley with his unique box-shaped guitar.

INTRODUCTION

Blues has been entertaining and inspiring listeners for just under a century. Its roots can be traced back to the 1920s and 30s in the Deep South. The African-American population still suffered terrible deprivation and savage racism, despite the fact that slavery had been abolished several decades before.

In earlier times exhausted slaves would comfort themselves by expressing their feelings in music. Farm laborers would often sing songs to the rhythm of their back-breaking tasks to help them cope with the tedium of the work. Rare free time was enlivened by social gatherings, where workers could relax by eating, drinking and entertaining one another with sorrowful songs, bewailing their fate.

However, by the 1930s and 40s, many talented performers had decided that there might be an audience for their music in the big cities. Musicians such as John Lee Hooker, Elmore James, Muddy Waters, Howlin' Wolf, Bo Diddley, Little Walter, B.B. King and hundreds more made the trip to Chicago or Memphis. The lucky ones were rewarded with fame, if not great fortune. The message spread to Europe, and blues music influenced a whole host of bands and musicians in the 1960s. The Rolling Stones, the Yardbirds, Fleetwood Mac, Eric Clapton, Led Zeppelin and the Who all acknowledged their American blues heroes. This support from the most popular musicians of the day encouraged millions of young listeners to explore authentic blues — many first-generation blues musicians suddenly started enjoying the success they had deserved for years.

It's important to remember that blues music is still with us today, kept alive in clubs and concert halls all over the world. Support and enjoy it!

Huddie "Leadbelly" Ledbetter was discovered in prison by Alan Lomax (see page 145), while serving a sentence for murder. He managed to sing his way out by writing a song for the governor of Texas, pleading for a pardon. He repeated this feat a few years later in a Louisiana prison!

BIG BILL BROONZY

Big Bill Broonzy was born in Mississippi in 1893. Brought up in a farming community, he endured segregation, racism and poverty, but he discovered that he could express his feelings in music in a powerful and moving way. Broonzy's first instrument was the violin, but he soon found that he could write and accompany himself more successfully on the guitar.

The Young Big Bill Broonzy
1991

Where The Blues Began
2000 (recorded 1928–46)

WARTIME

Big Bill Broonzy's army service in France during World War One made him realize that there was a bigger world out there, where black people could gain respect and prosperity. On his return to the U.S., he went to Chicago and started playing and recording with a number of contemporary blues artists.

FINGER PICKIN' GOOD

He also had a talent for playing jazz — a musical genre closely related to the blues — and by the late 1920s Broonzy was recording with small jazz groups in and around the Chicago area. Big Bill's superb finger-picking style (playing by plucking the strings with his fingers rather than with a plectrum, or "pick"), his expressive voice and his poignant songs soon brought him to the attention of ever wider audiences.

Big Bill was an early blues guitar hero.

Often known as the "'father of the blues," W.C. Handy was born in Alabama in 1873. He started out playing the cornet with touring bands, and it was during his travels that he first heard primitive blues music. Handy was the first person to publish a tune with the word "blues" in it — "Memphis Blues" in 1912. "Beale Street Blues" and "Yellow Dog Blues" followed. A movie of his life, *St. Louis Blues* was released in 1958, the year of his death.

A plaque marks the spot where W.C. Handy lived in Clarksdale, Mississippi.

BIG BILL BLUES

In 1927 Broonzy had his first hit. Recorded by Paramount, it sold almost exclusively to African-Americans. "Big Bill Blues" helped to put Broonzy on the musical map, and he started recording prolifically with many performers.

SPIRIT OF THE BLUES

A solo appearance at John Hammond's prestigious Spiritualists to Swing concert in 1938 saw Bill harking back to the traditional musical roots from which he had come. His subsequent huge success in Europe on the back of that "country blues boy" image tended to obscure the wide and diverse contribution he made to the blues. He wrote many classic songs, including "Key to the Highway," "All by Myself" and "Wee Wee Hours" which would later be recorded by major blues artists.

Big Bill died in 1958, just as his music was being discovered by young white musicians.

ALBERT COLLINS

Albert Collins was brought up in Texas and started his musical career there, playing keyboards in the late 1960s. He relocated to California, switched to guitar and teamed up with the renowned American blues/rock band Canned Heat, and made several albums.

Ice Pickin'
1978

Showdown
1985,
with Robert Cray and Johnny Copeland
Deluxe Edition
1997

ICE COOL
Going solo, Collins developed his trademark "ice cool" guitar style — every album title reflected this theme: *Frostbite*, *Frozen Alive*, *Cold Snap* and *Ice Man*, for example.

LIVE AID
Collins's career continued to flourish through the 1970s, 80s and 90s. He recorded and toured relentlessly, often in collaboration with other blues stars, such as John Lee Hooker and B.B. King. In 1985 Collins played before the biggest audience of his life — he was one of the few blues musicians to be invited to play at the monumental Live Aid charity concert. His performance with slide guitar hero George Thorogood was seen by a TV audience of two billion.

Unusually, Collins hangs his guitar over his right shoulder.

ROBERT CRAY

Robert Cray was born in Georgia, but he spent most of his childhood accompanying his military family all over the United States and Germany. Growing up in the 1960s, Cray listened to a huge number of rock, blues and soul artists. He would skillfully weave all those diverse influences into his later work.

Robert Cray playing the ever-popular Fender Stratocaster guitar.

Many critics think that Cray is more accomplished on stage than on record.

FATE LENDS A HAND

Cray was a huge fan of Albert Collins, and fate intervened when Collins played at Cray's high school prom. Cray was bowled over by Collins's precise, ice-pickin' style, and along with his friend bass player Richard Cousins he talked his way into the Albert Collins band. Cray learned a great deal from Collins over the next two years, and Collins much appreciated Cray's beautiful, soul-tinged voice.

SOLO SUCCESS

Cray went solo in 1975 — his album *Strong Persuader* is one of the biggest-selling blues albums ever. He and Collins joined forces again in 1985 for a monster album, *Showdown*.

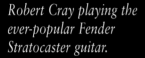

Who's Been Talkin'
1980
Strong Persuader
1986

Don't Be Afraid of the Dark
1988
Take Your Shoes Off
1999

BUDDY GUY

Legend has it that when George "Buddy" Guy made the trek to Chicago in search of fame and fortune, times were so hard that he practically starved to death. However, blues star Muddy Waters heard about his skills, gave him food to eat and helped to start his long career.

EARLY YEARS

Guy was born in 1936 in Louisiana. Like so many bluesmen before him, he was brought up in a farming community. He roamed around the South before making the move to the home of urban blues, Chicago, Illinois.

THE CHESS YEARS

Eventually he was signed to Leonard Chess's label. As he searched for his own voice, he developed a high-energy, heavy version of the blues.

Buddy Guy started out as a sideman for other musicians.

Guy was cautious during his stint with Chess, hanging on to his day job. This was a wise move because his career was slow to blossom, but he was persistent, optimistic and worked hard at his craft.

130

Buddy Guy in concert at London's Royal Festival Hall.

The Complete Chess Studio Recordings
1992, recorded 1960–67
Damn Right, I've Got The Blues
1991

Buddy's Blues
1997
Buddy's Baddest
1999, recorded 1991–99

FAMOUS FRIENDS

After his time at Chess, Guy made some excellent albums with harmonica player Junior Wells and started to make waves in Europe on the burgeoning festival scene. His flamboyant approach certainly suited a big stage with massive amplification. Things went a bit quiet on the recording front for a while, until Silvertone signed him in the early 1990s. Buddy recorded the fine album *Damn Right I've Got the Blues*, featuring UK heroes Mark Knopfler, Jeff Beck and Eric Clapton, who is a big fan of Buddy Guy. Other successful albums followed, including *Heavy Love* and *Real Deal*.

TRIBUTE

He continues to tour the world, often paying musical tributes to the blues giants of the past. But Buddy Guy is a fine and original bluesman in his own right, one who has influenced a new generation of musicians.

ERIC CLAPTON

One of the most successful blues musicians of all time was not born in the Deep South, but in the south of England. Eric Clapton only took up the guitar in his late teens, but within two years he was the hottest player in London. Eric was the star of the Yardbirds, John Mayall's Bluesbreakers, Cream, Blind Faith and Derek and the Dominoes, before he launched a solo career which has lasted for over 30 years.

Eric Clapton learns some licks from Buddy Guy.

JOHN LEE HOOKER

Along with B.B. King, John Lee Hooker was one of the last surviving Mississippi bluesmen who made the journey to the northern cities in the 1930s and 40s. Twenty years later, his music was embraced by white pop musicians, who recorded his songs and brought him the international fame he deserved. Unintentionally, he changed the face of modern music, helping to give it the blues roots that can still be heard today.

John Lee Hooker, pictured in the 1990s.

CLARKSDALE TO DETROIT

John Lee Hooker was born in Clarksdale, Mississippi, in 1920. His stepfather, an accomplished guitarist, encouraged him to play the blues and taught him the guitar by the time he was 12. In the late 1930s Hooker migrated — but not to Chicago like so many other bluesmen. He went first to Memphis and ended up in Detroit in 1943.

On stage with Carlos Santana.

BOOGIE MAN

Hooker was given his first electric guitar in 1947 by the legendary Texan bluesman T. Bone Walker. During the day he worked as a janitor in a car factory, and by night he performed in blues clubs. Gradually he made a name for himself, developing his glorious, gravelly voice and his boogie guitar style, with its insistent and mesmerizing rhythm. Hooker's refusal to be constrained to the traditional 12-bar blues format singled him out, and in 1948 he signed to a tiny record company, who leased his recordings to a much bigger label — Modern. Jackpot! His first single for Modern, "Boogie Chillen," sold more than a million copies. John Lee Hooker was suddenly a star.

FOOT TAPPER

Hooker accompanied himself on these early recordings, on guitar and foot! He would stamp his foot on the studio floor, and producer Bernie Besmen would record the results. Besmen became irritated by Hooker's habit of moonlighting for other record labels under various pseudonyms, such as John Lee Cooker and Texas Slim. They parted company but not before another million-seller, "I'm in the Mood," in 1951.

LATE BUT SWEET SUCCESS

After 40 years of hard work, most musicians would think about retiring, but not John Lee Hooker. He had his biggest successes in the late 1980s and 90s, with the albums *The Healer*, *Chill Out* and *Don't Look Back*. He was still thrilling audiences just weeks before his death in June 2001, aged 80.

The Healer
1989
The Ultimate Collection
1991
Mr. Lucky
1991
The Legendary Modern Recordings
1994, recorded 1948–54

The Early Years
1994
The Very Best of John Lee Hooker
1995, recorded 1948–87
Chill Out
1995
Don't Look Back
1997

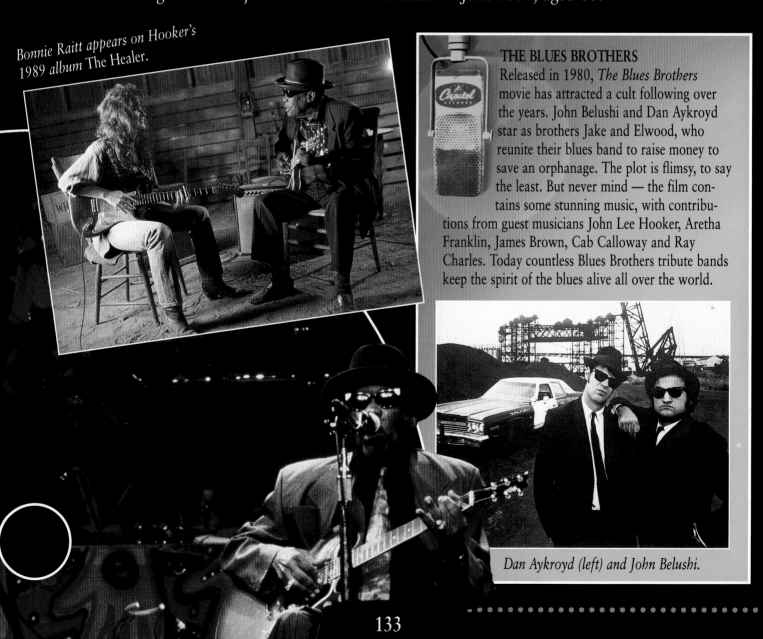

Bonnie Raitt appears on Hooker's 1989 album The Healer.

THE BLUES BROTHERS

Released in 1980, *The Blues Brothers* movie has attracted a cult following over the years. John Belushi and Dan Aykroyd star as brothers Jake and Elwood, who reunite their blues band to raise money to save an orphanage. The plot is flimsy, to say the least. But never mind — the film contains some stunning music, with contributions from guest musicians John Lee Hooker, Aretha Franklin, James Brown, Cab Calloway and Ray Charles. Today countless Blues Brothers tribute bands keep the spirit of the blues alive all over the world.

Dan Aykroyd (left) and John Belushi.

ELMORE JAMES

Apart from being an inspiration to thousands of slide guitarists, Elmore James will always be remembered for one of the most memorable riffs in blues history (a riff is a short repeated musical hook in a song). Countless blues bands all over the world have played the unforgettable, pulverizing introduction to "Dust My Broom." Many musicians would say that learning that riff is part of your apprenticeship if you want to take the blues seriously.

LISTENING AND LEARNING

Elmore James was born in that fertile breeding ground for blues performers, Mississippi, in 1918. He learned his craft in the same way as so many others had before him, by listening to the many traveling musicians who played in clubs, at parties and on the streets. Of course, to be a successful performer you had stand out from the crowd and offer something a little different.

BLUES GOES ELECTRIC

James bought an electric guitar in the mid 1940s, when the instrument was still in its infancy. He realized its potential immediately. You could cut right through the noise of a raucous crowd and produce all sorts of effects by cranking up the volume, creating distortion and feedback. Coupled with that, James decided to play slide guitar to add to the drama. Also known as bottleneck, this technique involves placing a piece of pipe, or the neck of a bottle, or one of the fingers of the left hand (if playing right-handed) to turn the guitar's string into a chord. The slide is then dragged across the strings, creating a wonderful, fluid sound.

BRIAN JONES

Like so many other Mississippi bluesmen, Elmore James had a huge impact on white musicians in the 1960s. Founding member of the Rolling Stones, Brian Jones, was such a big fan that he used the stage name Elmo Lewis for a time. Jones was himself a fine slide guitarist — just listen to the Stones' "Little Red Rooster" or "No Expectations" from the *Beggars Banquet* album to hear Elmore James's influence.

Brian Jones did much to popularize the slide guitar.

Let's Cut It
1987

The Sky Is Crying:
The History of Elmore James
1993, recorded 1951–61

Elmore James certainly didn't invent this technique — "Dust my Broom" was recorded by, amongst others, Robert Johnson — but he perfected and honed this style, and he wrote and recorded some classic blues songs, that use it to great effect. Luckily he recorded prolifically, though he never stayed with one record company for long. The lure of another advance payment was too strong, and the fact that he might be contracted to another label didn't seem to worry him!

CLASSIC COMPOSITIONS

Charging around the South in his new car and playing regularly on Sonny Boy Williamson's King Biscuit Time radio show, James rapidly built up an enthusiastic following, helped in no small measure by the release of some of the best blues records of all time — "The Sky Is Crying," "It Hurts Me Too" and "Shake Your Moneymaker" are just three examples. Sadly, James suffered from serious heart problems and died in Chicago at the age of 45.

Elmore James and one of his many fans in the 1950s.

135

ROBERT JOHNSON

Robert Johnson is universally acknowledged to be one of the most important blues performers to have ever lived. But he certainly didn't enjoy fame and fortune during his lifetime, which was tragically cut short when he was just 27 years of age.

The Complete Recordings 1990, recorded 1936–7

King of the Delta Blues 1999

COUNTRY BLUES

Robert Johnson was born in 1911 in Mississippi. From a very early age he listened avidly to the blues musicians wandering from town to town in the Deep South. This was true "country" blues — traditional work songs, with a battered guitar or well-worn harmonica for accompaniment.

Singer and guitarist Steve Miller was hugely influenced by Robert Johnson.

MASTER OF THE GUITAR

Robert Johnson was quick to learn and rapidly developed a guitar technique that to this day baffles listeners who listen closely to his (all too few) recordings. At times you would swear that you were hearing not one but two guitarists accompanying his quavery but hugely emotional singing.

The Rolling Stones recorded Johnson's "Love in Vain" in 1969.

CREAM

The leading British blues band of the 1960s was Cream. Each member was a virtuoso on his chosen instrument — Eric Clapton on guitar, Ginger Baker on drums and Jack Bruce on bass guitar, harmonica and vocals. Cream only lasted for two years, between 1966 and 68, but they recorded four superb albums. The highlight of their double album *Wheels of Fire* is a blistering version of Robert Johnson's "Crossroads," recorded live in San Francisco. Many listeners think the song features Eric Clapton's best-ever guitar solo.

Eric Clapton, Ginger Baker and Jack Bruce.

A DEVIL OF A TALENT

A colorful and enduring myth exists to explain exactly how Johnson acquired this impressive skill — a pact with the Devil no less! It is said that he met with the Devil himself at a remote crossroads, he granted Johnson his genius in return for his eternal soul. Well, you can believe that if you choose, but what is in no doubt is his enormous talent. He managed somehow to combine traditional country blues with the more urgent, dramatic sounds that were emerging from the cities that he visited.

THE LEGEND BEGINS

Robert Johnson's songs were often sad, haunting tales that reflected his restless and financially unrewarding lifestyle. He only ever recorded 41 tracks, in San Antonio and Dallas between 1936 and 1937. But the end came in 1938, when he was given a poisoned drink in a Mississippi club, probably by the husband of a woman he had made advances toward. After several days' illness, Robert Johnson died.

B.B. KING

Many listeners consider B.B. King to be the best lead guitarist in the world. Yet this remarkable blues veteran freely admits that he cannot play chords. Nor can he sing and play at the same time. Certainly he is one of the hardest working and most accomplished blues performers of all time — "King of the Blues."

Together Live
1987, with Bobby Bland
Indianola Mississippi Seeds
1989, (recorded 1970)
Blues Is King
1990

Singin' the Blues'/the Blues
1993, (recorded 1951–61)
Live at the Regal
1997, (recorded 1964)
His Definitive Greatest Hits
1999

A SOULFUL SINGER

B.B. King possesses a powerful and rich voice that might have been well-suited to soul, gospel or even operatic music. In addition, his clean, expressive and deeply emotional guitar playing is the envy of virtually every blues guitarist in the world.

EARLY INFLUENCES

Riley "Blues Boy" King was born near Indianola, Mississippi, in 1925. As a teenager he was heavily influenced by gospel music, but he also revered guitarist T. Bone Walker's subtle string-bending technique. Memphis, Tennessee, not Chicago, was King's first port of call after a spell in the army. In 1949 his career took an unexpected turn — he became a successful radio disc jockey.

THE OTHER KINGS

B.B. King is not the only blues star called King. Albert King was born in Indianola, close to B.B.'s birthplace. Journalists assumed that they must be related (particularly as B.B.'s father was called Albert), and neither bluesman denied this false rumor. Albert mastered the guitar, despite the fact that he was left-handed and strung the instrument upside down. Texan Freddy King moved to Chicago in the 1950s and recorded prolifically. Rock star Leon Russell signed him to his Shelter label in the early 70s and turned him into a superstar. Sadly, Freddy died young, after a heart attack on stage in Dallas on Christmas Day 1976.

Freddy King shortly before his death.

Albert King with a personalized guitar.

A LIFE ON THE ROAD

But performing was his first love, and it was inevitable that he would come to the attention of a record company. When he signed to Modern in the early 1950s, B.B. King found success — at a price. He had to tour relentlessly in order to bring in the income to support himself and his band. He was still performing over 300 concerts per year into his 70s.

LIVE AT THE REGAL

In 1961 King signed a contract with ABC. In 64, the company decided to record him in the environment in which he excels — on stage in front of an enthusiastic audience. The resulting album, *Live at the Regal*, is hailed by many critics as the finest live blues album of all time. King recorded more excellent albums in front of live audiences — one audience was the inmates of Cook County Jail!

A STRING OF HITS

King's long run of hits began in 1969, when "The Thrill Is Gone" entered the Top 20, and he often collaborates with younger musicians. A recent partner was Eric Clapton on the Grammy award-winning album *Riding With The King*, recorded in 2000.

B.B. King in the studio with Peter Green of Fleetwood Mac, himself a superb blues guitarist.

A live performance with Bono of U2.

JIMMY REED

Jimmy Reed was one of the biggest influences on younger blues artists, notably the Rolling Stones. He also played a major part in starting one of the most important blues record labels, Vee-Jay. Yet his reputation is often over-shadowed by other Mississippi blues stars, such as John Lee Hooker and B.B. King.

VEE-JAY IS BORN

Born in 1925, Jimmy Reed moved to Chicago from Mississippi in the mid 1940s and teamed up with the excellent guitar-player Eddie Taylor. When they were about 26 years old, Reed and Taylor went to the home of urban blues, the legendary Chess Records in Chicago — and were turned down. Undeterred, Taylor went across town to a record store owned by Vivian Carter and her husband Jimmy Brackent and begged them to help him cut a record. The results were issued on Chance, but when that label went out of business Vee-Jay was founded. For Reed, it was the start of a recording career that would see the release of such classic records as "You Don't Have To Go," "Bright Lights, Big City," "Baby Please Don't Go," "Hush Hush," "Big Boss Man" and many more.

Jimmy Reed with his harmonica around his neck.

The Masters
1998, (recorded 1953–64)

Big Boss Man
1999

MAMA KNOWS BEST

Reed owed a lot of his success to his talented and supportive wife, Mama Reed. She wrote most of the lyrics and helped Jimmy (who couldn't read or write) by quietly prompting him, a line at a time, in the studio. He achieved chart success in the R&B *and* popular listings, no mean feat for a blues performer, although Reed never received the income he deserved from his huge record sales.

Reed was always well turned out on stage.

ONE OF A KIND

It was the laid-back, slurred, almost gruff delivery of his songs that characterized Reed's work, which was punctuated by sharp, high-pitched harmonica licks — another of his trademarks. Eddie Taylor's unfussy guitar work also contributed to his unique sound. But sadly, Reed was not able to sustain his career for as long as he deserved. Like so many other performers before and since, he turned to alcohol to relieve the hours of tedium on the road.

BEGINNING OF THE END

Reed's career suffered a real setback when Eddie Taylor stopped playing with him. His unobtrusive contribution to the sound had been crucial to Reed's success. Reed was left high and dry, and he never again attained the artistic heights of his previous work. He continued recording and touring, but sadly his illnesses took their toll. Jimmy Reed died in 1976, aged just 51.

MEMPHIS SLIM

Like Jimmy Reed, pianist Memphis Slim was one of the first artists to record with the newly formed Vee-Jay label. Slim was born in Memphis and carved out a career as Big Bill Broonzy's invaluable accompanist. After a tour of Europe with bassist Willie Dixon in 1962, he settled in Paris, where he lived until his death in 1988.

Memphis Slim was revered in his adopted Paris.

141

BESSIE SMITH

Very few recording artists can claim to have sold over three-quarters of a million copies of their debut single. It is quite extraordinary, then, that a relatively unknown singer from the Deep South could achieve that milestone back in 1923. It is particularly impressive when you consider that the marketplace for such artists was restricted to the African-American population and the massive national radio airplay, enjoyed by pop stars today, simply wasn't available. But this was no ordinary performer. This was Bessie Smith, the "Empress of the Blues."

RAGS TO RICHES

Born in Chattanooga, Tennessee in 1894, Smith was orphaned at a very early age. Life was tough, but with her awesome voice she found that she could earn nickels and dimes by singing on street corners. Her's wasn't the only talent in the family. Her brother Clarence joined the fearsome "Ma" Rainey in her travelling show, and Bessie soon followed suit. After her apprenticeship with "Ma," Bessie went solo. Her debut, "Downhearted Blues," was soon followed by the classic "'Tain't Nobody's Business If I Do." The publicity she received from these huge hits meant that she could demand fees of between $1,000 and $3,000 per week — a fortune in those days.

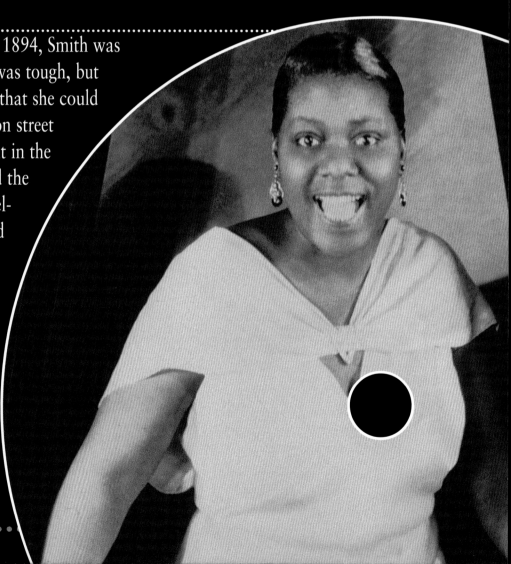

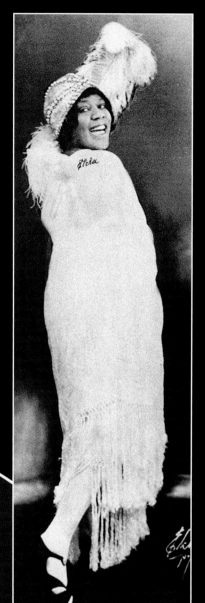

Smith starred in Pansy on Broadway.

SONGS WITH LOUIS

Life seemed rosy, and her collaboration with another superstar, Louis Armstrong, put the icing on the cake. Bessie Smith was a star the most successful female blues singer ever. New York's Broadway stage beckoned. She had just recorded the beautiful song "Nobody Knows You When You're Down And Out," when disaster struck.

THE CURTAIN FALLS

Following the Wall Street Crash, theaters closed all over the United States — nobody could afford to visit them. Suddenly Smith's lucrative career vanished. Reduced to singing for a few dollars in cheap nightclubs and increasingly dependent on drugs and alcohol, her decline was as spectacular as her rise to fame had been. But although Smith was down, she wasn't out. In 1933 she recorded with Benny Goodman and seemed to be inching her way back to her former glory. Sadly, though, Smith was killed in a car crash in 1937.

THE WALL STREET CRASH

The 1929 collapse of the New York stock market was one of the most devastating events of the 20th century. Many experts considered the value of public companies (their stock prices) to be grossly over-priced, and they began to sell their shares in the market. This caused panic as count-less investors followed suit. Stock prices tumbled, numerous businesses closed down and mil-lions of people became unemployed. The Great Depression which followed, caused misery and hard-ship throughout the 1930s.

There was mayhem on Wall Street when stocks collapsed in 1929.

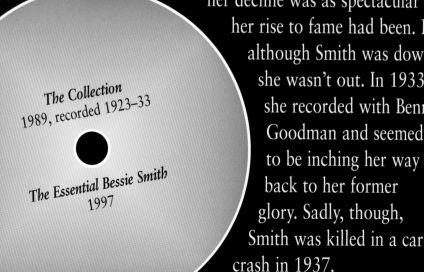

*The Collection
1989, recorded 1923–33*

*The Essential Bessie Smith
1997*

Smith was killed in Clarksdale, Mississippi.

143

MUDDY WATERS

One of the roles of the American Library of Congress is to record for posterity the history of American music, art and other areas of culture. Researchers record interviews with performers, writers, historians — in fact anybody who can help them to construct this gigantic body of information.

A JOURNEY DOWN SOUTH

In 1941 Library of Congress folklorist Alan Lomax traveled to Mississippi to research "country" blues music, which was usually performed by solo musicians roaming the South in search of a few dollars. He was particularly interested in Robert Johnson's work, and his trail led him to the primitive home of McKinley Morganfield, better known as Muddy Waters.

MUSICAL HERITAGE

Lomax immediately realized that he had stumbled upon a giant among blues players.

Waters, by then 26 years old, was a farm laborer who had been playing blues music for over 15 years. Lomax hastily recorded him on his trusty government tape recorder. Waters performed several songs, including an interesting (and perhaps surprising) song praising his farm boss! Lomax was back in 1942 to record more material, but Waters would not be found in the Deep South for much longer. In 1943, like so many bluesmen, he made the trek to Chicago.

The Best of Muddy Waters
1987, recorded 1948–54
Hard Again
1987
Muddy Waters at Newport
1988, (recorded 1960)

The Complete Plantation Recordings
1993, (recorded 1941–42)
First Recording Sessions 1941–46
1993
His Best 1947–55
1997

MAKING A NAME FOR HIMSELF

Muddy Waters hit town and started a day job driving a truck. By night he played in clubs and at parties, powerfully accompanying himself on amplified slide guitar. He worked for a while with Big Bill Broonzy and quickly established a reputation around town. Waters also met bass player and songwriter Willie Dixon, who would have a huge influence on his career.

Waters quickly came to the notice of Leonard Chess, owner of the Chess label, and his career took off.

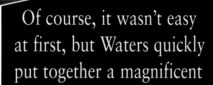

Waters and his Fender Telecaster electric guitar.

ALAN LOMAX

Alan Lomax is one of the great unsung heroes of modern music. He recorded Mississippi blues at its most raw and saved its traditions from being lost forever. Without Lomax's detective-work there might have been no blues explosion in the 1960s, no Beatles or Rolling Stones and, in turn, most of the pop acts of today would not exist.

Alan Lomax — savior of the blues.

Muddy Waters in performance in the 1970s.

Of course, it wasn't easy at first, but Waters quickly put together a magnificent band, featuring Dixon, Little Walter on harmonica and Otis Spann on piano. Dixon wrote many songs for Waters that would become classics of the genre — "Hoochie Coochie Man," "I Just Want to Make Love to You" and a blues anthem if ever there was one, "I've Got My Mojo Working."

AN IDOL TO YOUNGER MUSICIANS

By the 1970s Muddy Waters and his band were international stars, and Waters loved every minute of it. His recording career was given some much-needed help by guitarist Johnny Winter, who enthusiastically produced some stunning albums with Waters on the Blue Sky label, featuring some wonderful rerecordings of his previous hits. In 1981 Waters was joined on stage by the Rolling Stones, who took their name from his first Chess single, "Rollin' Stone." Waters died in 1983, and the world lost one of the greatest blues performers of all time.

SONNY BOY WILLIAMSON

The first question must be "Which one?" There were two harmonica players who used the name, both talented in their different ways. Let's start with Sonny Boy Williamson I.

The first Sonny Boy Williamson.

Sonny Boy Williamson I:
The Bluebird Recordings 1937–38
1996
Shake the Boogie
1999 (recorded 1937–47)

Sonny Boy Williamson II:
Down and Out Blues
1988 (recorded 1955–58)
King Biscuit Time
1989 (recorded 1951–65)
Goin in Your Direction 1994
His Best 1997

Sonny Boy Williamson II had a moody personality.

HARP HERO

His real name was John Lee Williamson. Born in Jackson, Tennessee, in 1914, he moved to Memphis in his 20s. The harmonica was not yet accepted as a credible lead instrument in blues ensembles, playing more of a supporting role for frontline performers. But Williamson wanted to thrust his harp to the forefront, and he vigorously developed his own technique, playing melody lines and sophisticated solos.

Sonny Boy Williamson II.

A CAREER CUT SHORT

Williamson struck lucky in 1937, when he teamed up with musical giants Big Joe Williams on vocals and Robert Nighthawk on guitar to make his first recordings. These included the songs "Good Morning Little Schoolgirl" and "Sugar Mama Blues." He would go on to record and perform with other great artists such as Willie Dixon and Muddy Waters. Tragically, his life was cut short when he was murdered outside a nightclub in 1948.

MAN OF MYSTERY

The second Sonny Boy Williamson's real name could have been Rice Miller or Alex Ford or Willie Williams — take your pick! Nobody knows where or when he was born, but we do know that by 1930 he was working as a musician under the name Little Boy Blue and that he probably played with Robert Johnson. When the first Sonny Boy was murdered, he took his name, claiming to be "the original Sonny Boy." Although his fellow musicians still referred to him as Rice Miller, nobody else seemed to notice!

FATHER FIGURE

Sonny Boy enjoyed his greatest successes in the 1960s, when he went to Britain and bands such as the Animals and the Yardbirds fell over themselves to play with him. He died in 1965, the last link between ancient and modern blues.

BLUES HARP

There can't be many blues singers who don't also play the harmonica, or harp. Howlin' Wolf, Jimmy Reed and rock musicians, such as Robert Plant of Led Zeppelin and Mick Jagger of the Rolling Stones, have all complemented their vocals with the harp. It has always been a popular instrument amongst blues singers – it's cheap and portable – but don't let anyone tell you it's easy to master. Both Sonny Boy Williamsons, for example, spent years practising and perfecting their style.

Robert Plant on the harp.

Sonny Boy Williamson II (center) was a regular on the King Biscuit Time radio show in the 40s.

HOWLIN' WOLF

Howlin' Wolf didn't get his nickname without good reason — a feature of his awesome singing style was his howling, just like an injured, angry wolf! He could be terrifying to watch. He was a huge man, aggression was never far from the surface, and woe betide any sideman or audience member who crossed him. You didn't argue with the Wolf — one look at those fists, the size of small hams, would frighten the most courageous critic.

THE SINGING FARMER

Chester Arthur Burnett was born in 1910 in West Point, Mississippi, a small farming community. Indeed, although he played with Robert Johnson and Sonny Boy Williamson II from his late teens, he remained a farmer until around 1940, and he never did learn to read, write or count. Like B.B. King, Howlin' Wolf headed to Memphis rather than Chicago to find fame and fortune and, like King, became a radio disc jockey. His vocal talents were discovered by Ike Turner.

CHESS SUCCESS

In 1951 the Wolf cut a record at the Sun studios in Memphis. Turner was astounded by the sheer power and pain in his astonishing voice. A contract with Chess Records soon followed.

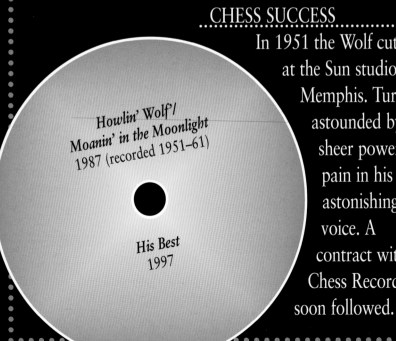

Howlin' Wolf/
Moanin' in the Moonlight
1987 (recorded 1951–61)

His Best
1997

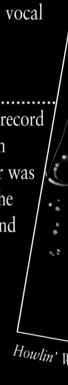

Howlin' Wolf was built more like a bear than a wolf!

A FEARSOME BLUESMAN

Howlin' Wolf was a very difficult man to work with, but several notable sidemen stuck with him, including Hubert Sumlin and the man who played on more Chess sides than any other musician, bass-player and writer Willie Dixon. The Wolf deeply distrusted Dixon, jealous of the songwriting royalties Dixon earned from tracks such as "Little Baby," "Wang Dang Doodle" and the classic "Spoonful." It was the hurricane force of his vocal delivery, with its chilling wails and howls that made Howlin' Wolf the unique bluesman that he was. He often toured scaring the pants off the hapless young musicians who accompanied him.

Howlin' Wolf also played the harmonica.

LEONARD CHESS

The legendary Chess Records was co-founded by two brothers, Leonard and Philip Chess, who had immigrated to Chicago from their native Poland as children. They took over the Aristocrat label in 1950, renaming it Chess. Their roster of artists represented the blues aristocracy — Howlin' Wolf, Jimmy Rogers, Little Walter, Muddy Waters, Bobby Bland, Buddy Guy, Otis Rush, Sonny Boy Williamson, Bo Diddley, Etta James, Little Milton, Rufus Thomas and Chuck Berry all recorded for the Chess label.

Leonard Chess, shortly before his death in 1969.

FRIENDS IN THE UK

The Wolf traveled to London in 1971 to record with a superstar lineup of British musicians, including Eric Clapton. The resulting *London Howlin' Wolf Sessions* is a classic. His final years were clouded by ill-health and a car crash. He died in 1976.

GAZETTEER

"Ma" Rainey was a hugely talented, loud and risqué singer.

People have been singing and playing the blues for the best part of a century now, and the influence of those wandering Mississippi musicians has stretched all over the world. The musicians on the previous pages are just some of the major figures in blues. The following artists have also played a part in shaping this unique musical genre.

Stevie Ray Vaughan (right) was more famous than his brother Jimmy (left).

INVENTOR OF THE BLUES?

Gertrude Pridgett became "Ma" Rainey when she married "Pa" Rainey, a comedian whose speciality was stuffing a saucer into his mouth! "Ma" claimed to have invented the word "blues." Perhaps, but what is beyond doubt is her stunning vocal technique, even heard years later.

BLUES BASS PLAYERS

As well as being Howlin' Wolf's longtime partner, Willie Dixon was a fine bass player and songwriter. His compositions include the Rolling Stones' hit "Little Red Rooster." Another bass master was Eddie Taylor, who joined Jimmy Reed and John Lee Hooker on the fledgling Vee-Jay label.

Willie Dixon playing a double bass, not an electric bass guitar.

Eddie Taylor was one of the first artists on Vee-Jay records.

RHYTHM AND BLUES

The closest relative to the blues is its faster and livelier cousin, rhythm and blues. Its greatest exponent was Chuck Berry, still wowing audiences into his 80s, with his original vocal and guitar style. His songs include "Maybelline," "Sweet Little Sixteen" and "No Particular Place To Go" (which he is said to have written during a spell in jail).

Chuck Berry always plays a Gibson guitar.

John Mayall (far left) with his Bluesbreakers, including Eric Clapton (second from right) and John McVie (far right).

GODFATHER OF BRITISH BLUES

Manchester-born keyboard player John Mayall has been flying the flag for blues since the 1950s. His band, the Bluesbreakers, variously featured esteemed guitarists Eric Clapton, Peter Green of Fleetwood Mac and Mick Taylor of the Rolling Stones. Now an American citizen, he toured the world with a new generation of Bluesbreakers until 2008.

BLUES BROTHERS

Stevie Ray Vaughan was the undisputed king of Texan blues in the 1980s. His blisteringly fast guitar sounded like nothing that had come before. Just check out *Live Alive*, or the studio album *Texas Flood*. He also teamed up with his brother Jimmy to make up the Vaughan Brothers. Tragically, Stevie's career was cut short in 1990, when he was killed in an air crash, along with a number of colleagues, while touring with Eric Clapton.

BLUES DESTROYER

Delaware guitarist George Thorogood has been leading his band the Destroyers for over three decades. An excellent slide-guitarist, his heavy blues style came to wide attention in 1985, when he jammed with Albert Collins at the Live Aid concert in Philadelphia. Artists such as Thorogood are working hard to keep the blues alive and well. Let's hope it stays that way for a very long time!

George Thorogood leading the Destroyers.

Heavy Metal

CONTENTS

On these disks is a selection of the artists' recordings. Many of these albums are now available on CD and MP3. If they are not, many of the tracks from them can be found on compilations.

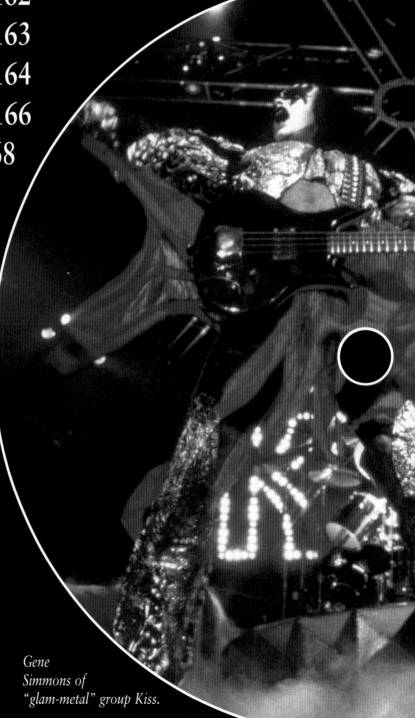

These boxes give you extra information about the music, the artists and performers and their times. Some contain anecdotes about the artists themselves or the people who helped — or occasionally exploited — them. Others provide historical facts and fascinating insights into the music, lifestyles, fans, fads and fashions of the day.

Gene Simmons of "glam-metal" group Kiss.

INTRODUCTION

Some say that heavy metal is the easiest style of modern music to identify. But those closer to Heavy Metal — or "metal" — say that it's the most difficult. So what, in general, are they talking about?

First, the name. *Heavy metal* was a phrase in a 1959 novel (see page 157). "Heavy" means the sounds are loud and deep. "Metal" is the metallic crashing of guitar strings.

Phil Lynott of "folk metal" Thin Lizzy.

Metal is usually guitar led, often with fast, highly technical playing. Songs may be ponderously slow or thrashingly fast with forceful, dramatic vocals, yells and roars.

Next, equipment. Guitars and drums are often customized (see page 167). The back line (on-stage amplifiers and speakers for the band itself) is towering. The public address (sound system for the audience) is mountainous. Power = volume = energy.

Third, image. It often consists of long hair, leather jackets and scruffy jeans, with plenty of macho posing, guitar waving and clenched fists. Some metal bands prefer extravagant theatrics, colorful makeup and glamorous costumes — or sinister darkness.

Metal grew out of progressive and heavy rock from the late 1960s, with bands such as Cream, Led Zeppelin and Deep Purple. From 1976 punk brought a competing type of loud, brash music. In the 1980s some saw metal as "dinosaur rock." But its bands and fans have fought back, and heavy metal remains popular, proud and loud.

AC/DC

Most young people cannot wait to get out of their school uniform. Angus Young, guitar-thrashing frontman from one of the first true heavy metal bands, did the reverse. He wore his uniform on stage, even short trousers and a cap! But then, AC/DC always stood by their own decisions. Their classic metal sound has endured for over 20 years.

THE WIZARDS FROM OZ

Often hailed as an Australian band, three key members of AC/DC were actually born in Scotland. Brothers Angus and Malcolm Young founded the band in Sydney in 1973. Members came and went until 1976, when singer Bon (Ronald) Scott stabilized the lineup. Another Young brother, George — who had achieved success with the Easybeats' pop classic "Friday on My Mind" — helped set up a recording contract with Australian company Albert. But the first three albums and seven singles, released only in Australia, hardly set the rock scene on fire.

Angus Young plays lead guitar.

ROCK THE WORLD

Nevertheless, the band had confidence in its loud, high-energy stage act. To achieve true stardom they decided to spread out from Australia. In 1977, with Mark Evans (bass) and Phil Rudd (drums), they recorded "Let There Be Rock."

Then, with Cliff Williams (of Romford, England) replacing Evans, they toured Europe and North America. Success! The album entered the Top 20 in December. *Powerage* (1978) did less well, but the next year's *Highway to Hell* blasted into the Top 10. However, disaster struck on February 20, 1980 when Scott choked to death after heavy drinking. After some soul searching, the rest of AC/DC bravely decided to carry on and signed up Brian Johnson, whose vocals were uncannily like Scott's.

A LIKING FOR LEATHER
The phrase *heavy metal* was derived from a quote by William Burroughs about "heavy metal thunder," in his 1959 novel *The Naked Lunch*. Soon metal became associated with other dark, strong, tough, powerful, macho-style "heavy" subjects, such as motorcycles, leather clothes, chrome, chains and semi-military uniforms. The 1970s trend towards "glam" brought sparkle, glitter, makeup and a slightly more camp or effeminate image. This was adopted by some metal performers. But the basic heavy leather look is still generally popular with metal artists and followers alike.

Judas Priest, popular from the late 70s to about 1990, model the metal leather look.

Johnson's trademark is a flat cloth cap.

Let There Be Rock
1977
Highway to Hell
1979
Back in Black
1980
For Those About to Rock (We Salute You)
1981

Flick of the Switch 1983
The Razor's Edge 1990
Ballbreaker 1995
Stiff Upper Lip 2000
Black Ice 2008

BACK TO BLACK HITS
1980 also saw AC/DC's first number one album, *Back in Black*. In 81 *For Those Who Are About To Rock (We Salute You)* sold massively, and established AC/DC as one of the world's top heavy metal bands. There have been personnel changes since, but Top 10 albums continue to flow, including *Live*. AC/DC are still hard at work. They were inducted into the Rock 'n' Roll Hall of Fame in 2003 and released an album of new material in 2008, their first in eight years.

AEROSMITH

Any type of music has its purer and simpler styles and its more complicated, involved ones. Aerosmith combine both. They are one of the cleverer, more tricksy metal bands, with lengthy songs arranged into various linked sections and rapid changes of pace and rhythm that swap keys and riffs at speed. Some people would argue that they are not truly metal. They are heavy rock, and too clever for their own good ...

EARLY PROBLEMS

Joey Kramer, Aerosmith's drummer from the beginning, came up with the band name by mixing letters in the style of the board game Scrabble. Kramer, with vocalist Steven Tyler and guitarist Joe Perry, considered two possibilities — Songsmith and Aerospace. They mixed the two and luckily chose the better combination. The band's first incarnation was as a fairly standard heavy rock outfit in the late 1970s. But alcohol and drugs took their toll. Aerosmith's career began to falter during the 1980s. The songwriting duo of Tyler and Perry lost their knack of creating songs that were tough yet smart.

Substance abuse earned songwriters Tyler (left) and Perry (far right) the nickname of "Toxic Twins."

WAKING UP

Despite their problems, Aerosmith have boasted an exceptionally stable lineup over many years. Natural frontman Tyler on vocals, keyboards and other instruments, and the thoughtful Perry and super-fast drummer Kramer are accompanied by Brad Whitford on rhythm guitar and Tom Hamilton on bass. In 1987 *Permanent Vacation* showed a newer, sharper version of the band. The same year rappers Run DMC had a huge hit single with "Walk This Way." The song had been written by Tyler and Perry and had featured on an earlier Aerosmith recording.

Permanent Vacation
1987
Pump
1989
Get A Grip
1993

Big Ones
1994
Nine Lives
1997

METAL WOMEN

The place of females in heavy metal music has always been confusing. Pretty girls have been added to mainly male metal bands for decoration, presumably to lure more male fans. Several female vocalists have explored the heavy sound, notably Joan Jett and the Blackhearts who had a hit in 1982 with "I Love Rock 'n' Roll," and UK band Girlschool. Alannah Myles' 1989 album of the same name boasted her smouldering, bluesy hit "Black Velvet," but most of the rest was raucous and metal-like. However, in the area of sexual equality, it could be argued that metal still has a long way to go.

Girlschool charted in 1981 with "Hit 'n' Run."

BETTER, BETTER

Aerosmith developed their theme of heavy-but-clever songs with a vengeance, assisted by a colorful stage show topped by Tyler's tall hat. Their 89 album *Pump* included the 5-minute-21-second "Love in an Elevator," an established classic in mini-opera format. It often appears on lists of all-time great rock songs.

The band's fortunes soared with a guest appearance at Waynestock in the movie *Wayne's World 2*. In 1994 a release of earlier tracks reminded listeners that Aerosmith had always harbored talent and showmanship. As some areas of heavy metal become musically more complex, but without losing the essential strong riffs and pounding beats, Aerosmith are elder statesmen who lead from the front.

BLACK SABBATH

Heavy metal is sometimes linked with black magic, curses, spells and the Devil. Partly responsible are one of the "founding fathers" of metal, who are still regarded as being among its loudest and heaviest bands. Black Sabbath can hardly argue against the case. Their name was inspired by bassist Terry "Geezer" Butler's interest in Dennis Wheatley's 1960s novel *The Devil Rides Out*.

CHANGE OF TUNE

Ozzy Osbourne is still successfully solo.

In 1967 singer John Michael "Ozzy" Osbourne joined up with guitarist Tony Iommi, Butler on bass and drummer Bill Ward. Known by various hippie-inspired names such as Mythology and Whole Earth, they dabbled in musical styles such as jazz and blues. But as their own ponderous, riff-laden, pile-driving sound took shape, they adopted the name Black Sabbath, and in 1970 they moved to the progressive Vertigo label. Their powerful dark image, immensely loud stage show and relentless touring paid off, and the first album, *Black Sabbath* made the UK Top 10. The single "Paranoid" from the second chart-topping album of the same name has become a metal classic.

Black Sabbath
1970
Paranoid 1970
Master of Reality 1971
Sabbath Bloody Sabbath
1973
Sabotage 1975

Technical Ecstasy 1976
Heaven and Hell 1980
Live at Last 1980
Born Again 1983
Dehumanizer
1992

COURTING CONTROVERSY

Wakeman brought the organ sound.

The Birmingham-based quartet's controversial approach to musical content, including substance abuse and mental illness, led to widespread criticism. The band were accused of encouraging drugs and even suicide. Nevertheless, their first six albums (to 1975) made the charts, and in 1973 they were joined by ex-Yes keyboardist Rick Wakeman. Gradually success waned, despite exhausting global tours. Musical differences surfaced, and Ozzy Osborne left temporarily in late 1977 then for good in 78. American Ronnie James Dio sang on 1978's *Never Say Die!* In spite of his impressive track record (see page 165), he was gone by 1982, replaced by Ian Gillan. Ward also left, and in came Vinnie Appice, brother of Carmine Appice, acclaimed drummer in Vanilla Fudge. Keyboard player Geoff Nichols, vocalist Glenn Hughes, bassist Dave Spitz and drummer Eric Singer arrived in 1983.

REGROUPING

The musicianship was still first-class, but the magic and fan base were evaporating, with only Tony Iommi from the original lineup. Another drummer who passed through Sabbath's ranks was the hugely experienced Cozy Powell (see panel at right). In 1991 Iommi attempted to recreate the band's original lineup and persuaded Butler, but drummer Ward refused. Ward also held out when Iommi, Powell and Ozzy Osbourne got back together in 1997 to co-headline Osbourne's successful Ozzfest tour. Despite their 90s fade-out, Black Sabbath richly deserve their place as one of metal's all-time greats.

POWELL POWER
Cozy Powell became Black Sabbath's drummer during the late 1980s. In April 1998 he sadly died in a car crash near his home. Cozy was a phenomenally fast, energetic drummer with a pivotal role in British heavy metal music. In addition to Black Sabbath, he played and recorded with Whitesnake, Rainbow, Emerson Lake and Powell, Jeff Beck, the Michael Shenker Group, Roger Daltrey and, perhaps surprisingly, 60s folk singer Donovan. He also had single hits — featuring massive drum sounds, of course — including "Dance with the Devil" in 1973. Powell could be argumentative, arrogant and opinionated, which often helps in the music business. Yet he could also be kind and considerate. He shared his vast experience and understanding with many younger drummers and percussionists.

Powerhouse drummer Cozy Powell.

ALICE COOPER

From the name Alice Cooper, you might picture a quiet lady singing folksy ballads. Instead you got a deafeningly heavy rock band, screams and wails, piercing guitar feedback and a horrific stage show featuring zombies, axes, chainsaws and dripping blood. The lead singer even pretended to saw off his own arm or fry in his on-stage electric chair.

Killer 1972
School's Out 1972
Billion Dollar Babies 1973
Welcome to My Nightmare 1975
Alice Cooper Goes to Hell 1976
Constrictor 1986
Trash 1989
The Last Temptation 1994

FROM VINCENT TO ALICE

For "Alice" was a he — Vincent Damon Furnier. At first the band was called Alice Cooper. They began as a reasonably successful heavy group, but by about 1970 they needed a kick-start. In came glam-horror, with ghoulish makeup, sinister lyrics about murder and mutilation and a fright-a-minute stage act with snakes and other sinister symbols. There were reports of Alice beheading live chickens (actually fakes) and ripping blood-spurting limbs off toy dolls on stage. Members of the audience fainted, vomited or walked out.

THEATER, NOT MUSIC

But the shock tactics worked. After a low-20s hit in early 1972, the follow-up, *School's Out* made the Top Five in the albums chart, and the single of the same name went to number one. In 1973 the fourth album of this period, *Billion Dollar Babies*, was a number one. In 1975 Furnier took the group's name for himself. Critics suggested his music needed the shock-horror theatrics for success. In reply, Alice has continued his themes and songs, though more tongue-in-cheek. In the 1990s he released several albums, the most successful of which was 1991's *Hey Stoopid*.

CREAM

Cream were born out of the "blues boom" in mid-1960s Britain. They took blues, made it into loud rock, added power chords, riffs and lengthy solos and helped to forge the sound of heavy metal.

Fresh Cream
1966
Disraeli Gears
1967
Wheels of Fire 1968

Goodbye Cream 1969
Live Cream 1970
Strange Brew: Best of Cream
1983

THE POWER TRIO

Cream's bassist, Jack Bruce, and drummer, Ginger Baker, came from jazz backgrounds, while blues fan Eric Clapton became the UK's first guitar hero in John Mayall's Bluesbreakers. Clapton wanted to experiment and, impressed by their skills, invited Bruce and Baker to form a new style of band — the power trio. Cream was born in 1966.

TRIALS AND TENSIONS

The band's first album *Fresh Cream* peaked at number five in the UK album charts. A furious touring schedule ensued, but problems soon developed. Bruce and Baker had a history of arguments and even fist-fights. Yet on stage these tensions seemed to help their music. The trio constantly extended and improvized their basic songs in the style of jazz musicians, with screaming notes from Clapton, Bruce playing bass like a lead guitar and Baker developing 20-minute drum solos.

But it was very short-lived. Cream released seven singles and only three studio albums plus various "live" versions. Thankfully their last concert, at London's Albert Hall, was captured on film. The inevitable split came on November 26, 1968, and left hordes of high-energy power-players heading toward true heavy metal.

After Cream, Clapton (right) and Baker (center-right) formed another "supergroup," Blind Faith.

DEEP PURPLE

In April 1968, after intensive rehearsals in a farmhouse, a new heavy band prepared to hit the road. But the members were cautious and decided to debut away from their native UK, in case they flopped. This is why Jon Lord, Ritchie Blackmore, Ian Paice, Rod Evans and Nick Simper played their first gig at a school hall in Tastrup, Denmark. Called Roundabout, the band soon changed its name. A heavy-metal legend was born.

CLASSICAL AND ROCK

That first 11-date Danish tour was a modest success, and Deep Purple signed to the Parlophone label. Heavily influenced by American band Vanilla Fudge, their first two albums, *Shades of Deep Purple* and *Book of Taliesyn*, featured extravagant re-workings of famous rock songs. Virtually ignored in the UK, they made the Top 10 in the U.S. By 1969 guitarist Blackmore and keyboardist Lord were writing their own songs. Evans and Simper departed, replaced by vocalist Ian Gillan and bassist Roger Glover. After an unsteady rock-classical fusion *Concerto for Group and Orchestra* came the metal classic, "Deep Purple in Rock." In 1970 the single "Black Night" went to

Shades of Deep Purple
1968
Deep Purple in Rock 1970
Fireball 1971
Machine Head 1972
Made in Japan 1972
Burn 1974

Stormbringer 1974
Deep Purple Live 1976
Deepest Purple 1980
Perfect Strangers 1984
The House of Blue Light 1987
The Battle Rages On
1993

Ritchie Blackmore used extensive effects, such as feedback and tremolo.

Purple lineup from left to right: Lord, Blackmore, Glover, Gillan and Paice.

number two in the UK. The next two albums, *Fireball* and *Machine Head*, both went one better. The latter included the enduring metal anthem with one of rock's most famous guitar riffs, "Smoke on the Water." However, egos clashed again. Gillan and Glover quit, replaced by singer David Coverdale — plucked from Lancashire obscurity — and bassist Glenn Hughes.

FADED PURPLE

In 1974 *Burn* made the Top 10, and Purple undertook massive world tours. But their direction and impetus were fading. In 1975 Blackmore left. In came jazz-influenced Tommy Bolin for the 12th album, *Come Taste the Band*. Tragically, he died of drug abuse two years later. Gillan, Lord, Blackmore, Glover and Paice reformed Deep Purple in the 1980s, with some commercial success, but the original fire and energy were lacking. Ian Gillan was soon on his way once more. Despite their many changes, Deep Purple richly deserve their status as one of heavy metal's most exciting and innovative bands.

PURPLE SPIN-OFFS

Various members of Deep Purple have enjoyed post-Purple success. Pyrotechnic guitarist Ritchie Blackmore founded Rainbow, whose first album of that name made the UK Top 10 in 1975. His scorchingly fast style, featuring notes from strings bent almost beyond belief, has been imitated but never bettered. A bewildering number of musicians passed through Rainbow, and their 1986 compilation *Finyl Album* reflects Blackmore's immense contribution to the heavy-metal scene. Ian Gillan formed his own band Gillan, and also sang with Black Sabbath. In 1978 David Coverdale founded yet another long-lasting metal outfit, Whitesnake.

Rainbow featured Ronnie James Dio on vocals.

GUNS N' ROSES

William Bailey, born in 1962 in Lafayette, Indiana, started his performing career at the tender age of five — singing in his local church choir. However, the church's influence faded as Bailey became immersed in the loud, fast, exciting rock music broadcast by innumerable radio stations. In 1984 he teamed up with like-minded guitarist Jeffrey Isbell in Los Angeles. The two decided to form a band. First on the list were stage names. William and Jeffrey just would not do ...

GETTING THE NAMES RIGHT

So Bailey became Axl Rose, and Isbell renamed himself Izzy Stradlin. With Tacii Guns on guitar and Rob Gardner on drums, they needed a band name. First it was Hollywood Rose, then LA Guns, but neither seemed quite right. In any case, Guns and Gardner left. Drummer Steven Adler joined, along with guitarist Saul Hudson, a native of Stoke-on-Trent, England. More name changes followed. Hudson became Slash, and the band became Guns N' Roses. With Duff McKagan on bass, "Gee-En-Arr" hit the road with a vengeance.

Slash has guested with many singers and bands. His stage name comes from his energetic habit of dashing around.

ON THE ROAD

G N' R delivered fast, loud, high-energy rock and a flamboyant, colorful stage act and soon attracted legions of fans. However, recording was less successful. Their first four-song release, on the tiny Uzi label, hardly sold. But it attracted the attention of famed record company boss David Geffen, who signed the band. Their first full album was *Appetite for Destruction*. An apt title, since the band seemed bent on causing huge problems for themselves through drugs, alcohol, sexist and racist comments, swearing and generally offensive behavior, which brought enormous and justified criticism. The first album took a year to reach number one in the U.S., although it has since sold more than 20 million copies. The next release was the live *G N' R Lies*, which captured the band's electrifying stage performance. In 1990 further alcohol problems forced Adler to leave. He was replaced by Matt Sorum, with Izzy Stradlin still on rhythm guitar.

Appetite
for Destruction
1987
G N' R Lies
1988

Use Your Illusion I and
Use Your Illusion II
1991
The Spaghetti Incident?
1993

NUMBERS ONE AND TWO

However, there were positive signs. Slash's reputation as a highly skilled guitarist gained recording invitations from Michael Jackson and other respected performers. In 1991 *Use Your Illusion I* reached number two — beaten to the top spot by its co-release *Use Your Illusion II*. However, tensions in the band continued to mount, particular between Axl Rose and the other members, who all left in the mid-1990s. Rose has continued to tour under the name Guns N' Roses with various lineups.

Axl Rose cultivated his "bad boy" image.

CUSTOM-MADE

Many heavy metal musicians have their instruments changed and modified to their own specifications, both in looks and sound. This is known as customizing. Slash of Guns N' Roses prefers a fairly basic Les Paul model (left), named after guitarist and recording innovator Les Paul, who designed the instrument in the 1950s for the Gibson company. Customizing can be as simple as changing the pickups on the guitar body to give a different type of sound. Gibson "Humbucker" pickups are renowned for their thick, fat sound, while Fender pickups produce sharper, slightly thinner tones. Or customizing may involve a guitar created entirely from specially designed parts, with a body in the shape of a moon, arrow or almost any other object. Some guitars become almost as famous as their players. Heavy rock band ZZ Top are renowned for their fur-covered "axes."

The "Super Yob" guitar built for Dave Hill of UK band Slade.

IRON MAIDEN

An iron maiden was a body-shaped cage used in medieval times, to restrain and torture victims. Iron Maiden the band played its first gig much later, in 1976. Bassist Steve Harris has recruited Paul Di'Anno on vocals, Dave Murray on guitar and drummer Doug Samson.

Iron Maiden
1980
The Number of the Beast
1982
Piece of Mind 1983
Powerslave 1984

Somewhere in Time 1986
Seventh Son of a Seventh Son 1988
Fear of the Dark 1992
A Real Live One
1993

CONTINUING CHANGES

Over the years Iron Maiden have changed their lineup regularly. The first album in 1980 saw Dennis Stratton on guitar and Clive Burr on drums. It reached number four in the UK. Maiden worked hard to promote it, and three of its tracks made Top-40 singles. But Harris was still not convinced. For the next album, *Killers*, out went Stratton and in came Adrian Smith. British fans flocked to the band's gigs, but the U.S. took little notice.

NUMBER ONE, TIMES THREE

In 1980 Di'Anno left to form Lone Wolf. Sheffield-born Bruce Dickinson took over vocals, and the band had a UK Top 10 single "Run To The Hills" and their first of three chart-topping albums, *The Number of the Beast*. At last the U.S. also took notice. In 1983 drummer Nicko McBain replaced Burr. Maiden toured extensively and between 1983 and 90, and six of their albums made the UK Top 10. After a break in 1988 guitarist Janick Gers replaced Adrian Smith. In 1993 Bruce Dickinson went solo. Yet more changes did not dent Iron Maiden's momentum, and the the band continued to hit the charts.

Steve Harris (left) is Maiden's founder member.

KISS

Kiss were outrageous and glamorous. The name refers to the act between romantic lovers, but written in capital letters, it stood for the band's approach to their music, as in "keep it simple, stupid."

Destroyer 1976
Dynasty 1979
Creatures Of The Night 1982
Lick It Up 1983

Animalise 1984
Asylum 1985
Crazy Nights 1987
Revenge 1992
Alive III 1993

WALKING TALL

In the early 1970s "glam rock" swept the modern music scene. Performers wore vivid makeup, glittering costumes and platform boots. The trend spread to heavy metal, and one band in particular took it to heart. They were Kiss, founded by bassist Gene Simmons (whose real name of Chaim Klein might seem more suited to the stage) and drummer Peter Criss.

KISS'S CRAZY NIGHTS

Kiss hit the charts with *Destroyer* in 1976. Simmons took the platform boots fashion to new heights — about 23 inches (60 cm). After moderate successes, the 1983 album *Lick It Up* achieved Top 10 status in the U.S. and the UK. Kiss took their high-powered brand of glam-metal around the world on extensive tours.

In 1987 the album *Crazy Nights* was another huge hit, while the single from it, "Crazy Crazy Nights," has become a heavy-rock classic.

LED ZEPPELIN

On the list of all-time greats in heavy music, Led Zeppelin would be near — or at — the top. They were born out of UK band the Yardbirds, whose lineups had featured guitarists Eric Clapton and Jeff Beck.

Page (left) and Plant (right) still perform.

In 1968 bass player John Paul Jones joined the band and became friends with its guitarist at the time, Jimmy Page. The two decided to form a new group.

SECOND-CHOICE SINGER

Page and Jones' first choice for a singer was Terry Reid. He was tied up by contracts, but he recommended the virtually unknown Robert Plant. He, in turn, suggested immensely powerful drummer John "Bonzo" Bonham. The band name was provided by the Who's drummer, Keith Moon, who joked that they would "go down like a lead (leaden) zeppelin," referring to the famous ill-fated German airships.

SPEEDY SUCCESS

Lead became Led, and the quartet signed with Peter Grant, a manager with a fearsome reputation. As musicians, the band were already experienced. Jimmy

Led Zeppelin
1969
Led Zeppelin II
1969
Led Zeppelin III 1970
Led Zeppelin IV 1971
Houses of the Holy 1973

Physical Graffiti 1975
Presence 1976
The Song Remains the Same (live) 1976
Remasters
1990
Boxed Set II
1993

170

The first album with a Zeppelin airship.

Page was a veteran of dozens of recordings, including Van Morrison's, as an anonymous session guitarist. Jones had played with ex-Shadow Tony Meehan and also with Plant in the Birmingham-based Band of Joy. But the sheer speed of Led Zep's success surprised everyone. The first album, released in March 1969 on the huge Atlantic label, shot into the Top 10 in Europe and the U.S. It featured Page's stunning blues-influenced playing, Plant's tortured vocals, Jones's solid bass and organ work and Bonham's massive drumming. Just eight months later *Led Zeppelin II* topped charts around the world. It redefined heavy rock music and is often quoted as the first true riff-laden heavy metal album. Zeppelin toured continually in their customized Boeing jetliner, performing spellbinding shows all over the world. Their anthem, the blues-rooted "Whole Lotta Love," was re-recorded by CCS and became the signature tune of the UK's long running TV show *Top of the Pops*.

The second album has the band members "pasted" into the photograph.

STAIRWAY TO GREATNESS

By 1971 Led Zeppelin were demonstrating a more subtle, delicate approach. The album often referred to as Led Zeppelin 4 or Symbols, but with the official title of four squigglelike runes (ancient symbols), includes one of rock's greatest works. "Stairway to Heaven" begins with acoustic guitar and recorder. Zeppelin's second to sixth albums went straight to number one in the UK and U.S., a feat equalled by few others. Their 1976 the Song Remains the Same concert at New York's Madison Square Gardens was captured on film. However, on Christmas Day 1980, John Bonham died after a drinking session. Zeppelin immediately disbanded, although Page and Plant revisited their music in the 1990s.

MASTERS OF THE RIFF

Led Zeppelin, like many heavy-metal and heavy-rock bands, based their songwriting around riffs. A riff is a fairly short sequence of notes that is repeated many times through the song. The openings of Zep's "Whole Lotta Love" and Metallica's "Enter Sandman" are classic examples. The riff is usually played by the guitarist, and perhaps keyboardist, and often by the bassist, too, for that "heavy" sound. It may be extended and developed in middle sections of the song then restated in the closing sections. In a band with two on-stage guitarists, one may play the basic riff while the other chooses notes in harmony and improvizes around it.

Page with twin-necked guitar (6 and 12 strings).

METALLICA

In 1981 Danish-born drummer Lars Ulrich and local guitarist-vocalist James Hetfield placed almost identical ads in a Los Angeles music paper. Each wanted a "soul mate," a like-minded partner to develop a new metal band which would have the heaviest sound of all time. The two got together, clicked at once and even agreed on the name for their new group.

A SHARED VISION

Hetfield and Ulrich began the search for band members to share their ideas. Ron McGovney joined on bass, but first guitarist Lloga Grand was quickly replaced by David Mustaine. By 1982 Mustaine also left, to develop his own career with thrash-metal band Megadeth. The next year Cliff Burton came in as bassist. With Kirk Hammett on lead guitar, Ulrich and Hetfield were at last beginning to achieve the sound they wanted.

Ride the Lightning
1984
Master of Puppets
1986
And Justice for All
1988

Metallica (The Black Album)
1991
Live Sh*t — Binge and Purge
1993
Reload
1997

SUCCESS AND DISASTER

Metallica moved to the East Coast and John Zazula's Mega Force label. The first albums, in 1984 and 86, caused few waves. But the band persevered, honing their extravagant and incredibly loud stage show.

Their songs were immensely powerful, dark and brooding, and they drew musical comparisons with Black Sabbath. In 1986 *Master of Puppets* broke into the Top 50. It seemed that five years of hard work were paying off at last. But in September 86, on tour in Sweden, the band's bus crashed and bassist Cliff Burton died. Hetfield and Ulrich were tempted to finish, there and then. But they came around to the opinion that Burton would have wanted them to continue.

Cartoon heroes Beavis and Butthead are devoted Metallica fans.

Lead guitarist Hammett (above) and main singer Hetfield (left).

THE BLACK ALBUM

Metallica recruited Jason Newsted on bass. He did not try to copy his predecessor, Burton, but brought his own voice, songwriting ideas and style of playing. In 1988 *And Justice for All* broke into the Top 10 album charts in the U.S. and the UK. In 1991 the band struck gold, or rather, black. The black cover of the album *Metallica*, with the snake logo in dark silver, meant that this recording is known simply as "The Black Album" (a great honor, derived from the Beatles' "White Album"). It made number one in the U.S., UK and most of Europe.

IN THE STUDIO

Heavy metal is sometimes seen as a simple wham-crash-thud type of music. But for most metal bands, nothing could be further from the truth. Metallica's founders could hear the distinctive sound they wanted in their heads, but it took several changes of band membership to come close to it. A final piece of the puzzle was record producer Bob Rock. His sympathetic ear and wide experience helped to knit together the deep guitar and bass riffs and pounding drums into one of metal's weightiest sounds.

BENDING THE RULES

Metallica went on to bend and even break a few metal rules. They featured delicate harmonies and quiet passages. Their lyrics showed an open-minded, caring approach. They wrote protest songs against political and social injustice, while many other heavy bands refused to condemn such problems. In the early 2000s Metallica made more headlines for their hard stance on Napsters than their music. Newsted left the band in 2001, but the remaining members headed back to the studio. Their most-recent releases topped the charts, showing Metallica are not slowing down.

The recording studio, where a band's "sonic signature" is developed.

MOTÖRHEAD

Colorful characters abound in heavy metal. After all, the music itself is larger than life, with its sheer power and intensity and sometimes aggressive style. Metal is rarely used as background music for a quiet dinner party! And characters are rarely more colourful than Motörhead's founder, bassist and singer, Lemmy.

A SHAKY BEGINNING

Ian Kilmister was born on Christmas Eve 1945 in Stoke-on-Trent, England — the son of a vicar. His nickname, Lemmy, came from his frequent pleas for money loans: "Lemme (lend me) a fiver!" Once a roadie for Jimi Hendrix, Lemmy was the bass player in hippie-rock band Hawkwind in 1971. In 1975 he was fired after drug charges and keen for revenge, so he formed his own band to play heavier, faster rock. The band name is slang for a person who takes amphetamine.

FAST AND ANIMAL

After a false start with Larry Wallis and Lucas Fox, Lemmy's casual friend Phil "Animal" Taylor — limited experience but the right image — became his drummer. The power trio format was completed by experienced guitarist "Fast" Eddie Clarke. Motörhead would certainly not achieve overnight success, and they're only achieved cult status in the U.S.

Motörhead
1977
Overkill 1979
Bomber 1979
Ace of Spades 1980
No Sleep til Hammersmith 1981
Ironfist 1982

Another Perfect Day 1983
No Remorse
1984
Orgasmatron 1986
1916
1991

174

But their frantic, energetic and sometimes deafening performances steadily built up large, enthusiastic audiences in the UK. In August 1977 their first album scraped into the UK Top 50. Three singles sold modestly, and Motörhead's reputation slowly grew. In 1979 they made the UK Top 30 with the aptly named *Overkill*.

FINALLY NUMBER ONE

In October of the same year, the third album *Bomber* peaked at number 12. Each release fared better until the band's second live album, *No Sleep til Hammersmith*, made number one. The 1980 single "Ace of Spades," from the same-name album, has become a metal classic. In 1982 Clarke went off to form Fastway. Ex-Thin Lizzy guitarist Brian Robertson (see page 176) stepped in. However the success of *Hammersmith* was never recaptured.

THE "TAP" ON TOUR

Heavy metal often seems to make fun of itself. Performers totter about on huge-heeled shoes with theatrical stage makeup and extravagantly customized guitars. The carnival feel and tacky showmanship contribute to the sheer fun of it all. However in 1984 an achingly amusing film, *This Is Spinal Tap*, provided the ultimate spoof on heavy rock. It is a fictional account of distinctly fading band Spinal Tap, and it sends up all aspects of the rock world. Ridiculously inflated egos, stupidly grandiose ideas, crooked managers, awful songwriting and dreadful record deals conspire to bring disaster at every turn. Like all good satire, the fiction is only slightly removed from the reality. Spinal Tap even turned themselves into a real band and toured to promote their spoof (but excellent) album *Break The Wind*.

Actors turned heavy rockers of Spinal Tap.

In 1983 Robertson left. Guitarist Michael Burston, nicknamed Wurzel because of his resemblance to the children's fictional character Wurzel Gummidge, joined Phil Campbell and Lemmy. Taylor moved on, and drummer Pete Gill moved in. Lemmy thought another live album might provide a boost, but 1988's *No Sleep at All* only managed to scrape into the Top 100. Original drummer Taylor returned and through the 1990s, Motörhead have continued their full-tilt approach — still one of British metal's best-loved bands.

THIN LIZZY

Thin Lizzy began in Dublin in 1969 — the brainchild of lanky, exotic-looking bass player and singer Phil Lynott. Guitar player Eric Bell and drummer Brian Downey completed the trio. Lynott had previously played in another Irish outfit, Skidrow. They were led by a 16-year old guitar star who would later achieve international fame and be part of Thin Lizzy for a time. His name was Gary Moore.

MELODY TO METAL

Thin Lizzy started as a distinctly non-heavy band, playing a melodic mix of songs that reflected Lynott's Irish-Brazilian parentage. By 1972 the trio had two interesting but unsuccessful Decca albums behind them. Then came their tuneful but strong single "Whiskey in the Jar." It echoed their increasingly forceful direction, due in no small part to Lynott's powerful stage presence. It entered the UK Top 10 in January 1973, peaked at number six, and is still heard regularly. Lizzy moved further into heavy-metal land, but the third album did not match the single's success. A succession of changes happened in 1974. Bell left and in came Phil Lynott's old Skidrow chum, Gary Moore. Not for long.

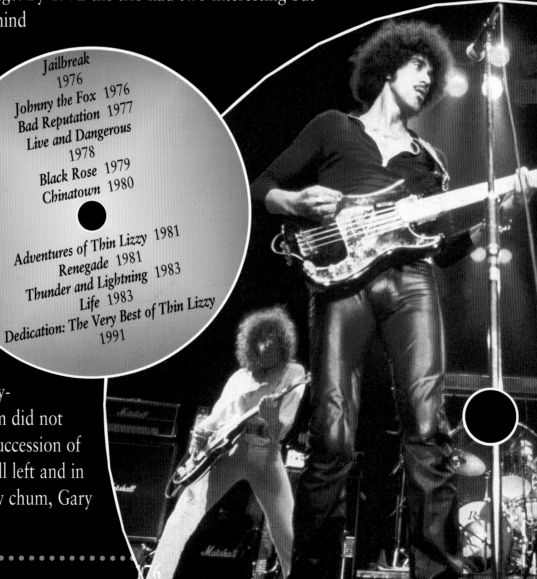

Jailbreak 1976
Johnny the Fox 1976
Bad Reputation 1977
Live and Dangerous 1978
Black Rose 1979
Chinatown 1980

Adventures of Thin Lizzy 1981
Renegade 1981
Thunder and Lightning 1983
Life 1983
Dedication: The Very Best of Thin Lizzy 1991

The band regained its balance when Lynott took on Scott Gorham and Brian Robertson as twin lead guitarists. A lengthy tour of the UK enhanced Thin Lizzy's reputation as one of the more imaginative heavy bands. *Fighting* (1975) was a minor hit, but the next one was massive. *Jailbreak* reached number 10 in the UK and stayed in the album chart for a year. In May 1976 the single "The Boys Are Back In Town" went four places better — and also made the Top 20 in the U.S.

Phil "Johnny the Fox" Lynott's heavy rock songs had romantic, folksy influences.

LIVE AND DANGEROUS

In 1977 Brian Robertson was forced to take time out with a hand injury. Back came Gary Moore. The album *Bad Reputation* got to number four, and the follow-up *Live and Dangerous* (1978), one of heavy rock's classic live performances, reached number two. However, bewildering personnel changes continued. Robertson left again; Moore returned again. In September 1979 he was replaced by guitarist Midge Ure from Ultravox. In turn, he was replaced by Snowy White. Out came the excellent album *Chinatown*, and the single of the same name gave Thin Lizzy their first number one. *Adventures of Thin Lizzy*, a compilation album, was yet another hit, but membership changes followed.

AN EARLY LOSS

Thunder and Lighting was released in 1983 and reached number four. However, in 1984 Phil Lynott decided that his band had run its course. He dissolved Thin Lizzy. Tragically, just two years later he was dead. A charming and enigmatic man, and an intelligent song-crafter, Lynott sadly succumbed to drug and alcohol addiction. He was just 35 years old.

DRUMS GALORE

Vocalists and guitarists often dominate the stage shows of heavy metal bands. Drummers are hidden behind their huge kits, unable to pose or run around. Yet loud, solid drumming is the backbone of heavy rock. Rick Allen of Def Leppard is a fine example, but with a difference. He lost an arm in an accident. However, his specially customized kit enables him to carry on playing. Def Leppard have enjoyed more success in the U.S. than in their native UK.

Def Leppard are from Sheffield, England.

VAN HALEN

The riverside town of Nijmegen in Holland is the birthplace of two of the best-known heavy metal performers, Eddie (guitar) and Alex (drums) Van Halen. The brothers immigrated to the U.S. in the 1960s.

BORN TO ROCK

The Van Halen boys loved rock music and teamed up with Chicago-born bass player Michael Antony and singer David Lee Roth as Mammoth. Right from the start they put everything into their loud, powerful, uncompromising metal music, performing in any Los Angeles venue, no matter how small. In the audience one night was Gene Simmons of Kiss (see page 169). He was impressed, especially with David Lee Roth's singing, and decided to help. But the name Mammoth was already taken by another band. After dismissing Rat Salade, the band decided that they would be known simply as Van Halen. Simmons introduced them to producer Ted Templeman, who quickly signed them to Warner Brothers. Van Halen's first album, released in early 1978, entered the Top 40 on both sides of the Atlantic. Over the following year it sold more than two million copies around the world.

THE HEAVY BASS
One of the defining sounds of heavy metal music is the low notes of the bass guitar, often thudding in time to the bass drum. The bassist can repeat the basic notes of the key for a solid, unfussy foundation to the song or follow the notes of the other guitarists to emphasize the riffs. Playing bass may seem an easy option compared to a front man vocalist or guitarist. But the bassist must stay in perfect synchrony with the drummer, or the bedrock of the metal sound loses its kick and punch.

Rick Savage plays bass in Def Leppard.

The success of Van Halen was due partly to David Lee Roth's stunning singing and outrageous stage presence. He captivated audiences with his wild-man antics and over-the-top performances. More importantly, his vocals also sounded great in the more demanding environment of the recording studio, where small variations in tone and key become far more obvious. In 1978 Eddie Van Halen was named as Best New Guitarist by the influential American magazine *Guitar Player*. But the band's early singles did less well. They had to wait until the release of their second album, in April 1979, before their fifth single made the Top 20 in the U.S.

Van Halen
1978
Van Halen II 1979
Women And Children First 1980
Fair Warning 1981
Diver Down 1982
1984 1984

5150 1986
OU812 1988
Live: Right Here, Right Now
1993
Balance 1995
Van Halen III 1998

David Lee Roth had a hit solo album in 1991 with A Little Ain't Enough.

JUMPING INTO THE CHARTS

In 1979 the group's spectacular rise to fame moved into top gear. *Van Halen II* sold better than their first album. The momentum continued for six years, with four more Top-50 albums. Only five of their 13 singles cracked the Top 20, but one was "Jump" — their first number one. The album that carried it, *1984*, stayed in U.S. Billboard charts for a year. However, in 1985 the band reverted to a trio when dynamic David Lee Roth left to try his luck solo. Next year a new singer appeared — Sammy Hagar from metal band Montrose. The first single featuring Hagar went to number three. The album *5150* (which is the police code for prisoners considered insane) became their first of four number ones. Sammy Hagar left Van Halen in 1996, Gary Cherone, formerly of Extreme, came in. Cherone released one album with Van Halen, *Van Halen III*, before their amicable split. After a brief hiatus Van Halen returned to touring in 2004 with Hagar back on vocals. The long-awaited reunion tour with Roth took place in 2007–08, with Eddie's son Wolfgang on bass.

GAZETTEER

Since the 1960s, heavy metal music has diversified into many different forms. A book like this cannot detail the hundreds of top-class metal performers through the years. Selected bands shown here demonstrate the many styles of heavy rock music.

The Gibbons brothers of ZZ Top.

HEAVY BOOGIE

The term "heavy rock" includes a wide variety of loud, energetic music styles, featuring mainly guitar, bass guitar and drums and perhaps keyboards. Texan band ZZ Top play "heavy metal boogie," based around the 12-bar blues format widely used in boogie and rock 'n' roll. Their 1983 album *Eliminator*, with their trademark red custom car, sold millions. In the 1970s British group Nazareth also played a basic rock beat with plentiful slide guitar. They had a UK Top 10 album, *Loud 'n' Proud*, in 1973.

HEAVY ROCK

More varied and theatrical is the music of Meatloaf. Working with acclaimed record producer and songwriter Jim Steinman, his recordings have long songs

Meatloaf's original name was Marvin Lee Aday.

with many different sections, changing in pace and rhythm and featuring piano passages, trumpets and even violins. His massive seller *Bat Out of Hell*, released in 1978, has spent a total of nine years in the Top 100 album chart. The follow-up *Bat Out of Hell II — Back Into Hell* reached number one in 1993.

Another hugely successful band are Rush, from Canada. They had six Top 10 albums in the 1980s. Their style is loud and heavy yet melodic. The tunes

Rush hit the big time with Permanent Waves *in 1980.*

Nazareth's 1973 single "Broken Down Angel" made the UK Top 10.

are catchy, and some have a quieter, more romantic feel. This type of music, with a wider appeal, is sometime termed adult-orientated rock. One of its most popular performers is former recording studio gofer, Jon Bon Jovi. He is the lead singer, songwriter and guitarist in the band that bears his name. Since *New Jersey* in 1988, each Bon Jovi album has reached the top 10. Jon has also written movie soundtracks such as *Young Guns II.*

John Francis Bongiovi Junior – alias Jon Bon Jovi.

GRUNGE

A new type of heavy music appeared in about 1990. Known as grunge, it is weighty but generally fairly slow, with a scowling, grinding feel, very distorted guitar sounds, growled vocals and angry lyrical content. Widely successful grunge bands included Seattle-based Nirvana, whose 1991 album *Nevermind* helped to define the sound, and Smashing Pumpkins. Sadly Nirvana's vocalist-guitarist Kurt Cobain shot himself in 1994 in a fit of deep depression.

OTHER METALS

There are many other kinds of metal-based heavy music. Thrash metal is played almost excessively fast. Death metal, whose performers

Smashing Pumpkins

include Brazilian band Sepultura, is obsessed with dying, skulls, skeletons, coffins and graveyards. No doubt other exciting, energetic "metals" will appear in future years.

Sepultura wrote about social issues in their homeland.

Jazz

CONTENTS

On these disks is a selection of the artist's recordings. Many of these albums are now available on CD and MP3. If they are not, many of the tracks from them can be found on compilations.

These boxes give you extra information about the artists and their times. Some contain anecdotes about the artists themselves or about the people who helped their careers or, occasionally, about those who exploited them.
Others provide historical facts about the music, lifestyle, fans, fads and fashions of the day.

Jazz evolved from the slave-rhythms of the South.

INTRODUCTION

Imagine if somebody asked you to explain exactly what rock music is. It would probably take you several hours to describe all the different styles and trends of the last 50 years. But jazz is even more varied — its history stretches back for a century. Jazz can mean anything from a solo barroom pianist or the highly orchestrated big bands of the 1930s to the "cool" ensembles of the 50s and 60s or the raging electric bands of today.

Scott Joplin played an early version of jazz in the first years of the 20th century called ragtime — music played in a "ragged" time or rhythm.

Jazz was the first all-American art form. It was entirely invented by African-Americans, with no outside influences, except perhaps for the rhythms that slaves had introduced from Africa in previous centuries. No one doubts that there have been many distinguished non-African and non-American jazz musicians, some of whom are featured in this book. But unlike the blues, which was adapted and stylized by white performers in the 1960s, jazz remains the authentic music of African-Americans.

It is impossible to make any serious study of jazz without understanding how most African-Americans lived 100 years ago. They were subjected to bitter racism, segregation and poverty. Through music they could attain dignity, a voice of their own and have a lot of fun at the same time! And because jazz proved popular with affluent white audiences, canny musicians could also earn a good living. The future of music was there for the taking.

LOUIS ARMSTRONG

It could be argued that Louis Armstrong was the most important figure in 20th-century music. Single-handedly, he introduced improvisation to jazz and invented many of the musical phrases that are taken for granted today. But Armstrong was not just a jazz musician. He was an all-around entertainer and singer who enchanted millions the world over. And he achieved all this from a background of almost unimaginable poverty.

BORN ON THE FOURTH OF JULY

Armstrong claimed that he was born on Independence Day 1900, a date that was patriotic, easy to remember and (conveniently) might have excused him from military service. Abandoned by his father, he grew up in the infamous Storyville ghetto in New Orleans. He was sent to reform school in his early teens for firing a handgun during a New Year's Eve celebration, and this punishment changed his life — the music teacher in the "Colored Waifs Home" taught him to play the bugle and cornet. Armstrong was hooked. Free again, he started earning money as a musician, borrowing instruments and playing with any band that would have him. In about 1917 he joined the hottest and most successful band in New Orleans, which was led by cornetist King Oliver.

Hot Fives and Hot Sevens
1925
Satchmo at Symphony Hall
1947
Louis Armstrong Plays W.C. Handy
1954
Satch Plays Fats
1955
The Great Chicago Concert 1956
Ella and Louis 1957 (with Ella Fitzgerald)
Ella and Louis Again 1957 (with Ella Fitzgerald)
Ultimate Collection 2000

THINGS "HOT" UP

He moved to Chicago with Oliver and married the pianist in the band, Lillian Hardin. She encouraged him to head for New York. Over the next few years, Armstrong switched to the trumpet and made classic recordings with his Hot Five and Hot Seven bands.

Louis played trumpet, not piano, with his Hot Five band.

There are few trumpeters who have not been influenced by Louis's unique style.

HIGH SOCIETY
Louis Armstrong wasn't just a trumpeter and singer — he was an actor too. His best-known screen appearance was in the 1956 movie *High Society*, which also starred Bing Crosby, Grace Kelly and Frank Sinatra. Armstrong memorably sang "Now You Has Jazz." Other songs included"Well, Did You Evah" and "Who Wants To Be A Millionaire?."

Armstrong on the set of High Society *with stars Grace Kelly and Bing Crosby (far right).*

ALL STARS
Nicknamed "Satchmo," Armstrong fronted larger and larger bands over the next few years to great acclaim and introduced his unique, gravelly singing to his act. By the 1940s he was leading his All Stars, an ever-changing lineup of musicians, which over the years included Jack Teagarden, Earl Hines, Velma Middleton and countless others. Louis would continue to lead a succession of All Stars for the rest of his life.

Armstrong's funeral brought the streets to a standstill.

SATCHMO SELLS OUT?
As well as touring triumphantly, Armstrong made several film appearances and had a number of hits in the pop charts, with songs such as "Mack the Knife," "Hello Dolly" and "Cabaret." Some jazz purists accused Armstrong of selling out, because of his popular appeal to white audiences, but the fact remains that he was a consumate performer. In 1968, he had a UK number one hit with "What A Wonderful World." Against doctors' orders, Louis continued singing and playing into his seventies. He died in his sleep on July 6, 1971.

ORNETTE COLEMAN

In the 1920s, Louis Armstrong changed the face of music by inventing phrasing and styles that were imitated and adopted by everyone in jazz. Many artists have pushed jazz forward, but there is probably only one other musician who can claim to have changed jazz single-handedly — Ornette Coleman. By carefully studying the music, Coleman tore up the rulebook that had governed jazz for 30 years, much to the horror of traditionalists!

JAZZ REBEL

In 1944, aged 14, Ornette Coleman acquired his first alto saxophone. At first he thought that the low C on the instrument was the A in his instruction book, and although he realized his mistake in time, it made him examine new ideas in harmony and pitch. By 1946 he was playing tenor sax in various blues and R&B bands and even with a touring minstrel show. So unusual was his style that Coleman gained a bad reputation, and in 1949 he found himself stranded and jobless in New Orleans. Eventually Pee Wee Crayton took him into his band. When Coleman stubbornly refused to play traditonal blues, Crayton took him aside and told him in no uncertain terms that that was what he was being paid for!

Ornette Coleman switched back to alto saxophone from the larger tenor instrument.

Coleman played trumpet on Jackie MacLean's Old and New Gospel.

THE ARRIVAL OF FREEFORM
Coleman took a number of day jobs, studying musical theory whenever he could. In the mid-1950s he made contact with a number of musicians who sympathized with his ideas, and he established a quartet. A meeting with John Lewis of the Modern Jazz Quartet led to a two-week engagement at New York's Five Spot Café. Two weeks turned into a legendary 54-month stay, during which Coleman developed free-form, jerking jazz, marking a shift away from jazz's 30-year love affair with chords. The Five Spot engagement saw him regularly vilified by the press and musicians, and even physically assaulted by an angry drummer. But enough people understood Ornette Coleman to turn him into a jazz hero.

Roland Kirk also played tenor saxophone, clarinet, flute and trumpet.

STILL SHOCKING
In the 1960s Coleman wrote some memorable film scores, notably *Chappaque Suite*. The influence of rock began to creep into his work in the mid-1970s, as Coleman introduced electric guitars and basses into his band, Prime Time. Even in the 21st century many people consider free-form jazz to be outrageous and difficult on the ear. Others recognize Ornette Coleman's unique role in changing musical history, like it or not.

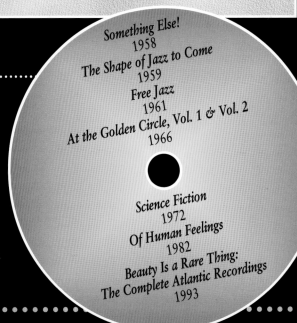
Something Else!
1958
The Shape of Jazz to Come
1959
Free Jazz
1961
At the Golden Circle, Vol. 1 & Vol. 2
1966

Science Fiction
1972
Of Human Feelings
1982
Beauty Is a Rare Thing:
The Complete Atlantic Recordings
1993

JOHN COLTRANE

John Coltrane was one of the most gifted jazz musicians of all time. He was also an extremely intelligent and meticulous student of music, religion, philosophy, physics, mathematics and chess. Between his studies, he was a huge force for change in jazz, recording some seminal albums and fronting the most acclaimed quartet in postwar jazz. He was already achieving legendary status when his career was cut short at the age of 40.

EARLY PROMISE

John Coltrane was born in 1926 and was brought up by his grandfather the Reverend William Blair. Coltrane's religious faith remained very important to him throughout his life. He started out on clarinet but rapidly switched to alto sax. After finishing high school Coltrane won scholarships for performance and composition to a music school in Philadelphia, but it was in a navy band in 1945–46 that he honed his craft. Out of uniform, Coltrane had spells in various big bands, notably Dizzy Gillespie's, and began to adopt the larger tenor saxophone. A job in Miles Davis's classic 1955 quintet really got him noticed.

Giant Steps 1959
My Favorite Things 1961
John Coltrane and Johnny Hartman 1963
Impressions 1963
Crescent 1964
A Love Supreme 1965

Ascension 1965
Transition 1965
Meditations 1966
Expression 1967
The Impulse! Years 1993

John Coltrane played the straighter high-pitched soprano sax on My Favorite Things.

DOWN, BUT NOT OUT

Coltrane's tenor perfectly complemented Davis's trumpet, but Davis was forced to fire his sideman in 1957 because of his drug addiction. However, with admirable strength and personal courage, Coltrane managed to kick drugs and alcohol permanently in just two weeks. The change was remarkable, and "Trane" was able to develop his fluid, but rasping, style. He was back with Davis in 1959 for the classic album *Kind of Blue*.

THE PINNACLE

In 1960 Coltrane formed his famous quartet, with Jimmy Garrison on bass, Elvin Jones on drums and McCoy Tyner on piano. They recorded *My Favorite Things*, *Impressions* and his finest album *A Love Supreme*, a musical celebration of the faith that had enabled him to overcome his addictions.

THE FINAL YEARS

After *A Love Supreme*, Coltrane embellished his band with more saxophonists, trumpeters and percussionists. To many his music became increasingly inaccessible — Elvin Jones and McCoy Tyner both quit the fold. But Coltrane was keen to push the frontiers of jazz. He was still doing it just weeks before his death in 1967.

AFRICAN BEAT

John Coltrane strongly believed that the origins of jazz were in Africa, and that African slaves had brought its percussive rhythms and harmonies with them to America in previous centuries. Coltrane helped to found the Olatunji Center of African Culture in New York City and played at its opening in 1967 (pictured below), complete with an ensemble featuring an African drummer. Coltrane was planning to make his first trip to Africa, to research its music and culture, shortly before his death.

John Coltrane embraced African sounds, such as the bata drum, pictured above.

Free-form saxophonist Archie Shepp (left) was a regular with "Trane" in the mid-1960s.

Coltrane collaborated with Thelonious Monk and Duke Ellington over the years.

191

MILES DAVIS

When Dr. Miles Davis gave his son a trumpet for his 13th birthday, could he have imagined that the boy would go on to be a master of the instrument and a jazz superstar? For over 40 years Miles Davis junior proved himself to be one of the most versatile and imaginative musicians ever and perhaps the greatest bandleader in jazz. And he was responsible for an album that is still hailed as the greatest jazz record ever — *Kind of Blue*.

Birth of the Cool
1957 (recorded 1949–50)
Miles Ahead 1957
Milestones 1958
Porgy and Bess 1959

Kind of Blue 1959
Sketches of Spain 1960
In a Silent Way 1969
Bitches Brew 1970
Tutu 1986

A PRICELESS EDUCATION

Born in 1926, Davis did not suffer a life of poverty or deprivation like so many of his peers. His dentist father was easily able to support his son through the prestigious Juilliard School of Music when he was 18, but the lure of New York's exciting jazz scene proved too strong, and he soon joined up with the legendary Charlie Parker. By 1948 Davis had worked with some of the greatest names in jazz — Coleman Hawkins, Benny Carter, Dizzy Gillespie, Gerry Mulligan and John Lewis.

Davis's 1968 band included Wayne Shorter (sax), Chick Corea (keyboards) and Dave Holland (bass).

MILES AHEAD

Unfortunately, in the early 1950s Davis became addicted to heroin, and his career stalled for a few years — there would be other lengthy periods of inactivity throughout his career. Back again in 1955, he formed a series of quintets and sextets, which included, among others, John Coltrane and Charles Mingus. *Milestones* and *Kind of Blue* are essential listening for any serious jazz fan. He also recorded *Porgy and Bess* with arranger Gil Evans.

During the 1980s Davis was a regular at jazz festivals, such as this one at Montreux, Switzerland.

ELECTRONIC JAZZ

Miles Davis was one of the great pioneers of electronic jazz. As early as 1968 he had electrified his band and was playing his trumpet through an effect called a wah-wah pedal, just like rock guitarists Eric Clapton and Jimi Hendrix. Davis was dismissive of many rock musicians, but he influenced rock almost as much as jazz. On his disco-inspired album *Tutu*, he played his trumpet through a synthesizer.

Miles Davis also played electronic keyboards.

COOL JAZZ

Davis's restrained and economical style was given the label "cool," to distinguish it from the pacy and furious playing of other artists. In 1965 Davis formed another fine band, which recorded *E.S.P.*, *Miles Smiles* and *Nefertiti*.

BUILDING ON A LEGEND

Davis continued to experiment through the early 1970s, constantly changing band members and embracing new sounds. After a six year hiatus he returned in 1981 with *The Man With the Horn*, and tackled pop and disco songs on his later albums. Davis spent the rest of his life recording and touring only when he felt like it, knowing his legendary status was assured. Despite his well-known health problems, the jazz world was shaken when Davis died in a Californian hospital in 1991.

DUKE ELLINGTON

Edward Kennedy Ellington was a pianist, composer, lyricist, bandleader and icon of the 20th century. Leading a succession of big bands for over 50 years, he brought sophistication and intricacy to jazz, which had mostly been thought of as rather shallow, lightweight music. Today critics often compare the Duke with the greatest classical composers of the day.

CHILD PRODIGY

The Duke was born in 1899 and had a relatively comfortable upbringing — his father was a butler and had served at the White House. His mother played the piano, and she encouraged him in his musical studies. By his mid-teens he was writing tunes and playing for a living. By the age of 18, sharp-dressed and handsome, Duke Ellington was leading his first bands!

The Duke often used to shout "everybody look handsome" at his band!

194

The Duke owed much to his arranger, Billy Strayhorn.

THE COTTON CLUB

Duke Ellington moved to New York in 1923 and soon formed the Washingtonians, who made a name for themselves in several nightclubs. In 1927 his band secured a residency at the Cotton Club in Harlem, which led to regular radio and recording sessions. Duke wrote some immortal tunes over the next few years, including "In a Sentimental Mood," "Satin Doll," "Take the 'A' Train" and "Don't Get Around Much Anymore," which influenced generations of musicians.

THE NEWPORT JAZZ FESTIVAL

Big bands seemed very old-fashioned by 1956, and Duke Ellington was struggling to keep his band going by the time of that year's Newport Jazz Festival. His musicians were in a stubborn mood when they took the stage at about midnight. Angry with them, Duke announced "Diminuendo and Crescendo in Blue," a tune they hardly ever played. Something magical happened. Tenor sax player Paul Gonsalves played no fewer than 27 solos, and the crowd went wild. Until his death in 1974 the Duke was showered with awards, and hailed as a genius, all over the world.

Newport 56 didn't just change Duke Ellington's life — it changed the course of jazz.

THE FALL AND RISE OF THE BIG BANDS

The popularity of the big bands waned during the 1950s, but the Duke managed to keep his band on the road using his songwriting royalties. A triumphant performance at the 1956 Newport Jazz Festival brought him renewed success, and he was able to spend the rest of his life working on increasingly sophisticated orchestral suites with his loyal arranger Billy Strayhorn.

Duke Ellington was the ultimate showman, even in his 70s.

Ellington Plays Ellington
1953
Ellington at Newport
1956
Three Suites
1960
Duke Ellington Meets Coleman Hawkins
1963
Far East Suite
1966
70th Birthday Concert
1969
The New Orleans Suite
1970

ELLA FITZGERALD

Dubbed "America's First Lady of Song," Ella Fitzgerald gave the definitive performances of the work of America's foremost songwriters. Countless singers have tackled these songs, many of them successfully, but what singled Fitzgerald out was the young, fresh quality of her voice. And Fitzgerald was a jazz singer, first and foremost, as proven by her work with Louis Armstrong, Duke Ellington and Count Basie.

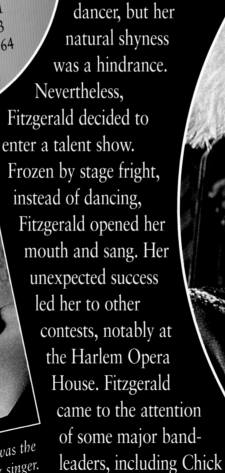

Live From the Roseland Ballroom 1940
The Ella Fitzgerald Set 1949
The Cole Porter Songbook 1956
The Rodgers and Hart Songbook 1956
Porgy and Bess 1956 (with Louis Armstrong)

The Irving Berlin Songbook 1958
The George and Ira Gershwin Songbook 1958
The Harold Arlen Songbook 1961
The Jerome Kern Songbook 1963
The Johnny Mercer Songbook 1964

BASHFUL BEGINNINGS

Fitzgerald was born in 1917 and moved to New York as a child. She showed early promise as a dancer, but her natural shyness was a hindrance. Nevertheless, Fitzgerald decided to enter a talent show. Frozen by stage fright, instead of dancing, Fitzgerald opened her mouth and sang. Her unexpected success led her to other contests, notably at the Harlem Opera House. Fitzgerald came to the attention of some major bandleaders, including Chick Webb, who took her on.

Among non-jazz audiences, Fitzgerald was the best-known and most popular jazz singer.

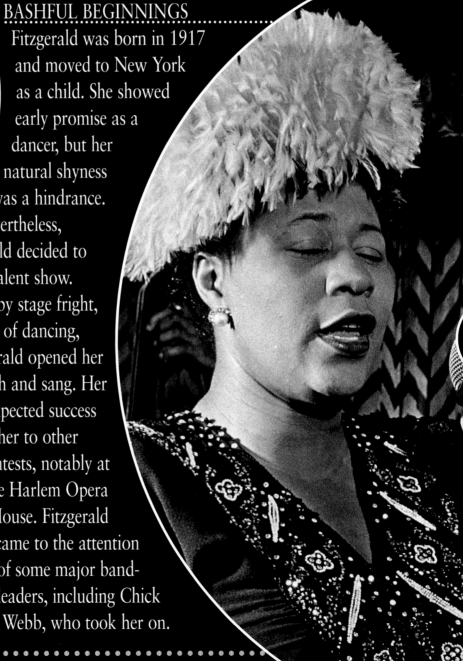

196

ELLA SPREADS HER WINGS

Fitzgerald became the star attraction in Webb's band, and after his death in 1939 she took over as leader. She felt confident enough to start a solo career in 1942 and made some classic recordings. Along with Louis Armstrong, Fitzgerald developed "scat" singing, an improvized vocal technique that uses a stream of syllables, not words, to imitate musical instruments.

Fitzgerald died at home in Beverly Hills in 1996.

THE VERVE YEARS

In the late 1950s Fitzgerald recorded a series of "songbook" albums for the Verve label, which were interpretations of classic American songs, or "standards," which will probably never be bettered. She also recorded three joyous (and often hilarious) albums with Louis Armstrong, although the straight-laced Fitzgerald did not always appreciate Armstrong's larking about in the studio!

AUTUMN YEARS

Fitzgerald continued to perform in concert halls and at festivals all over the world. Her health deteriorated in the mid-1980s, and she stopped recording and performing in the early 1990s.

Ella had many collaborators, including Dizzy Gillespie.

NORMAN GRANZ

Norman Granz was one of the most powerful figures in jazz, yet he wasn't a musician. As a manager and producer, he always fought hard for the music he loved and for the rights of his artists. A fierce opponent of racism, he was instrumental in opening up concert venues that had previously been closed to African-American artists. Granz was Ella Fitgerald's manager and started the Verve label largely to promote her work. Other Verve artists included Oscar Peterson, Stan Getz, Dizzy Gillespie and Ben Webster.

Norman Granz started the successful Jazz at the Philharmonic series of concerts.

DIZZY GILLESPIE

Along with Charlie Parker (see page 206), Dizzy Gillespie was a pioneer of a new kind of jazz in the mid-1940s, which was to influence the music for decades to follow. "Bebop," or just plain "bop," was truly revolutionary stuff. Characterized by fast and furious improvization, bebop owed little to traditional blues and jazz phrasing. It both enraged and thrilled audiences.

THE ORIGINS OF BEBOP

John Birks Gillespie began playing the trumpet in his early teens. Despite being mostly self-taught, he won a scholarship to study music, but he preferred the life of a jazzman and quit university in 1935. He was nicknamed Gillespie by a fellow trumpeter because of his bubbly character. Gillespie's dazzling technique brought him plenty of work, and in 1937 he joined Teddy Hill's big band for a European tour. Back home, in 1939 he joined up with drummer Kenny Clarke, who was also becoming disenchanted with the traditional big bands. Gillespie began to experiment with new jazz sounds, and in 1940 he recorded "Hot Mallets" with Lionel Hampton's band — perhaps the first example of what would later be known as bebop.

Dizzy conducts his mid-1940s big band, which was not a great success.

NEW JAZZ, NEW TRUMPET

In 1940 Gillespie met Charlie Parker, and they became friends over the next few years. Gillespie played with a huge variety of musicians, including Parker, until the early 1950s, constantly developing the bebop sound. Fate lent a hand in 1953, when his trumpet was accidentally damaged during a party and the bell was bent at an upward angle.

Amazingly, Gillespie found that when he played it, he preferred it that way because his ear could pick up the notes more quickly. The bent trumpet became Gillespie's trademark.

JAZZ AMBASSADOR

Gillespie was highly respected, and not just in jazz circles. In 1956 U.S. President Eisenhower sent Gillespie and his band on goodwill tours of Africa and South America. For the next 35 years Gillespie led dozens of bands, big and small, around the world and cemented his reputation as one of jazz's finest composers — "Salt Peanuts," "Hot House" and "A Night in Tunisia" are all Gillespie originals. Gillespie died in 1993, aged 75.

Gillespie was loved for his jovial character as well as for his music.

CHET BAKER

Much of Dizzy Gillespie's success over half a century can be put down to his strength of character. Despite his clowning, Gillespie was an astute businessman with a stable family life, who rejected the drug-fuelled lifestyle of many musicians. Trumpeter Chet Baker showed the same early promise as Gillespie, playing "cool" jazz in the style of Miles Davis, but Chet developed a heroin addiction in his early 20s, which would haunt him for the rest of his life. He died in 1988, aged 58.

Chet Baker fell to his death from an Amsterdam hotel window.

Live at the Downbeat Club 1947
School Days 1951
At Newport 1958
Electrifying Evening 1961
Swing Low Sweet Cadillac 1967

Oscar Peterson and Dizzy Gillespie 1974
Trumpet Kings at Montreux 1974
Summertime 1980
To a Finland Station 1982
To Bird with Love 1992

WYNTON MARSALIS

Every now and then, a group of musicians comes along to sweep away the movements of the last few years. Jazz in the 1970s was dominated by electric ensembles who played a fusion of rock and jazz. Even Miles Davis sometimes sounded as if he was playing pop music. Many fans thought it was time for jazz to get back in touch with its roots. Wynton Marsalis was the young trumpeter who spearheaded that change.

Straight Ahead
1981 (with Art Blakey)
Think of One
1982
Black Codes (From the Underground)
1985
J. Mood
1985

Standard Time
1986
Blue Interlude
1992
The All American Hero
2000
The Marciac Suite
2000

Wynton Marsalis has recorded the classical works of Haydn and Mozart.

OFF TO A GOOD START

Wynton Marsalis and his saxophonist brother Branford came from an exceptionally talented family. Born in New Orleans in 1961, Marsalis took up the trumpet aged six, encouraged by his father Ellis, a pianist, composer and teacher. Marsalis studied classical music but also developed an interest in jazz. In his teens he was playing with both a marching band and the New Orleans Philharmonic Orchestra. By the age of 19 he was a virtuoso, as well as a keen student of musical theory, jazz history and culture.

JAZZ PURIST

Marsalis and Branford spent much of the early 1980s with Art Blakey's Jazz Messengers and gained invaluable experience on the road. Marsalis also played with jazz veterans Herbie Hancock and Ron Carter, and he felt confident enough to form his own band, with Branford on tenor and soprano sax and Kenny Kirkland on piano, both of whom would go on to play with the rock star Sting. But unlike Branford, Marsalis was dismissive of rock music and jazz-rock fusion, and he strictly adhered to the "hard bop" traditions of the 1950s and 60s.

DOUBLE AWARD WINNER

Marsalis continued to play classical music, and in 1984 he became the first person to win Grammy Awards for jazz and classical recordings in the same year. Marsalis continues the fight to preserve jazz's heritage, while Branford presses ahead with experiments in jazz, hip-hop, blues and rock music.

ART BLAKEY AND THE JAZZ MESSENGERS

The Jazz Messengers, led by drummer Art Blakey, served as a university for young jazz musicians for over 30 years. Blakey had an uncanny knack of hiring young musicians who would stay with him for a couple of years then go on to stardom. Apart from the Marsalis brothers, ex-Messengers include Freddie Hubbard, Wayne Shorter, Herbie Hancock and Woody Shaw.

Art Blakey also guested with Thelonious Monk, Miles Davis and Charlie Parker.

Branford Marsalis (left, with Wynton) was very influenced by John Coltrane.

Ellis Marsalis (above left) has become well-known through his sons.

CHARLES MINGUS

Jazz is full of contradictions. In the mid-1950s bands were getting smaller — it was unusual to hear an act with more than six players. It seemed certain that the big bands of the 30s and 40s were on their last legs. Then along came an extraordinary bass player, composer and arranger, who expressed himself not through a trio or quartet but a big band — with a difference.

ANGER AND ALIENATION

Charles Mingus was born in 1922 into a mixed-race family — his grandparents were British, Chinese, Swedish and African-American. This ancestry gave him feelings of persecution and paranoia, which would stay with him all his life. Influenced by European classical music and the sounds he heard in church, Mingus went to study bass in New York.

BIG BANDS

The heyday of the big bands was in the 1930s and 40s. But although they went out of fashion, many of the big bands survived — even after the deaths of their leaders! Charles Mingus's big band continued under the name Mingus Dynasty long after he had died. Count Basie's band carried on for a long time after his death in 1984. The bands of Glenn Miller and Duke Ellington each continued under the leadership of a relative. Glenn Miller's brother took over the famous wartime band for the next 50 years, and the Duke was succeeded by his son.

Count Basie with Duke Ellington (right), whose son, Mercer, led the band after the Duke's death.

JAZZ WORKSHOP

Mingus secured some dates with Kid Ory, Louis Armstrong and Red Norvo and stunned audiences with his virtuosity. After a brief stint with Duke Ellington, he started his own record label, Debut, in 1953 to give African-American artists the exposure they deserved. In 1955 he organized the first of his experimental big bands, under the banner "Jazz Workshop."

Charles Mingus played at the Montreux Jazz Festival in 1975 with Gerry Mulligan on baritone sax (far right).

NOT-SO-SWEET SUCCESS

Charles Mingus's big-band music differed from that of, say, Duke Ellington. It interspersed intricate, almost classical, passages with manic improvisation from the whole band. He mixed all manner of jazz styles, from New Orleans sounds to gospel, bebop and free-form. His amazing recordings brought him accolades and fame, but Mingus remained bitter. He recalled how, after a show at New York's Carnegie Hall, he was unable to get home because white taxi drivers refused to take him in their cabs.

STRUGGLING TO THE END

From the mid-1960s the financial problems of running a big band started to affect Mingus's mental health. *Beneath the Underdog*, his remarkable autobiography, revealed his inner turmoil when it was published in 1971. He continued to tour, until an incurable wasting illness prevented him from playing. In 1978, U.S. President Carter honored Mingus with an all-star concert at the White House. The event moved him to tears. Early the following year, Charles Mingus was dead.

Mingus Plays Piano, *from 1963, is one of Charles's most interesting albums.*

Jazz Composers Workshop 1954
Pithecanthropus Erectus 1956
The Clown 1957
Mingus Ah Um 1959
Pre-Bird (Mingus Revisited) 1960

Oh Yeah 1961
The Black Saint and the Sinner Lady 1963
Mingus In Europe 1964
Let My Children Hear Music 1971
Cumbia and Jazz Fusion 1976

THELONIOUS MONK

Teachers of classical music are always telling their students that they must learn certain rules and stick by them. Perhaps it was because Thelonious Monk only received formal piano tuition when he had already been playing for five years that he never took the rules too seriously, playing with flat fingers, often hitting neighboring keys at the same time. But if Monk had done as his teachers told him, he might never have become a genius of modern music.

DIVINE INSPIRATION

It was in 1924 that six-year-old Thelonious Sphere Monk took up the piano. He was a bright student, excelling in math and physics, as well as playing the organ in church. It was while touring with a gospel group that jazz beckoned, and he established a name for himself in the clubs, playing in Dizzy Gillespie's big band and with Coleman Hawkins.

Thelonious Monk led a string of quartets in the 1960s.

THE BLUE NOTE YEARS

In 1947 Monk entered the studios of Blue Note Records and recorded some inspirational sessions with, amongst others, Art Blakey on drums. These recordings were eventually released as *Genius Of Modern Music*, and it's easy to see why. They contain the first versions of Monk compositions that went on to be jazz standards — "In Walked Bud" and "Ruby My Dear," for example. "'Round Midnight" is possibly the most widely recorded song in jazz. Monk's unconventional piano style puzzled many listeners, but he was just trying to force sounds out of the instrument that were usually only heard in eastern music.

Saxophonist Gerry Mulligan helped to promote Monk's music.

OUT OF THE PICTURE

In 1951 Monk was charged (probably falsely) with drug possession and was banned for six years from playing in New York. This undoubtedly harmed his career, although he did find work outside the city. In 1957, back in New York he found the public more sympathetic to his music, and his career really took off in the 1960s. But ill health and natural shyness restricted his playing in the 70s. When Monk died in 1982, he had not played in public for six years.

Genius Of Modern Music
Vol. 1 (1989) Vol. 2 (1998)
(recorded 1947–52)
Monk's Music 1957
Monk's Dream 1962
Big Band and Quartet in Concert 1963

Solo Monk 1964
Live at the Jazz Workshop 1964
Straight No Chaser 1966
Underground 1967
Blue Monk (released 1996)

BUD POWELL

Bud Powell was another of bebop's supreme pianists. He was influenced by Monk's unusual style, but he quickly developed a sound of his own. Powell played with all the major figures in bebop, including Charlie Parker and Dizzy Gillespie. But as a youth he suffered a savage beating at the hands of the police, and this, coupled with his addiction to drugs and alcohol, triggered a number of mental breakdowns. Powell was just 41 when he died in 1966.

Like Monk, Bud Powell recorded for the Blue Note label.

CHARLIE PARKER

Bebop's tragic hero, Charlie "Bird" Parker set the jazz world alight when he emerged in the mid-1940s. Fellow musicians recalled the magical experience of hearing his alto saxophone for the first time. No one had imagined that one man could produce such amazing sounds. Bird has influenced every saxophonist who has come since. But his career hardly got off to a good start.

Yardbird Suite
1945
Live at Rockland Palace
1952
Charlie Parker at Storyville
1953

Bird at the Hi-Hat
1953
Complete Dial Masters
released 2000
Complete Savoy Masters
released 2000

PARKER PERSEVERES

Born in Kansas City in 1920, Charles Christopher Parker was given an alto sax by his mother when he was 11. He dropped out of school at 14 to concentrate on the instrument, but his early stage performances were dogged by nerves. He froze during a solo at the Hi-Hat Club, and the humiliation prompted him to give up music for three months. In 1937 he was ordered off stage by drummer Jo Jones, but this time he resolved to practice harder. His efforts paid off, and by 1942 he was with Earl Hines's big band, along with his soul mate Dizzy Gillespie.

Bird formed a band with Miles Davis in 1947.

BIRD TAKES FLIGHT

Now known as Bird, he moved to Harlem in 1944 and hooked up with a number of like-minded musicians, including Thelonious Monk and, of course, Dizzy. Bird's playing was so unusual because of the complex chords and rhythms his saxophone followed, his unbelievably fast solos and his use of the higher end of the instrument. Nothing like it had been heard before. After a handful of records were released, bebop became a national trend and a celebration of everything young and fashionable.

OFF THE RAILS

But Bird was now an alcoholic and heroin addict, and, after setting a hotel room on fire in 1946, he was imprisoned in the psychiatric wing of Los Angeles County Jail. Freed in 1947, he made some classic recordings and toured abroad for the first time, in France and Scandinavia. Bird even had a brief flirtation with classical music, as heard on the *With Strings* albums. But ulcers and liver disease were the legacy of his hard lifestyle. Bird gave his last performance at Birdland, the club named after him, just a week before his lonely death in March 1955.

"BIRD"

The 1988 movie *Bird* is a good starting point for anyone wanting to learn about the life and music of Charlie Parker. The star of the film, Forest Whitaker, had to take saxophone lessons so that he could mime accurately to the music. The film pulls no punches in depicting Bird's genius, his downward spiral into drug addiction and his squalid death. *Bird* was directed by actor-turned-director Clint Eastwood.

Forest Whitaker won the best actor award at the Cannes Film Festival for his performance in Bird.

Tommy Potter (bass) played with Bird in the mid-1940s, along with Max Roach (drums).

Bird was given his nickname because he loved fried chicken!

WEATHER REPORT

The rock 'n' roll explosion of the 1950s and 60s passed jazz by. Jazz had Coltrane and Davis — why would it need Elvis and the Beatles? But by the late 1960s, rock music was so huge that it could no longer be ignored. Maybe jazz could learn from rock after all.

BEST OF BOTH WORLDS

Weather Report was one of the groups that invented jazz-rock fusion. It was formed in 1970 by Austrian keyboard player Joe Zawinul and saxophonist Wayne Shorter, who had both played on Miles Davis's electric album *Bitches Brew*. Realizing the potential of a rock-based rhythm section, they recruited Airto Moreira on percussion and Miroslav Vitous on bass. Their first album was a big hit, as were the group's high-energy live performances. Two more percussionists joined the band for their next album.

Joe Zawinul needed plenty of keyboards to produce the sounds he wanted.

BLUE SKIES AHEAD

By the time of the *Sweetnighter* album, Joe Zawinul began to impose more structure on the group, moving away from free-form sounds and emphasizing melody. But Weather Report's live shows continued to be freewheeling displays of virtuosity, with each musician trying to outdo the others. The group was a revolving door for new jazz talent, as members came and went, with founders Zawinul and Shorter still at the core.

EVER-CHANGING, JUST LIKE THE WEATHER

Weather Report entered its most successful phase in 1976, when the flamboyant electric bass player Jaco Pastorius joined the band. Instead of just providing rhythm, Pastorius's bass served as a third lead instrument, as Zawinul experimented with the sophisticated electronic technology of the day. Their album *Heavy Weather* even provided a hit, "Birdland," which has become a jazz standard. With the arrival of Peter Erskine on drums in 1978, the group even had a stable lineup for a while. After another change of personnel in 1982, Weather Report continued for three years, before Zawinul and Shorter parted company, to pursue solo success.

Jaco Pastorius died a violent death outside a Florida nightclub in 1987.

STING

The rock star Sting had a problem in 1984. His band the Police was the biggest in the world and had just completed a record-breaking world tour, but the band was effectively finished. How could he follow that? Sting decided to wipe the slate clean and get back to his jazz roots — he had started his career as a jazz bassist in Newcastle. He assembled the finest collection of young American jazz musicians he could find, including Omar Hakim, drummer with Weather Report, and Branford Marsalis. The resulting album, *The Dream of the Blue Turtles*, was a worldwide smash, and it opened people's ears to a new sound — modern rock music played by jazz musicians. Sting continued the theme with *Nothing Like the Sun* in 1987.

Sting played electric guitar, not bass, on his first solo album.

Weather Report 1971
I Sing the Body Electric 1972
Sweetnighter 1973
Tail Spinnin' 1975
Black Market 1976

Heavy Weather 1977
Mr. Gone 1978
8:30 1979
Night Passage 1980
This is This 1985

GAZETTEER

One of the most exciting things about jazz is its sheer variety. One person might adore the big bands. Another might go for 1970s free-form. They can fight like cats and dogs about which is better, but they are both jazz fans. Music by all the following artists is waiting to be discovered.

Bix Beiderbecke was rejected by his parents when he took up jazz.

Fats Waller made over 150 records.

WHITE JAZZ
Born in 1903, cornetist Bix Beiderbecke played with Paul Whiteman's orchestra but only achieved true recognition after his early death from chronic alcoholism in 1931.

STAR OF THE SLIDE TROMBONE
Trombonist Kid Ory was the first African-American New Orleans musician to make a record, in 1922. He was a champion of traditional jazz until his retirement in 1966.

Kid Ory quit music in 1933 but returned in the 1940s.

Grappelli was playing into his 80s.

Milt Jackson (far right) played vibraphone in the Modern Jazz Quartet.

Dave Brubeck worked with baritone sax-player Gerry Mulligan.

TRUE ORIGINAL

"Ain't Misbehavin,'" "Honeysuckle Rose," "Your Feet's Too Big" — just three in the long list of classic compositions by Thomas "Fats" Waller. His lighthearted songs brought some welcome relief during the dark days of unemployment and economic depression in the 1930s.

FOREIGN STARS

It's not just America that's produced some great jazz. Parisian violinist Stéphane Grappelli and Belgian guitarist Django Reinhardt formed the Quintette du Hot Club de France in the early 30s. Their style of jazz has been much imitated but never bettered. Gil Evans was born in Toronto, Canada. As well as his arrangements for Miles Davis (see page 192), Gil made a number of records under his own name.

Stan Getz was one of the most highly regarded tenor players ever.

JAZZ SAMBA

Tenor sax star Stan Getz brought the Brazilian samba style of music to jazz, through his work with Antonio Carlos Jobim. "The Girl from Ipanema" became a worldwide hit for them.

Gil Evans worked with Sting.

MODERN JAZZ

The expression "modern jazz" was first coined in the 1950s, and people have been struggling to think up a more up-to-date term ever since! Dave Brubeck irritated some jazz purists by putting a modern jazz tune into the Top 10 in 1961, but "Take Five" remains instantly recognizable all those years later. Milt Jackson, John Lewis, Percy Heath and Connie Kay — the Modern Jazz Quartet — performed their brand of (not so modern) music for 35 years. Today jazz is still a modern and evolving art form. Who knows what's around the corner?

Reggae

CONTENTS

On these disks is a selection of the artists' recordings. Many of these albums are now available on CD and MP3. If they are not, many of the tracks fromthem can be found on compilations.

Dennis Brown

These boxes give you extra information about the artists and their times.

Some contain anecdotes about the artists themselves or about the people who helped their careers or, occasionally, about those who exploited them.

Others provide historical facts about the music, lifestyles, fans and fashions of the day.

INTRODUCTION

It is astonishing that one tiny Caribbean island, Jamaica, should be the main source of a style of music that is known all over the world: reggae.

Of course, the history of reggae is complex. As with blues and jazz, reggae's roots can be found in Africa. It is generally considered that reggae itself developed from mento, a traditional form of Jamaican folk music. Folk music has traditionally been a vehicle for protest songs, and mento was no exception,

A reggae band plays at Reggae Sunsplash, the annual Jamaican Song Festival.

railing against injustice, racism and corruption. But, as with the blues music that developed in the U.S. under similar circumstances, the strong message was made palatable by its powerful, danceable beat.

Reggae has a serious side that sets it apart from other popular music. It has close links with Rasta, a religion based around the Bible but reinterpreted from a black perspective. Its followers consider Africa their spiritual home. Reggae songs also deal with more down-to-earth problems, such as unemployment, education, poverty… and affairs of the heart!

In defining reggae, "Toots" Hibbert of the Maytals puts it: "Reggae means coming from the people. Everyday things, like from the ghetto. We put music to it, make a dance out of it. I would say that reggae means coming from the roots, ghetto music. Means poverty, suffering and in the end, maybe union with God if you do it right."

ASWAD

Aswad were one of the most important and influential UK reggae bands and popularized political black music. Even their name is political, taken from the Arabic for "black." Inspired by the success of Bob Marley, the band aimed to combine their Rastafari beliefs with comment on social issues of the 1970s and 80s, such as racism and poverty.

BACK TO AFRICA

Formed in 1975 by Brinsley "Dan" Forde and drummer Angus Gaye, the band also featured George Oban on bass and the Jamaican singer Donald Griffiths. Aswad soon found a voice of their own and approached the premier UK "black" label, Island, with their demos. Executive Leslie Palmer was interested enough to take a chance with Aswad and released their first single, "Back to Africa" in 76. Although not a major hit, this debut sold enough to encourage Island to release another single in the same year. The band's first album, *Aswad*, followed a few months later.

LIFE IN THE GHETTO

Aswad were based in West London. Living in poor-quality accommodation, the band experienced at first hand the realities of racial harassment and relative poverty. They were fiercely determined to express these experiences through their music.

Aswad
1975
Hulet
1978
New Chapter of Dub
1982

To the Top
1986
Crucial Tracks: The Best of Aswad
1989
The Wicked
1990

MUSICAL DIFFERENCES

But before long, there was conflict within the band. Keyboard player Courtney Hemmings left, and in came Tony "Gad" Robinson. The friction cost the band some time.

In 1978 the band released the album *Hulet*, to the delight of their loyal followers. However, the band members were still at odds over the musical direction they wanted to take. Frustrated, founding members Oban and Griffiths left the band.

SOUND TRACKERS

But Aswad were about to enjoy an unexpected lift to their career. Brinsley Forde landed the lead in *Babylon*, Franco Rosso's film about reggae music that was released in 1980. The accompanying soundtrack album featured two of Aswad's most impressive singles: "Rainbow Culture" and "Warrior Charge."

SUCCESS

After two albums for CBS Aswad returned to Island for their first live album, recorded in 1982 at the Notting Hill Carnival, the UK's biggest black festival. Two moderately successful singles followed: "54-56 Was My Number" (originally recorded by Toots Hibbert), and "Chasing the Breeze." In 86 Aswad recorded an acclaimed album, *To The Top*. Not before long, they enjoyed their first number one hit with "Don't Turn Around" in 88. The band remains one of the UK's most exciting reggae outfits.

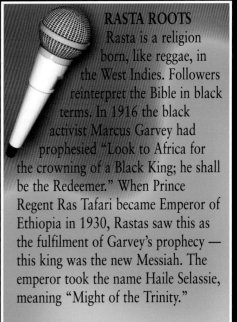

RASTA ROOTS
Rasta is a religion born, like reggae, in the West Indies. Followers reinterpret the Bible in black terms. In 1916 the black activist Marcus Garvey had prophesied "Look to Africa for the crowning of a Black King; he shall be the Redeemer." When Prince Regent Ras Tafari became Emperor of Ethiopia in 1930, Rastas saw this as the fulfilment of Garvey's prophecy — this king was the new Messiah. The emperor took the name Haile Selassie, meaning "Might of the Trinity."

According to Rastafari belief, Haile Selassie I (right) is the living God.

Aswad is just one of many reggae bands to combine Rastafari beliefs and social commentary in its music in the hope of promoting racial tolerance.

217

DENNIS BROWN

People tend to assume that reggae artists come from deprived backgrounds. How else can they write genuine songs of protest, highlighting poverty and prejudice? Yet one of the finest and best-loved reggae singers, Dennis Emmanuel Brown, came from a respectable middle-class household. Born in 1957, son of a TV scriptwriter, Brown stayed at school until he was 17 years old — later than average for Jamaican youngsters of the time.

CHILD STAR

However, as for many reggae artists, Brown's musical career started early. He was writing and singing at the age of 11. By the time he was 13, Brown was signed to the prestigious Studio One record label based in Kingston, Jamaica, owned by Clement Coxsone Dodd.

MUSIC LESSONS

But Brown never felt that music got in the way of his education: "Working with Downbeat (Dodd's sound system) was like going to a college because you had all the people that was happening at the time there. They had people like Alton Ellis, the Heptones, Lascelles Perkins, Lloyd James and John Holt. Coxsone was the ace producer at the time."

Producer Clement Coxsone Dodd, owner of Studio One.

No Man Is an Island
1970
Super Reggae and Soul Hits
1972
Wolf & Leopards
1978

Money in My Pocket
1979
Super Hits
1983
The Prime of Dennis Brown
1993

NO BOY IS AN ISLAND

In 1969 Dennis Brown released his first single, a version of the Impressions' "No Man Is an Island" — five years before he left school! It was a big local hit, as was its follow-up "If I Follow My Heart." The early 70s saw Brown flitting between record labels and working with a succession of excellent producers. In 74 he met the talented producer Winston "Niney" Holness. Together they made some of Brown's finest recordings, including the albums *Just Dennis* and *Wolf & Leopards*.

MONEY IN HIS POCKET?

As early as 1974 Brown had toured the UK with Toots and the Maytals, but he had to wait another five years before achieving international recognition — and even then some feel he never achieved the acclaim he richly deserved. Ten years into his career "Money in My Pocket" and "Ain't That Loving You" gave Brown the breakthrough he had been waiting for. He signed a deal with the huge record label A&M and moved to London. At the same time he became involved in the small Jamaican label DEB as a producer and writer.

ROOTS REGGAE

Not all of Brown's albums and singles were great commercial successes, but his heartfelt commitment to his Rastafari roots and his beautiful, soulful voice ensured the unfailing support of a large fan base. His concerts were always well attended, and he never performed a bad show.

CULTURAL HARMONY

Like so many other reggae artists and fans, Dennis Brown is a devout Rastafarian and considers Africa his homeland: "Africa? Africa? Just the mention of it, man, is like you call my name. Africa is the motherland and Africa is where we rightly belong. And that's where I want to be."

But it was Brown's time in London that really opened his eyes to how different communities could live together in harmony without sacrificing their own way of life. Says Brown, "In England you see that the Jews stick to their culture, the Greeks the same, the Pakistanis, the French, the Dutch. Well I saw it was possible and wise to identify myself with being a Rasta."

GONE TOO SOON

Dennis Brown's career slowed down in the late 80s, but he kept recording and touring until his death in 1999. The official cause was a collapsed lung, but some have reported Brown was addicted to crack cocaine, and that this precipitated his illness.

Brown in front of the Rastafari colors make up the Ethiopian flag.

BURNING SPEAR

Born Winston Rodney, Burning Spear took his stage name from the spiritual name of Kenyan statesman Jomo Kenyatta. He is arguably the most uncompromising of all the Rastafari reggae artists. From the very beginning of his career, Burning Spear distanced himself from what he saw as the frivolous, lighthearted, dance-based aspect of reggae music, preferring to leave that to other performers in the field.

SERIOUS STUFF

It is not surprising that Burning Spear's early recordings, which reflected his strong beliefs, were not commercially successful. They were more akin to traditional Rastafari chanting than rude-boy posturing, and their improvised, jazz-based approach to recording made his singles inaccessible to many listeners. Still, no one would deny the sheer quality of tunes such as "Foggy Road," "Swell Headed," "Ethiopians Live It Out" and "New Civilisation" and Spear did make the Jamaican Top Five with "Joe Frazier."

MARCUS GARVEY

The overpowering influence for all Spear's writing came from the work of Marcus Garvey, the civil rights leader; Garvey's own words feature prominently in the songs. Following his departure from the Coxsone Dodd organization, Burning Spear and co-performers Rupert Wellington and

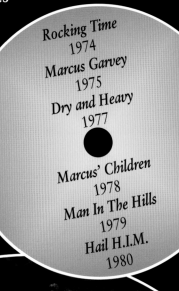

Rocking Time
1974
Marcus Garvey
1975
Dry and Heavy
1977

Marcus' Children
1978
Man In The Hills
1979
Hail H.I.M.
1980

Delroy Hines recorded the spell-binding "Marcus Garvey" in 1975 for producer Jack Ruby. The single, and album of the same name, brought Spear fame, and the album was released in the UK on Island. The word was that Burning Spear would shortly match Bob Marley's superstar status.

SOLITARY SPEAR

In fact, superstardom never came. Spear recorded one more album, *Man in the Hills*, with Jack Ruby then took control himself, splitting from Hines and Wellington. "Travelling," "Free Black People," "Spear Burning" and "Throw Down Your Arms" highlighted his mesmerizing vocal delivery and accomplished writing.

ENGLAND BOUND

In 1976 Spear teamed up with Aswad. In 77, after a frantic day's rehearsal, they tore apart London's Rainbow Theatre: this compelling performance was captured forever by Island's mobile recording studio. In 78 Spear left Island and recorded *Marcus' Children*, (titled *Social Living* in the UK). He had great respect for Aswad and took them back to Jamaica for the recording sessions.

ALBUM ARTIST

Burning Spear switched to EMI for his next classic, *Hail H.I.M.* Recorded at Marley's state-of-the-art Tuff Gong studio and produced by "Family Man" Barrett, it confirmed Spear's reputation as an artist whose work seemed better suited to albums than singles. Never one for the catchy hook or cheap lyric, Spear writes songs that are reflective, spiritual and thought provoking. One of the most important reggae artists, he still tours the world delivering his soulful music to his many fans.

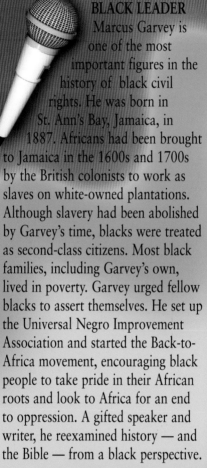

BLACK LEADER
Marcus Garvey is one of the most important figures in the history of black civil rights. He was born in St. Ann's Bay, Jamaica, in 1887. Africans had been brought to Jamaica in the 1600s and 1700s by the British colonists to work as slaves on white-owned plantations. Although slavery had been abolished by Garvey's time, blacks were treated as second-class citizens. Most black families, including Garvey's own, lived in poverty. Garvey urged fellow blacks to assert themselves. He set up the Universal Negro Improvement Association and started the Back-to-Africa movement, encouraging black people to take pride in their African roots and look to Africa for an end to oppression. A gifted speaker and writer, he reexamined history — and the Bible — from a black perspective.

Garvey proclaimed: "We are the descendants of a suffering people. We are ... determined to suffer no longer."

PRINCE BUSTER

Prince Buster came to ska and blue beat music relatively late in life — his 20s. He had earned the name "Prince" because of his ability to look after himself in boxing matches and street gang clashes. (The tough teen was also Coxsone Dodd's "minder," protecting the legendary Downbeat sound system.) Buster Campbell's unusual first name was his father's tribute to the founder of the Jamaican Labour Party, William Alexander Bustamente.

A DEBUT CLASSIC

In 1960 Prince Buster gave up boxing in favor of music and made his first record, "Oh Carolina" (the song that was to give Shaggy a chart-topping UK and U.S. hit 35 years later). Buster had split from Coxsone Dodd and set up his own business, the Voice Of The People, which ran record stores, sound systems and a record label. "Oh Carolina" was a hugely impressive debut for the young Prince Buster, and he was soon collaborating with talented artists such as Arkland Park's Drumbago All Stars, the Les Dawson Blues Unit, the Rico Rodriguez Blues Band, the Folks Brothers and Count Ossie. Buster's first album, *I Feel the Spirit*, came out in 63 and only added to his growing reputation.

BUSTING OUT

I Feel the Spirit
1963

Fly Flying Ska
1964

Fabulous Greatest Hits
1967

Prince Buster beat a lot of the competition by breaking into the international market. By the mid-1960s he was a cult figure in the UK. He was adored by the "mods", and the large Jamaican community in London.

Prince Buster poses for the cover of his debut album, I Feel the Spirit.

BLOCKBUSTER

Buster appeared on the popular 1960s TV music program *Ready, Steady, Go!* alongside such legends as the Rolling Stones, the Beatles and the Animals. He wrote about everything — Jamaican street violence, politics, his own childhood memories, and women. He had a huge influence on later reggae bands, including Madness (named after one of his songs), the Beat and UB40.

JUKE BOX JURY

In the 1970s Buster's income from his own recordings tailed off, but his canny investments in the outskirts of the music industry paid off. He monopolized the jukebox business in Jamaica, and his tough reputation helped him to retain an iron grip on his organization.

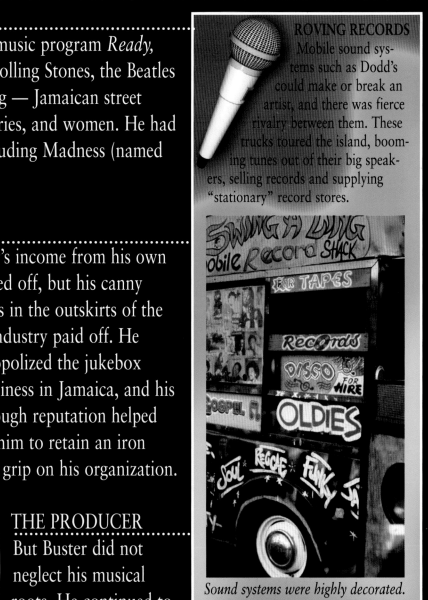

ROVING RECORDS

Mobile sound systems such as Dodd's could make or break an artist, and there was fierce rivalry between them. These trucks toured the island, booming tunes out of their big speakers, selling records and supplying "stationary" record stores.

Sound systems were highly decorated.

THE PRODUCER

But Buster did not neglect his musical roots. He continued to perform and turned producer for many well-known Jamaican artists. Big Youth, Dennis Alcapone (whose name was also inspired by one of Buster's songs), John Holt, Dennis Brown, Alton Ellis, the Heptones and the Ethiopians all worked with Buster in the producer's seat. He soon realized that his classic back catalog was his greatest asset, so he repackaged and re-released his earlier hits. Today Buster divides his time between his businesses and regular performances. He is enjoying new popularity. Following its use in a Levis ad, his single "Whine and Grind" hit the UK and U.S. the Top 10s in 1998.

Jukeboxes gave Buster a steady income in the 70s.

JIMMY CLIFF

Singer James Chambers' first venture into the recording business was not very encouraging, although his experience was not unique: "I made my first record for a tiny record company based in Kingston, Jamaica ...'Daisy Got Me Crazy' was never released and I got no money for it. All they offered me was a shilling for my bus fare home which I refused. I thought it was an insult."

BUT THEN

Jimmy Cliff persevered. At the age of 14 he had a Jamaican number one with "Hurricane Hattie," recorded for Leslie Kong's label, Beverley. It was young Cliff who had persuaded Kong to go into the record business. He had written a song called "Dearest Beverley" and he approached Leslie Kong to release it because he owned a Kingston restaurant called Beverley's.

NEW YORK, NEW YORK

Chris Blackwell, head of the Island record label and long a champion of ska and reggae, spotted Cliff performing at New York's World Fair in 1964. Impressed, Blackwell whisked him back to England. But Cliff did not achieve overnight success — he toured pubs and clubs, often on backing vocals. In 65 ska was unknown in the UK. "They didn't really know what Jamaican music was. So in my nightclub act, I did two thirds rhythm and blues and one third ska."

BEAUTIFUL BRAZIL

But success was just around the corner. Cliff submitted his song "Waterfall," written in 1968, to a song festival in Brazil. Cliff went for a week — and stayed for a year!

Always touring, Cliff often supports major acts.

HOUSE OF EXILE
Many reggae artists are Rasta, but in 1972 Jimmy Cliff turned to Islam — as the African-American activist Malcolm X had done before him. From then on, Cliff became an outsider in his native Jamaica.

Cliff became a big star in Africa. He was one of the first artists to record there. "In Africa, I got the greatest satisfaction I've ever had as an artist. The acceptance and appreciation I received there, it made me feel so good. After all, the first song I'd ever written was 'Back To Africa.'"

Perhaps Cliff's proudest moment was when he played to 75,000 people – blacks and whites — in Soweto, South Africa.

Hard Road to Travel
1967
Jimmy Cliff
1969
The Harder They Come
1972

House of Exile
1974
The Best of Jimmy Cliff
1976
Give the People What They Want
1981

Inspired by Brazil and its people, Cliff wrote "Wonderful World, Beautiful People," the song that brought him international fame. The single "Vietnam" followed, which was extravagantly praised by Bob Dylan and Paul Simon.

SUPERSTARDOM!

In 1972 Cliff starred in *The Harder They Come*, a box-office smash about the reggae music industry. Neither the film nor its soundtrack made Cliff's fortune, but the movie was a cult classic and is still screened today.

The Harder They Come *brought reggae — and Jimmy Cliff — to new audiences around the world.*

TROUPER

In the 70s Cliff made lengthy trips to Africa and Latin America, and the music and culture of these countries inspired and excited him. His music reflected these influences, and Cliff released dozens of singles during the 70s and 80s, though few were really successful. It would take "Trapped," Cliff's song performed and recorded by Bruce Springsteen, and "I Can See Clearly Now" to catapult Cliff back into the public eye. He continues to tour the world today, more than 40 years after refusing that shilling for his bus fare home.

DESMOND DEKKER

Could the glorious reggae that has poured out of Jamaica since the early 1960s have ever developed without the vision and talent of local producers? One of them, Leslie Kong, took on young Desmond Dacres (soon to be "Dekker"). Orphan Dacres grew up in Saint Thomas but went to Kingston to work as a welder. He used to sing while he worked — so well that his colleagues encouraged him to turn professional.

ACE RECORDINGS

Singing with the Aces, Dekker's first single, "Honour Your Father and Mother," was released in Jamaica and the UK in 1963. Dekker had no less than 20 number one hits in Jamaica during the 60s before making it in the UK charts with "007 (Shanty Town)" in 67.

THE PROMISED LAND?

Two years later Dekker's "Israelites" became the first reggae record to top the UK charts. It also entered the Top 10 in the U.S. — no mean feat as the U.S. was slow to appreciate Jamaican music. Dekker moved to England, where audiences lapped up his witty, observant songs. He came close to scoring another number one with "You Can Get It If You Really Want," written by Jimmy Cliff and featured in the film *The Harder They Come*.

Action!
1968
This is Desmond Dekker
1969
Israelites
1969
Black and Dekker
1980
King of Kings (with The Specials)
1993
The Best of Desmond Dekker
1993

KONG'S DEATH

In 1971 Dekker nearly gave up music when his long-time producer, Kong, died of a heart attack. He changed labels but never repeated his early successes. In 84 he declared bankruptcy. He complained bitterly that he had never received the royalties he was due from his hits. He died of a heart attack in May 2006.

GREGORY ISAACS

Originally a panel-beater, Gregory Isaacs was quickly discovered by renowned producer Rupie Edwards. Singing with the Concordes, he made "Another Heartbreak," "Each Day" and "Black and White." Isaacs also worked for Prince Buster on "Dancing Floor." Dozens of other singles were released in the late 1960s and early 70s.

CONTROL FREAK

By 1973 Isaacs was established as a tough, uncompromising member of the reggae "Mafia." He set up the African Museum label in order to have more artistic control, though he still recorded for other labels in his search for success. In 74 his single "Love Is Overdue" (on Trojan) entered the UK charts.

Extra Classic
1977
Slum Dub
1978
Soon Forward
1979

Out Deh
1983
The Cool Rider Rides Again –
22 Classic Cuts
1993

LIKE A VIRGIN

His reputation grew. In the UK Richard Branson, founder of Virgin Records, sat up and took notice. Virgin released Isaacs' *Soon Forward* and *Cool Ruler*.

BAD BOY

But then Isaacs' career suffered a setback. Personal and financial problems resulted in a jail sentence. His "bad boy" image had caught up with him. On his release he needed cash — fast. Isaacs recorded his new material with any label or producer who offered the right price. Luckily his talent ensured that there was no artistic compromise, and

Isaacs has worked for many producers in his long, distinguished career.

Isaacs, one of the great reggae artists, continues to produce reggae music of the very highest quality.

BOB MARLEY

Bob Marley was without a doubt the most famous figure to emerge from the Jamaica-based reggae community. Sadly, on May 11, 1981, 36-year-old Robert Nesta Marley died from lung cancer and a brain tumor. The talented superstar left behind hundreds of classic recordings for reggae fans to enjoy.

IN THE BEGINNING

Marley was born in 1945, the son of an English seaman and a Jamaican mother. At school he met Bunny Wailer and Peter Tosh, who were to join him as pivotal figures in the Jamaican "ska" movement. The trio went into the studio in 1965 to record the first of many singles as the Wailers. They enjoyed local success with 39 singles before finally producing their first album. Marley's music encompassed many styles during this period. He experimented with soul, rock-steady (romantic soul), ska and even close harmony "doo-wop" styles.

UNIQUE PARTNERSHIPS

The I-Threes — Rita Marley, Marcia Griffiths and Judy Mowatt — provided a gospel sound.

In 1966 Marley married Rita Anderson, a talented singer working with local group the Soulettes. She would later become a member of his own group of backing singers, the I-Threes. Devout Rasta, Marley and his wife lived on a commune.

Soul Rebel
1970
Catch a Fire
1973
Burnin'
1973

Natty Dread
1975
Exodus
1977
Legend
1984

For the time being, the Wailers were all-male. Joined in 67 by brothers Aston and Carlton Barrett, the group began to work with the talented producer Lee Perry. In his spare time Marley loved to play soccer and had his own team.

SUCCESS

In 1972 the owner of Island, Chris Blackwell, signed the band. Unconventionally, he gave them a large advance and trusted them to go back to Jamaica to record something for him. With their fixed lineup, the Wailers were the first reggae "band" and their tremendous *Catch a Fire* album of 1973 sold worldwide. The following year, UK guitarist Eric Clapton recorded Marley's witty but poignant song "I Shot the Sheriff," which helped to raise Marley's profile even further. Tosh and Wailer left the band to pursue their own careers.

PEACEMAKER

Bob Marley was as passionate about politics as he was about music. An attempt on his life in 1976 may have been due to his strongly held views. Marley, his wife, Rita, and his manager, Don Taylor, were all injured when gunmen burst into Marley's Kingston home and shot at them.

But political awareness brought about a proud moment in 78. Marley played the Jamaican One Love peace concert, where he persuaded Michael Manley, the Jamaican prime minister, and Edward Seaga, the opposition leader, to shake hands in front of the huge crowd.

Marley promoted political peace.

BLACK AND WHITE

Now backed by the I-Threes, Marley took his accomplished reggae music all over the world for the next five years and achieved superstardom. The gospel sound of the I-Threes was much more familiar to the rock-fed audiences of the day, and Bob Marley and the Wailers attracted new listeners to reggae. Reggae concerts no longer had an exclusively black audience — to the great delight of this peace-loving Rasta.

Just before his tragically early death, Marley headlined at a huge concert in the newly liberated Zimbabwe. He was extremely proud to be associated with such a momentous event in the struggle for black liberation. In fact, his entire career played its own important part in this struggle.

Marley released his first single under the name Bobby Martell.

LEE PERRY

One of reggae's most adventurous — and longest serving — producers, Rainford Hugh Perry was born in 1939 in Saint Mary's, Jamaica. He acquired a number of nicknames along the way: "Little" Lee Perry would later be known as the "Upsetter," "Gong" and, most famously, "Scratch."

STARTING OUT

Perry started out in the music business at the bottom, selling records for the legendary Clement Coxsone Dodd from the trunk of Dodd's car. Soon he was promoting and presenting Dodd's hugely successful Downbeat sound system. Coxsone recognized Perry's talents as a record producer and talent scout. Lee Perry would also become a prolific and popular recording artist in his own right.

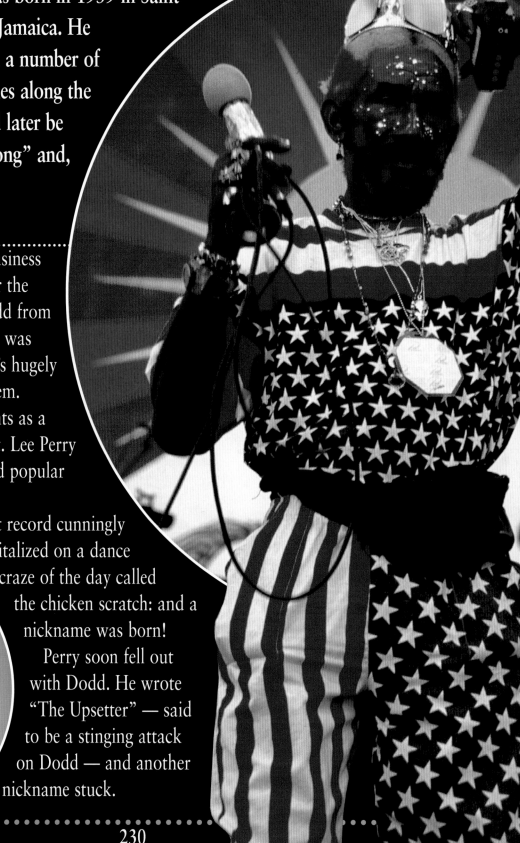

His first record cunningly capitalized on a dance craze of the day called the chicken scratch: and a nickname was born! Perry soon fell out with Dodd. He wrote "The Upsetter" — said to be a stinging attack on Dodd — and another nickname stuck.

The Upsetter
1969
The Return of Django
1970
Super Ape
1976

Scratch on the Wire
1979
The Upsetter Box Set
1985
Arkology
1997

BUILDING THE ARK

In 1968 Perry took an important step. His reputation as a producer had been growing, and he set up his own studio, the Black Ark, in his own backyard. Next came his own record label, Upsetter. He was astute. He encouraged and produced many unknown reggae artists. By 69, he had achieved success outside Jamaica. The Upsetters, a studio band assembled by Perry, had a Top 10 hit in the UK. However, his finest hour was to come.

Lee Perry worked with Bob Marley and the Wailers and significantly contributed to their success. (Marley named his label Tuff Gong after Perry's newest nickname, "Gong.")

END OF THE ARK

Upsetter released over 100 reggae singles and dozens of albums between 1969 and 74. But there were disturbing signs that all was not well. Perry had always been an eccentric, but something snapped. He burned down his studio and fled to Holland, a country known for its liberal attitude toward drugs. He soon relocated to London, where the punk scene was springing up, to work again with Bob Marley on "Punky Reggae Party," released in 77.

THE MAD GENIUS

Although marijuana is illegal in Jamaica, many Rasta smoke it as a sacrament. Some say it brings about spiritual experiences.

It is impossible to tell to what degree Lee Perry's use of drugs contributed to what many people saw as a sad mental decline in the late 1970s. He suddenly denounced Rasta and gave some puzzling interviews: "Good evening and greetings, you people of the universe. This is Lee "Scratch" Perry, madder than the mad, greater than the great, rougher than the rough, tougher than the tough and badder than the baddest. We are here at the turntable terranova — it means we are taking over."

Madder than the mad? Possibly. Genius? Certainly.

Lee Perry: "We're taking over the star!"

RESPECTED PRODUCER

Despite his bizarre behavior, Perry has a well-deserved reputation as one of the greatest producers of all time. The 1980s saw collaborations with talented UK dub producers the Mad Professor and Adrian Sherwood. Lee "Scratch" Perry is still recording, and has become a much-respected icon.

After giving up Rasta, Perry banned anyone with dreadlocks

SLY and ROBBIE

It's unusual for session musicians to make a name for themselves, but that is precisely what Sly and Robbie did. Record producers often bring in session musicians when they have a clear idea of the sound they want to create but neither the patience nor money to waste valuable studio time while band members practice on unfamiliar instruments. Enter the session musician: someone who can take one look at a written part then play it without a mistake. In fact, top-class session musicians throw the "dots" (printed music) out of the window and respond with their hearts rather than their heads. Sly and Robbie not only did that, but they created their own "sound" in the process.

STAR SESSIONISTS

Sly Dunbar is a genius on the drums.

Drummer Lowell Charles Dunbar got the nickname "Sly" because of his admiration for the American funk band Sly and the Family Stone. Dunbar was playing with Skin, Flesh and Bones when he met up with bass player Robbie Shakespeare in 1975. Their musical styles and approach to reggae gelled instantly. They made their name producing "The Right Time" for the Mighty Diamonds, and the word got around fast that Sly and Robbie were *the* rhythm section if you wanted to add gloss and panache to your recordings. Sly and Robbie have played on countless reggae records, working with the Upsetters,

Disco Dub
1978
Rhythm Killers
1987
Silent Assassin
1990

Reggae Greats
1985
Reggae Hits 1987-90
1991

Sly and Robbie with Black Uhuru, for whom they produced the groundbreaking Showcase.

U-Roy, Bunny Wailer, Peter Tosh, Black Uhuru, Burning Spear and many others. They became known as the "Dynamic Duo," or the "Rhythm Twins."

CALL A TAXI

The pair formed their own record label, Taxi, and produced many hit singles for Jamaican artists. In the late 70s Sly Dunbar recorded two solo albums, *Simple Sly Man* and *Sly, Wicked and Suck*, which featured — of course — Robbie Shakespeare on bass. Soon the pair were in great demand outside the close-knit reggae community. International pop superstars such as Joan Armatrading, Bob Dylan, Ian Drury and even John Lennon's widow Yoko Ono were lining up for their services. They also provided the beats for Jamaican-born singer Grace Jones's best-selling dance album *Nightclubbing*.

Sly and Robbie's mechanical beats were called robotic by some, and they certainly anticipated the sounds of the digital age of drum machines and sequencers.

Shakespeare provides innovative bass sounds for many artists.

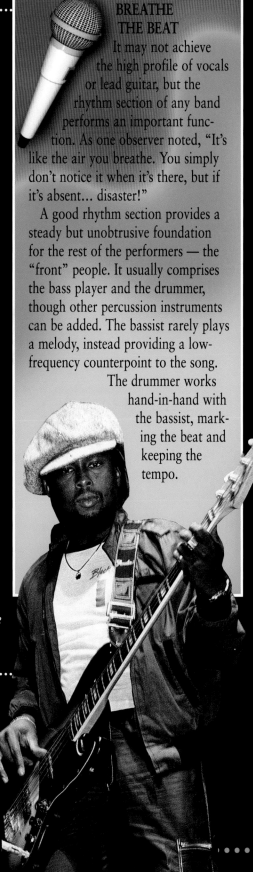

BREATHE THE BEAT

It may not achieve the high profile of vocals or lead guitar, but the rhythm section of any band performs an important function. As one observer noted, "It's like the air you breathe. You simply don't notice it when it's there, but if it's absent… disaster!"

A good rhythm section provides a steady but unobtrusive foundation for the rest of the performers — the "front" people. It usually comprises the bass player and the drummer, though other percussion instruments can be added. The bassist rarely plays a melody, instead providing a low-frequency counterpoint to the song.

The drummer works hand-in-hand with the bassist, marking the beat and keeping the tempo.

INTO THE DIGITAL AGE

New technologies did not deter Sly and Robbie. "Murder She Wrote" and "Tease Me" produced for Chaka Demus and Pliers, were both UK hits. Dunbar experimented, mixing in the Asian pop sound of bhangra to take ragga to new heights.

After a career spanning four decades, the best rhythm section in Jamaica can still produce the goods!

TOOTS and the MAYTALS

Frederick "Toots" Hibbert made history by releasing the first ever record to have reggae in its title — *Do the Reggay*. In the early 1960s he had formed a "ska" vocal trio along with Nathaniel "Jerry" Mathias and Henry "Raleigh" Gordon, for the influential disc jockey and recording company boss Coxsone Dodd. Toots had a very distinctive voice: strong, sometimes raucous, but very soulful. This voice launched him into a career that has so far lasted more than 40 years.

EARLY DAYS

Hibbert was born in May Pen, Jamaica, but in the late 1950s he moved to the notoriously tough Trenchtown district in Kingston. Hibbert was working as a barber: "I used to sing all the time, and people would come around and listen, and say I was good and I should go and record my voice. That's when I met Raleigh and Jerry. They came around and said they liked my singing and wanted to form a group."

The Maytals' first record, *Hallelujah*, was an instant success in Jamaica. More local hits followed, also on a religious theme, such as "6 & 7 Books of Moses," "Shining Light" and "He Will Provide." Then they moved to Dodd's rival, Prince Buster. Toots and the Maytals enjoyed several more hits, but in 1966 they switched labels again, this time to Byron Lee's BMN company.

The Sensational Maytals
1966
Never Grow Old
1966
Funky Kingston
1973

Reggae Got Soul
1978
Do the Reggae 1966–1970
1988
Sensational Ska Explosion
1993

RECORDING SENSATION

That same year they won the Jamaican Song Festival. These annual festivals showcased reggae bands. Like the sound systems, they played an important role in promoting reggae music.

After this success, the Maytals never seemed to be out of the Jamaican charts. "Bam Bam" was followed by "Fever," "It's You," "Never You Change" and "Daddy." The year also saw the release of their first album, *The Sensational Maytals*.

This rare debut album was later re-released as 'Sensational Ska Explosion'.

TIME INSIDE

However, a temporary halt to their growing success was just around the corner. Toots was jailed after being caught in possession of marijuana. On his release Toots moved to Leslie Kong's Beverley label and wryly enjoyed his biggest success to date with "54-46 That's My Number." It referred to his prison number!

MENTO MENTOR

Mento was the first recorded Jamaican music and had a big impact on many reggae artists. It drew on a mixture of musical genres, notably the traditional work songs sung by the plantation slaves and the music of the Pocomania Church, where Toots Hibbert had been a chorister as a boy. As in U.S. Baptist Churches, this music featured lots of percussion, clapping and foot stamping.

Mento also borrowed rhythms from the marching bands of carnival (Jonkanoo) and from the quadrille, a ballroom dance that had been popular with European settlers.

Other influences came from nearby Cuba, for example rumba, bolero and mambo, while from America came the big-band sounds of swing and, of course, rhythm and blues.

A traditional mento band performs on the streets of Kingston, Jamaica.

FAME AT LAST

Toots' records had been imported to the U.S. and the UK for many years for a small group of fans, but in 1976 Toots knew he had made it at last when he received this glowing review: "Toots Hibbert is unquestionably one of the greatest vocalists to appear in popular music in the past decade."

From then on, Toots and the Maytals could fill venues in major cities all over the world whenever they chose to jump on a plane. In 1980, Toots achieved another historic first, when *Toots Live*, recorded in London's Hammersmith Palais, went on sale in the stores — just 24 hours after it was recorded!

UB40

Reggae has had an enormous impact on the world of pop music. First came the "ska" sound of the Specials and the Beat then UB40's crossover pop. Artists such as Shaggy and Shabba Ranks explore dancehall ragga, while dub has spawned the likes of Dub Syndicate and US3. More recently, jungle and drum and bass tunes are popular in clubs across the world.

Sons of a respected Scottish folk singer, Ali and Robin Campbell looked beyond their father for their musical influences — to the West Indies, 6,500 km (4,000 miles) away. The Campbell brothers were joined by fellow reggae enthusiasts Earl Falconer, Mickey Virtue, Brian Travers, Jim Brown, Norman Hassan and Astro.

TRIBUTE TO THE KING

In January 1980 UB40 released "King," a tribute to the assassinated black civil rights leader Martin Luther King, Jr. The record went straight into the UK Top 10, and the band were on their way. They toured with pop group the Pretenders during that same year, which helped bring them to more fans. In August their first album was released.

BAND WITH A MESSAGE

The early 1980s was a time of severe unemployment in the UK, especially among the young. Previously out of work themselves, the band named themselves after the unemployment benefit (UB) form number 40. They were fiercely critical that the government of the day was unsympathetic to the unemployed and used their debut album as well as their choice of name to highlight the problem. The album was entitled *Signing Off*.

Signing Off
1980
Present Arms
1981
Labour Of Love
1983

UB40
1988
The Best of UB40: Vol One
1987
The Best of UB40: Vol Two
1995

This is the expression British people use when they gain full-time employment and no longer need to "sign on" each week to receive benefit. The album's cover featured a blow-up of the notorious form.

Chrissie Hynde (center) made two hit singles with UB40.

LITTLE LABEL

UB40 formed their own label, DEP International and, still highlighting the plight of the unemployed, released the single "One in Ten," which gave them their second Top-10 hit. The band didn't look back. Five singles later, 1983 brought them two number ones in the UK charts. The single "Red, Red Wine," and their album *Labour Of Love* sold worldwide.

SUPERSTARDOM

UB40 began to tour the world and concentrated more on their love of rasta.

Although the A-sides of their singles were always accessible pop songs, the band stayed true to their first musical love. They craftily promoted reggae sounds to their pop audience by featuring a heavy dub version of each song on their B-sides.

SELLING REGGAE TO THE WORLD

Born in Jamaica, Chris Blackwell moved to London in 1962. Noticing the large Jamaican community there, he licensed Jamaican artists on his own record label, Island. Blackwell is most famous for signing Bob Marley. It is due to his foresight and clever marketing that reggae became such a popular form of music around the world.

Chris Blackwell founded Island Records.

DRINKING IN SUCCESS

It was not surprising that UB40 wanted to take part in the 1988 Nelson Mandela concert with fellow reggae fans Special AKA. They played "Red, Red Wine." It gave them their first U.S. number one and they have never looked back.

The SPECIALS

Perhaps one of the pop bands that owes most to Jamaican music is the Specials. Formed as Special AKA in 1979, the band featured a multi-racial lineup.

INSTANT SUCCESS

The band formed their own label, Two-Tone Records, to release "Gangsters" in the UK — their first single. It was an instant hit "Too Much, Too Young" gave the Specials their first UK number one. As always, the song reflected their reggae influences. In addition to their own songs, they covered material by the Skatalites, Bob Marley and many other Jamaicans. But just four more hits followed, including the atmospheric "Ghost Town," before the band split.

The Specials
1979
More Specials
1980

In the Studio
1984
The Specials: Singles
1991

THE POWER OF MUSIC

Singer Jerry Dammers took the name Special AKA with him and became involved with Artists Against Apartheid. In 1988, to promote a concert in aid of their campaign to free the African National Council leader, Dammers rereleased his hit "Nelson Mandela," retitled "Free Nelson Mandela (70th Birthday Remake)." Perhaps in a small but important way Dammers helped to change history.

The Specials were Jerry Dammers, Terry Hall, Neville Staples, Lynval Golding, Roddy Radiation, Sir Horace Gentleman and John Bradbury.

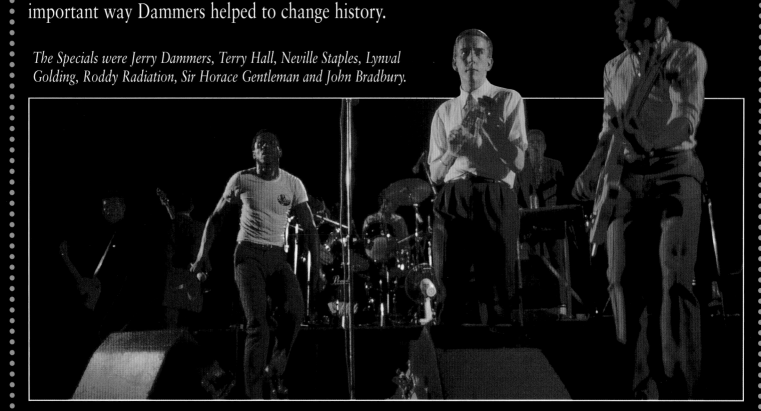

MADNESS

One of the most successful UK bands to embrace rasta music was Madness. Madness took their name from an early Prince Buster song, and their first single "The Prince" was their tribute to his influence. It was released in 1979 on the newly formed Two-Tone label.

PRINCE BUSTER'S CHILDREN

Madness didn't have to wait as long for success as their hero had. "The Prince" entered the UK Top 20, and within months Madness recorded their first album. Staying faithful to their mentor, their second single, "One Step Beyond" was a Prince Buster song — and it took them straight back into the charts.

Madness's entertaining, witty and astute ability to fuse their ska, blue beat, reggae and rock influences paid off. The band enjoyed 24 UK Top 20 singles between 1979 and 86. Most of their songs were tongue-in-cheek observations of ordinary life in the 70s and 80s. Despite their popularity, in 86 Madness called it a day.

One Step Beyond
1979
Absolutely
1980

Madness
1983
Keep Moving
1984
Madstock
1992

MORE MADNESS

However, 1992 saw a brief reunion of the whole band. They played at a festival in London's Finsbury Park, and, fueled by media interest, three reissues entered the charts: "It Must Be Love," "House of Fun" and "My Girl."

The band were understandably pleased when *One Step Beyond*, a musical which highlighted the plight of London's homeless, opened in London in 93. The show featured 15 Madness songs. A tribute indeed to a band that had always tried to be a voice for the poor and disadvantaged.

GAZETTEER

The previous chapters have only scratched the surface: dozens of other talented reggae musicians have been performing their inspiring music during the last five decades.

The Heptones

ISLAND SOUNDS

The Heptones, the Mighty Diamonds, Bunny Wailer, Peter Tosh and Big Youth are just some of the other classic reggae artists to achieve international success with their music.

The Skatalites were one of the most prolific and shortest lived reggae outfits, recording for producers Dodd, Prince Buster and Duke Reid. In the year they were together, 1964–65, the Skatalites backed most of the talented singers of the day — including the Maytals, Jackie Opel and the Wailers — and produced some fantastic instrumental tracks in their own right, such as "Tear Up," "Beardman Ska" and "Shot In the Dark."

The Mighty Diamonds

REGGAE WOMEN

Although Black Uhuru was fronted by the talented Puma Jones, women in reggae are few and far between. The I-Threes probably achieved the most success. However, one female pop (not reggae) star deserves a mention. Millie was the first Jamaican to have a hit outside her native island, with the phenomenally successful pop song "My Boy Lollipop," which sold seven million copies.

Millie

The Skatalites

240

MOVIES

Films such as *The Harder They Come* played an important part in popularizing reggae. The classic *Rockers* was made in 1977 and starred Gregory Isaacs, Burning Spear and Robbie Shakespeare, among others.

Black Uhuru

Steel Pulse

U.S. REGGAE

It was not until the 1980s that U.S. reggae stars appeared, such as Bobby Kondors ("The Heads") and Shinehead ("Pepper Seed"). The 90s brought reggae superstardom to Shaggy ("Boombastic").

REGGAE'S SECOND HOME

Reggae has always been particularly appreciated in the UK. In the 1960s Clement Dodd and Duke Reid regularly brought over their awesome sound systems.

Many British bands, including Misty and Roots, the Clash and Steel Pulse, took their inspiration from Jamaica. In the 90s Finlay Quaye recorded the excellent album *Maverick a Strike*. Renowned for his Bob Marley covers, Quaye picked up a Brit Award for his reggae-inspired sound.

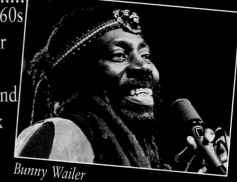

Bunny Wailer

Finlay Quaye

FESTIVAL OF BRITAIN

Back in 74 fans in the UK were able to sample the genuine article. London's Wembley hosted a Caribbean Music Festival. It featured Bob and Marcia ("Young, Gifted and Black"), Desmond Dekker, the Maytals, the Pyramids and Jackie Edwards (the singer who helped Chris Blackwell set up Island). Much of the film *Reggae* was shot there, "which captured the infectious happiness of the music and the artists."

Big Youth

Rock and Rap

CONTENTS

On these disks is a selection of the artist's recordings. Many of these albums are available on CD and MP3. If they are not, many of the tracks from them can be found on compilations.

These boxes give you extra information about the artists and their times.

Some contain anecdotes about the artists themselves or about the people who helped their careers or, occasionally, about those who exploited them.

Others provide historical facts about the music, lifestyle, fans, fads and fashions of the day.

Super Furry Animals are a Welsh band popular in the UK.

INTRODUCTION

Rap is a vocal style that has dominated urban American music for over 20 years. In the late 1970s young DJs discovered they could borrow, or "sample," excerpts of recordings and stitch them together to make a new song. Add some spoken or shouted lyrics (rap), and you have a new type of music. Rappers competed to come up with wittier and more rebellious lyrics.

The first rap hit was "The Message" by Grandmaster Flash and the Furious Five in 1982. Dozens of acts followed, venting their frustrations and obsessions in rap — poverty, politics, drugs and crime.

Grandmaster Flash samples records, spinning or scratching two records at once.

Influenced by rap, heavy metal, grunge and dance music, legions of white bands emerged in the mid-90s, playing nu-metal, hardcore rap, post-grunge, rap-metal, industrial metal — take your pick. These styles of music are as much about attitude as music. Provocative lyrics and maximum volume combine with an image of tattoos, dyed hair and pierced bodies to cause hysteria among teenagers, and outrage among their parents! Many rock and rap stars have ended up in court, owing to their violent lifestyles — which just makes them seem even more glamorous to some fans.

In Britain, rock bands, such as the Manic Street Preachers, are hardly short on attitude, fired by the same anger as their American counterparts. Other stars, such as Fatboy Slim, are exploring gentler territory, influenced by the rave scene which swept the country in the 90s.

EMINEM

The most talented and witty rapper to come out of America in the 1990s? Or a precocious and offensive product of the white establishment who makes a living out of making enemies? The choice is yours. Whatever you think of him, Eminem was the biggest-selling rapper to emerge at the turn of the new millennium. He has an infamous reputation, even among those who have no interest in modern music.

DOCTOR'S APPOINTMENT

Marshall Mathers, better know as Eminem, was 23 years old, homeless and broke when he accepted an invitation to perform at the 1997 Rap Olympics in Los Angeles. He sorely needed the $500 prize money, but despite a rapturous welcome by the mainly African-American and Hispanic crowd, he only came in second. Bitterly disappointed, Eminem was preparing for the lonely journey home when he was approached by two talent scouts from Interscope Records. After listening to a tape of Eminem's music, Interscope arranged an appointment with the doctor — Dr. Dre, the chief figure in West coast rap music.

CAUSING A STIR

The color of his skin led several less talented rappers to view Eminem with suspicion, but Dre had no such doubts. He signed Eminem, and they immediately began work on the *Slim Shady* album, which was a huge hit, helped by the singles "My Name Is" and "Guilty Conscience." But Eminem's violent and foul-mouthed lyrics stirred up controversy in the media. The single "Stan" was targeted for its graphic description of an obsessive and homicidal fan, though it made a star out of Dido, whose voice was featured on the track.

Eminem was fined for weapons offences in 2001.

GUILTY OR NOT GUILTY?

No stranger to the courts, Eminem has faced firearms and assault charges and has even been sued by his ex-wife and his mother! Just before a concert tour in 2001, Australian Prime Minister John Howard said that Eminem's songs are "sickening, demean women and encourage violence." But Eminem insists that his lyrics are strictly tongue-in-cheek, and he is only trying to cause debate, not offense.

DOCTOR IN THE HOUSE

Dr. Dre is the godfather of West coast gangsta rap music, which often contains violent and obscene lyrics. Along with Ice Cube, he was a member of the rap group NWA. His first solo album was called *The Chronic*, and it was a huge hit. He went on to produce the controversial rapper Snoop Doggy Dogg between spells in prison. Dre also founded the rap record labels Death Row and Aftermath.

Dr. Dre gave $1 million to charity following the American terrorist attacks in 2001.

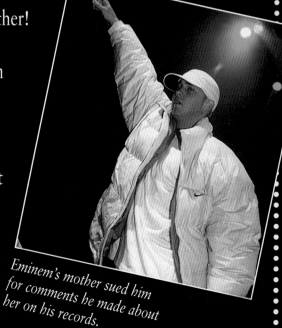

Eminem's mother sued him for comments he made about her on his records.

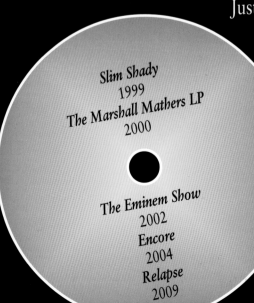

Slim Shady
1999
The Marshall Mathers LP
2000

The Eminem Show
2002
Encore
2004
Relapse
2009

247

FATBOY SLIM

Talk about a versatile star! Norman Cook has been in the music business for more than 20 years, during which time he has played bass guitar in a pop group, produced other artists, recorded samples and remixes, worked as a club DJ and created his own electronic sounds. Today he records under the name of Fatboy Slim, one of the new breed of "Brithop" dance producers.

ONE BAND TO THE NEXT

Cook joined the four-piece Housemartins in 1986 and played bass with the band until they split the following year. He then returned home to record with Beats International. They hit number one in the UK with "Dub Be Good to Me," but this was yet another short-lived collaboration. It looked as though everything Cook touched turned to gold — his next project was with the "acid jazz" act Freak Power, whose "'Tune In, Turn On, Drop Out" single hit number two in the UK.

MAN OF MANY PARTS

Cook's ambition was to enter the record books by scoring the most Top 40 hits under different names. He worked as a producer and DJ under the names Pizzaman, Fried Funk Food, Might Dub Katz and Norman Cook Presents Wildski. His latest incarnation is Fatboy Slim.

Better Living Through Chemistry
1996
On the Floor at the Boutique
1998
You've Come a Long Way Baby
1998

Halfway Between the Gutter and the Stars
2000
Palookaville
2004
Here Lies Love
2009

The Housemartins were well known for their left-wing political views.

RECORD BREAKER

Norman Cook achieved his ambition when Fatboy Slim's "Going Out of My Head" entered the UK charts in 1997. Tracks from Fatboy Slim's first album became club anthems, and Cook threw himself into his work, remixing Jean-Jacques Perrey's single "Eva" and Cornershop's "Brimful of Asha," which spent several weeks at number one. American success came with his second album, which provided the hit singles "The Rockafeller Skank" and "Praise You."

SCREEN STAR

Many Fatboy Slim tracks have ended up on movie soundtracks or in television commercials, which have yielded Norman Cook a large fortune. He now works from home, by the sea in Brighton. His music has been given a further boost by his work with Spike Jonze, who directed the video for "Weapon of Choice," starring Christopher Walken, which won an amazing six MTV Video Music Awards in September 2001.

Cook married the TV and radio presenter Zoe Ball in 1999. They have a son called Woody.

THE ART OF DJing

To be a successful club DJ takes years of practice, skill and imagination. DJs need technical know-how and an instinctive feel for the music and their audience. While a record blares from the speakers into one ear, DJs line up other records on separate turntables, listening with headphones on the other ear. These days some club DJs are as famous as the musicians whose records they play.

DJs create "scratching" effects by spinning records with their hands.

FOO FIGHTERS

Only rarely do drummers in major bands enjoy successful solo careers after their bands have split up. It's even more rare for a drummer to start a new band, that is just as big as the one he left. But Dave Grohl is no ordinary drummer.

SNUFFED OUT

Nirvana was the biggest band of the early 1990s, with singer and guitarist Kurt Cobain at the helm and Dave Grohl on drums. Grohl had been playing drums, guitar and writing songs since his early teens and had found long-awaited fame with Nirvana. But the band was in trouble, and it was clear to everyone close to it that Kurt Cobain was suffering from mental problems, made worse by his addiction to drugs. In early 1994 he committed suicide, and the band that had re-written rock history was no more.

On stage with Foo Fighters, Dave Grohl plays guitar and sings.

Foo Fighters
1995
The Colour And The Shape
1997
There is Nothing Left to Lose
1995

One by One
2002
In Your Honor
2005
Echoes, Silence, Patience & Grace
2007

WORD OF MOUTH

After several months of silence following Cobain's death, Grohl booked some studio time with his old friend Barrett Jones. Grohl had a large backlog of songs, and the two of them recorded an entire album in just a week, playing all the instruments themselves. Grohl made 100 cassette copies of the new album, giving them to friends and associates in the music business. Word of the tape spread like wildfire, and before he knew it, record companies were frantically bidding against each other to release the album.

OUT OF THIS WORLD

In the meantime, Grohl recruited a band, which he named Foo Fighters, after a World War Two special force that investigated UFOs. Capitol Records signed them and released Grohl's solo recordings under the group name, even though none of the rest of the band had played on it. The album was an instant success, spearheaded by the radio-friendly hit single "This is a Call."

WALKOUTS

Grohl did what he knew best and hit the road with his new band, touring throughout 1996. Late that year Foo Fighters began sessions for their second album, but quarrels led to the departure of drummer William Goldsmith, leaving Grohl to pick up the sticks himself. *The Colour and the Shape* was the first album Foo Fighters recorded as a band, although there would be more resignations — guitarist Pat Smear left soon after its release, and his replacement also proved short-lived. However, since 1999 the Foo Fighters lineup has not changed, and the band has released three more successful albums.

NIRVANA

Dave Grohl joined Nirvana in 1990, fresh from the punk band Scream. Nirvana was formed in Seattle and typified the "grunge" sound that came out of that city. Grunge was a raw mixture of angry and tortured lyrics, thunderous drumming and blaring guitars. Millions of teenage fans sympathized with Kurt Cobain's bleak view of the world and almost felt that he was writing about their own experiences. A decade later, Nirvana is still an enormous influence on bands.

Kurt Cobain married the singer from Hole, Courtney Love. They had a daughter together.

Foo Fighters are influenced by the punk scene of the late 1970s.

251

LIMP BIZKIT

Who says that rock stars shouldn't play businessman? With his angry look, tattooed limbs and burly physique, Fred Durst is the face of "rapcore" — a mix of hip-hop, heavy metal and punk. But Durst is also a video director, scriptwriter and a record company executive in charge of millions of dollars' worth of talent.

Three Dollar Bill Y'All
1997
Significant Other
1999
Chocolate Starfish
and the Hot Dog Flavored Water
2000

Results May Vary
2000
The Unquestionable Truth
2000

ALL AT SEA

Fred Durst had an unhappy childhood — he was bullied at school, partly because his fascination with black rap culture made him stand out from the crowd. Durst's stepfather, who had fought in the Vietnam War, was strict with him, and, in an attempt to please him, Durst joined the U.S. Navy when he left school. Life at sea didn't suit him at all, and he bitterly regretted his mistake. Out of uniform, he drifted between casual jobs, finally becoming a tattooist, while he developed an early version of Limp Bizkit in his hometown of Jacksonville, Florida. One day Fieldy, the bass guitarist with Korn, entered Durst's tattoo parlor, and rolled up his sleeve.

TATTOO AND A TAPE

Limp Bizkit headlined the Family Values Tour in 1999.

As well as several tattoos, Fieldy gained Durst's friendship and was happy to accept a cassette of Limp Bizkit's early recordings. The other members of Korn were so impressed that they passed the tape on to their producer Ross Robinson, who helped to secure Limp Bizkit a support slot on tour with House of Pain and the Deftones. Record companies vied to sign the band, and in 1998 Flip/Interscope released their debut album, which turned them into the most talked-about act on the rapcore scene.

THE DARK SIDE

The follow-up, *Significant Other* entered the U.S. chart at number one, and sold 4 million copies in its first six months. All the while, Fred Durst was proving himself a clever business-man, snapping up senior positions at the Flip and Flawless labels. But there was a dark side to this massive success. Limp Bizkit stirred up controversy at the 1999 Woodstock Festival, which culminated in riots. Although the band played the day before the worst of the violence, there were reports of rapes and numerous injuries during Limp Bizkit's set, and much of the media accused Durst of egging the crowd on to cause trouble.

Fred Durst worked as a gardener and store assistant after leaving the Navy.

NOT TO BE MESSED WITH

Fred Durst can be a forceful character and has sometimes clashed with his tourmates. He was also a supporter of the controversial Napster website, which allowed fans to trade music over the Internet, depriving performers and record companies of royalties.

Limp Bizkit played free concerts on a tour sponsored by Napster.

KORN

The Californian band Korn helped Limp Bizkit on their way in the early part of their career. Korn emerged in the wake of Nirvana, playing "funk-metal," and became one of the most provocative and popular bands of the mid-1990s. Korn made headlines in 1998 when a young student was sent home from school for wearing a T-shirt adorned with the band's logo.

Korn's biggest album was Issues, *released in 1999.*

MANIC STREET PREACHERS

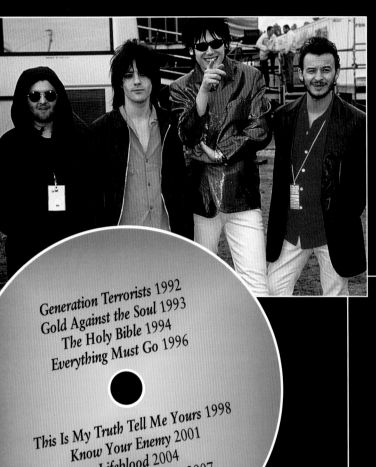

Wales has given the world some astonishing bands, none more so than the Manic Street Preachers. Their rebellious attitude, heavy guitar rock and dangerous image made them darlings of the British music press. But the Manics also had to overcome the tragedy of losing one of their key members.

Generation Terrorists 1992
Gold Against the Soul 1993
The Holy Bible 1994
Everything Must Go 1996

This Is My Truth Tell Me Yours 1998
Know Your Enemy 2001
Lifeblood 2004
Send Away the Tigers 2007
Journal for Plague Lovers 2009

START OF THE JOURNEY

For a group that once proclaimed that all bands should break up after releasing just one album, the Manics have lasted a long time! The band was formed in Blackwood, Wales, in 1988, featuring James Dean Bradfield on vocals and guitar, Nicky Wire on bass guitar, Sean Moore on drums and later, the band's driver, Richey Edwards, also on guitar. The band gained a reputation for its stunning live performances, and Manics' singles "Motown Junk" and "You Love Us" prompted plenty of adulation in the British press.

James Dean Bradfield and drummer Sean Moore are cousins.

TORTURED SOUL

Richey Edwards caused a sensation in 1991 when he sparked an argument with a music journalist, who had questioned the band's originality. Edwards produced a knife and carved the word "4Real" on to his own arm. Many people dismissed this as a publicity stunt, but it was in fact an early indication of Edward's mental instability. The Manics' first UK top-10 hit was a version of "Suicide Is Painless," the theme to the TV comedy series *M*A*S*H*. By 1993, it was clear that Edwards was suffering from alcoholism, anorexia and depression, which culminated in more acts of self-mutilation. He once appeared on stage with chest injuries, which he had given himself with knives a fan had given him. In 1994 he entered a private clinic to try to rid himself of his demons.

James Dean Bradfield plays a Gibson Les Paul guitar.

The Manics say they miss Richey Edwards most on stage.

WELSH ROCKERS

For years Wales was more associated with middle-of-the-road singers, such as Tom Jones and Shirley Bassey, than hard rock music. But in the 90s, a wealth of talent has come out of the principality. As well as the Manics, Wales has given us Stereophonics, Super Furry Animals and Catatonia, who sadly announced their split in September 2001. The singer and songwriter David Gray was born in Manchester, but he has lived in Wales for most of his life.

Cerys Matthews (second from left) was the flamboyant lead singer with Catatonia.

MISSING PERSON

The Manics' third album *The Holy Bible* was a bleak and somber record, but this didn't stop them from winning over more fans. Edwards briefly rejoined his bandmates, but the news they had been dreading finally came in February 1995. Edwards vanished, leaving behind his passport and credit cards. A week later his car was found near the Severn Bridge, a notorious suicide spot — he has never been seen since. Bravely, the band decided to carry on, using the lyrics Edwards had left behind. The Manics went from strength to strength, establishing themselves as superstars all over the world, although, like many British acts of the day, American success eluded them. Always a controversial band, in 2001 they became the first western act to play for the hard-line communist dictator of Cuba, Fidel Castro.

MARILYN MANSON

As long ago as the late 1960s, certain rock musicians adopted ghoulish images and flirted with the idea of devil-worship, or Satanism. But Marilyn Manson was the first major star openly to embrace Satanism, calling himself the "Antichrist Superstar." He is certainly an American anti-hero, who has won over millions of fans while enraging parents and conservative public opinion.

TRUE ORIGINAL?

Cynical rock critics often compare Manson with Alice Cooper, the 70s star who still dons zombielike makeup and sings of pestilence and death even though he is a respectable golf-playing family man these days! Like Alice Cooper, Manson also adopted a girl's name.

LONE WOLF

But while Alice Cooper's act is humorous, Manson seems serious in his beliefs. Brian Warner always considered himself an outcast as a youth, until he found a soulmate in guitarist Scott Mitchell. They formed a band in Tampa Bay, Florida, in 1989, with Warner changing his name to Marilyn Manson and Scott Mitchell to Daisy Berkowitz.

SPOOKY MUSIC

Marilyn Manson and the Spooky Kids became well-known for their elaborate makeup and homemade special effects. They found a friend in Trent Reznor of Nine Inch Nails, who offered them a contract with his record label and a support slot on his next tour. They didn't need asking twice! The group increased its fan base at every show, as word of mouth spread about their outrageous singer.

Marilyn Manson's band has seen a number of lineup changes.

ROCK IN THE COURTS

As well as Marilyn Manson, many metal acts have been accused of experimenting with the occult, including Black Sabbath and Led Zeppelin, although both acts deny the charge. Judas Priest were accused of putting hidden messages on their record *Stained Class*, which drove two fans to shoot themselves. The fans' American families took the band to court, though the case collapsed almost immediately.

Judas Priest suffered the indignity of having to perform their songs in court.

INTENDING TO OFFEND

Marilyn Manson sealed his reputation in Salt Lake City, home of the Mormon religion. He tore up a copy of the Mormons' Holy Book on stage and was given the title "Reverend" by the Church of Satan's founder. Marilyn Manson's shows have been picketed by religious activists ever since. A master of self-publicity, many people still accuse Manson of being a showbiz sellout, particularly since the publication of his best-selling autobiography, *The Long Hard Road*. But supporters of free speech praise him for his bravery. In an age where rock sets out to shock, Marilyn Manson is surely one of the most controversial stars to emerge over the decade.

Manson's fans are mostly urban white teenage boys.

Portrait of an American Family 1994
Antichrist Superstar 1996
Mechanical Animals 1998
Last Tour on Earth 1999

Holy Wood 2000
The Golden Age of Grotesque 2003
Eat Me, Drink Me 2007
The High End of Low 2009

MASSIVE ATTACK

Massive Attack were the pioneers of "trip-hop" music, a smooth mix of hip-hop rhythms, melodic tunes and samples. The band was also one of the most influential groups of its day, and paved the way for other acclaimed acts.

WILD NIGHTS

Massive Attack evolved from the Wild Bunch, which formed in 1983 on the Bristol, England, club scene. They astounded clubbers with the way they could move effortlessly between musical styles as varied as punk, soul and reggae, and their shows were so popular that bands playing in other parts of town found they were performing to empty halls.

FALSE START

The Wild Bunch folded in the mid 1980s, but two members, Adrian "Mushroom" Vowles and Grant "Daddy G" Marshall hooked up with Robert "3D" del Naja to form Massive Attack. Three years later they released their first single, "Daydreaming" featuring the cool vocals of Shara Nelson and the rapper Tricky. The British music press heaped praise on Massive Attack, particularly the single "Unfinished Sympathy," which became a club favorite. But their early records never sold in huge quantites, and after an unfulfilling American tour it looked as if the band might not survive.

3D is also a graffiti artist, whose work has been exhibited in galleries.

Blue Lines
1991
Protection
1994

Mezzanine
1998
Singles 90/98
1999
100th Window
2003

FAME AND RESPECT

Massive Attack took three years to lick their wounds before the release of *Protection* in 1994. The band has always been rated by fellow musicians as one of Britain's finest dance/rap outfits, and U2 and Madonna jumped at the chance to collaborate with them. They shared the band's philosophy that good dance music must also be fun just to listen to. Massive Attack's fans are a patient lot! The band only releases albums every few years, but every one is well worth the wait.

MICROCHIP MUSIC

Today anyone with a few pieces of simple hardware and software can make music in their own home. You don't need to be an instrumental virtuoso to cut a track — by sampling excerpts of other people's songs you can create a new one of your own. But is sampling a legitimate artform or just a lazy way of stealing other people's ideas? The debate rages on.

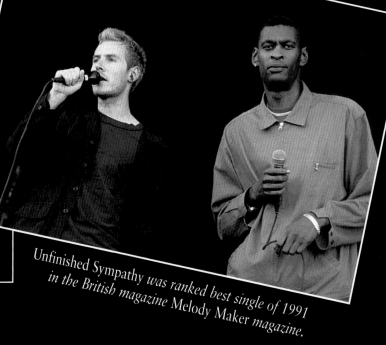

A computer can enable anyone to make electronic music anywhere, from a concert hall, to a club, to a bedroom.

Massive Attack briefly abbreviated their name to Massive in the early 1990s.

Unfinished Sympathy was ranked best single of 1991 in the British magazine Melody Maker magazine.

OFFSPRING

Californian band the Offspring was one of the biggest post-grunge bands to emerge after Nirvana. *Smash* sold over four million copies after its independent release in 1994.

MODERN METAL

The Offspring's music is often described as "punk-pop," although the group probably owes more to gritty, guitar-led heavy metal. Guitarist Kevin "Noodles" Wasserman's powerful riffs perfectly complement Dexter Holland's almost expressionless vocals. The band first came to light in 1989 and released a couple of low-key albums that won them some local success. The big break came with their album *Smash*, including the single "Come Out and Play," which became a big hit on MTV and radio. Offers from major labels flooded in, but the Offspring stayed loyal to their small indie label — for a while at least!

The Offspring's music, and that of similar bands, has been called "skate punk."

Offspring 1989
Ignition 1993
Smash 1994
Ixnay on the Hombre 1997

Americana 1998
Conspiracy of One 2000
Splinter 2003
Rise and Fall,
Rage and Grace 2008

Offspring touring in 2001.

MUSIC ON THE NET

Eventually the financial lure proved too strong, and the band left their label, Epitaph, and attracted criticism from some of the bands they left behind. The Offspring annoyed their new bosses at Sony by announcing in 2000 that they intended to offer their new album to fans as a free download on the Internet — a plan which was scrapped when Sony threatened to sue.

PAPA ROACH

Success rarely comes overnight in the music business, but Papa Roach had to wait longer than most for their first hit. The band formed at high school in California in 1993, but it was seven years before a major record label released one of their albums.

ALTERNATIVE METAL

The original members of Papa Roach were Coby Dick, Jerry Horton, Dave Buckner and Will James. Soon after forming they started to make short recordings of their own songs, which were dubbed "alternative metal" to distinguish them from the traditional heavy metal of the 1970s and 80s. Change arrived in 1996, when Will was replaced by their 16-year-old roadie Tobin Esperance, and a new manager encouraged them to release a full-length album.

Infest
2000
Lovehatetragedy
2002
Getting Away with Murder
2004

The Paramour Sessions
2006
Metamorphosis
2009

DREAM COMES TRUE

Local radio stations picked up on "Old Friends from Young Years," and the album became a surprise minor hit. The band hit the road, sharing the stage with Suicidal Tendencies, Sevendust and Powerman 5000. A record deal with Dreamworks led to their major-label debut. *Infest* finally gave them the success they had craved, and Papa Roach spent the next two years playing to ever-larger audiences.

Papa Roach appeared, along with Marilyn Manson, on the 2001 Ozzfest tour.

THE PRODIGY

Keith Flint of the Prodigy is one of the most recognizable faces in Britain, which is remarkable because dance acts tend to shun the limelight. The Prodigy's decision to focus on their image, as well as their music, saw them cross into the mainstream pop charts to become the biggest "electronica" act of the 1990s.

COTTAGE INDUSTRY

The origins of the Prodigy were in producer Liam Howlett's Essex, England, bedroom in the late 1980s. Howlett set up his own studio at home and came up with "What Evil Lurks," which was a big hit on the rave scene in 1990. Keith Flint and Leeroy Thornhill were regulars on the scene and they linked up with Howlett to form the Prodigy. The band was unusual from the start, mixing the atmosphere of a rave with the sort of showmanship more associated with arena rock bands.

DANCING UP THE CHARTS

In fact, Liam hardly changed the Prodigy's sound from their earliest efforts right through to their world-famous records, five years later. He mixed fierce metal chords with aggressive chanted vocals from Flint, sampling brief spoken words, usually from TV programs. The Prodigy put over a dozen singles into the UK Top 20, which made many serious clubbers reject them. In return, Liam cut an anonymous single to fool the DJs who had dismissed his band as being overcommercial.

Keith Flint (right) combines a pierced body with a punk hairstyle.

Experience 1992
Music for the Jilted Generation 1995
The Fat of the Land 1997

Experience Expanded 2001
Always Outnumbered, Never Outgunned 2004
Invaders Must Die 2009

Liam Howlett (center) is the brains behind the Prodigy.

CROWD PLEASERS

The Prodigy loved the publicity they gained as *Experience* hit the Top 10. *Music For The Jilted Generation* turned the band into superstars in Europe. The album entered the UK chart at number one and was nominated for the prestigious Mercury Prize. Instead of retreating to the clubs, the band hit the road and made a triumphant performance at the Glastonbury Festival, proving that their style of music suited a large outdoor crowd just as well as a club full of ravers.

LIGHTING THE FUSE

The single "Firestarter" was one of the biggest British hits of 1996. *The Fat of the Land* album also enthralled American music-lovers. It became the first British electronica album to top the U.S. chart.

AND THE WINNER IS...

Every year the music industry collectively pats itself on the back in a series of long awards ceremonies. The most famous are the Grammys, almost matched by the relatively new MTV awards. In Britain there are the Brits, the Mercury Music Prize, the MOBOs, the Q Magazine awards and numerous others. At least if you miss out at one set of awards you have a good chance of winning at another!

A major award can boost a band's record sales.

SEAN COMBS

In 1993 Sean "Puffy" Combs started working from home as a remixer. A decade later he was in charge of a multi-million dollar entertainment empire and had produced records for Notorious B.I.G., Boyz II Men, Mariah Carey, TLC and Lil' Kim. He is also a fine rapper in his own right, releasing material under the names Puff Daddy, P. Diddy and Diddy.

Combs was briefly a dancer before he joined Uptown Records.

GOING IT ALONE

Born in the New York borough of Harlem, the young Combs was a bright boy who eventually attended university in Washington D.C. An old friend, Heavy D, worked at Uptown Records and found Combs a traineeship there. Within months he was an executive, with ambitions to be a vice-president of the company. But when he was fired from his job, he decided to go it alone and set up his own company, Bad Boy Entertainment.

SUCCESS TURNS SOUR

A year of hard work gave Bad Boy its first big hit, when Combs's remix of Craig Mack's "Flava In Ya Ear" hit the Top 10. Notorious B.I.G.'s "Big Poppa" did even better, but as Bad Boy got bigger, it became involved in a bitter feud with the West coast label Death Row. Tupac Shakur, Death Row's biggest star, mocked Combs and Biggie in one of his videos and accused Combs of being involved in a shooting. In 1996 Shakur was himself shot dead by an unknown killer, and just six months later, Biggie met the same fate, just before his second album, *Life After Death*, hit number one.

TRIBUTE

Combs was distraught, but after a break he returned as Puff Daddy with "Can't Nobody Hold Me Down," which held the number one slot for two months. But his biggest hit was yet to come — "I'll Be Missing You," a heartfelt tribute to Biggie featuring his widow Faith Evans.

IMAGE CHANGE

Soon after, Combs found himself in trouble with the law, when he was arrested for allegedly firing a gun in a nightclub then fleeing the scene. He faced the prospect of a hefty jail sentence but was acquitted, though one of his associates was found guilty. More trouble followed, mostly for traffic offences. Combs shed his bad boy image, adopting a more mature, businesslike persona. He even changed his nickname to P. Diddy to distance himself from his past.

No Way Out
1997
Forever
1999
P. Diddy & The Bad Boy Family: The Saga Continues
2001
We Invented the Remix Vol. 1
2002

THE DARK SIDE OF RAP

Rap lyrics are often violent and obscene. They can also express a vicious hatred of women, white people, the police — in fact almost anyone. "Gangsta rap" can often spill over into real gang culture, as the murders of Notorious B.I.G. and Tupac Shakur demonstrated. But not all rap is so full of anger. Will Smith was a huge rap star who did not use bad language on his records, and Public Enemy supported rap's "Stop the Violence" movement in the late 1980s.

Notorious B.I.G. was also known as Biggie Smalls.

Combs's Bad Boy empire is worth hundreds of millions of dollars.

RED HOT CHILI PEPPERS

The Red Hot Chili Peppers are a revolving door of a rock band. Members have been and gone, returned and died, ever since they formed in 1983. They were ahead of their time — one of the first bands to mix punk, funk, rap and metal into an intense brand of heavy rock. It took a few years for the music business to catch up with them.

SCHOOL BUDDIES

Michael "Flea" Balzary, Hillel Slovak and Jack Irons played in a band together at high school. Anthony Kiedis was a fan who used to open their shows by reciting poetry and gradually became part of the band. News of their performance at a drug-fueled party spread like wildfire, and within six months they had an eight-album deal with EMI.

Anthony Kiedis (above) has admitted to serious drug problems in the past. He cut his hair and dyed it blond in the late 1990s (right).

IN AND OUT

The band gained a reputation for its outrageous stage shows, which they often performed virtually nude! The first major lineup change came before the band's first album was even released — Hillel and Jack departed, to be replaced by Jack Sherman and Cliff Martinez. In early 1984 Sherman was out of the band, and Hillel was back in, and in 1985 Martinez was dumped to be replaced by Jack Irons, the drummer he had replaced. Confused? So were the Chilis — their heavy drug-taking and rigorous life on the road were affecting their judgment and threatening the survival of the band.

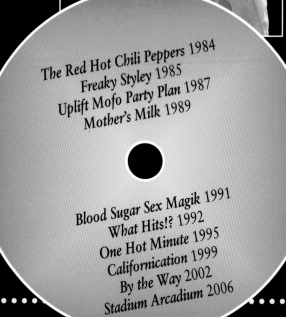

The Red Hot Chili Peppers 1984
Freaky Styley 1985
Uplift Mofo Party Plan 1987
Mother's Milk 1989

Blood Sugar Sex Magik 1991
What Hits!? 1992
One Hot Minute 1995
Californication 1999
By the Way 2002
Stadium Arcadium 2006

DOWN AND OUT

Most worryingly, Hillel was sliding into a life of heroin addiction, and although the Chilis' records were beginning to sell in large quantities, on stage he often forgot the notes and let the rest of the band down. A decision was made to fire Hillel, but, in typical Chilis fashion, they changed their mind. It was hardly surprising when Hillel fatally overdosed in 1988, but the band was badly shaken. Worst affected was Jack Irons, who left the group.

BACK AGAIN

After a break the band reconvened with John Frusciante on guitar, and finally entered the premier league of rock with *Blood Sugar Sex Magik*. But in 1992 Frusciante was out, and, after several replacements had come and gone, Dave Navarro settled into the job. The Chilis were plagued by ill-health and traffic accidents in the 1990s. Flea and Navarro joined Jane's Addiction, and after a brief tour Navarro decided not to return to the Chilis. John Frusciante was back in the band for *Californication* and the tour that followed it. The band's lineup finally remained unchanged — until they went on hiatus in 2008.

JANE'S ADDICTION

Dave Navarro joined the Chilis from Jane's Addiction, one of the most unusual bands to emerge in the mid-1980s. Fronted by the flamboyant Perry Farrell, the band combined pure rock with metal, punk, folk and even jazz music. Jane's Addiction split in 1991 but invited Navarro and Flea to join their reunion in 1997. Afterward, Navarro realized that he never wanted to tour again and left the Chilis for good.

Perry Farrell used to design his band's album covers.

SHAGGY

Shaggy is one of the biggest stars of contemporary reggae music, following in the footsteps of such greats as Bob Marley and Lee Perry. But Shaggy doesn't sing tortured songs of resistance like other reggae greats — his style veers from pop and R&B to good-time dancehall tunes, and back to reggae again, making him a favorite with a huge range of music fans. And he got his break in music while he was in uniform.

Pure Pleasure 1993
Boombastic 1995
Midnite Lover 1997

Hotshot 2000
Lucky Day 2002
Clothes Drop 2005
Intoxication 2007

MILITARY MAN

Orville Richard Burrell was born in Kingston, Jamaica, in 1968. He was nicknamed Shaggy by friends, after the greedy character in the *Scooby Doo* cartoon. When he was 18 Shaggy joined his mother in Brooklyn, New York, and decided to pursue a career in music. He hit number one on the reggae charts with "Mampie" and "Big Up," but the hits soon dried up. Frustrated by his lack of mainstream success, Shaggy enlisted with the U.S. Marines.

LIVE ON STAGE

Many samplers and rappers are only used to making music in studios or small clubs. When it comes to playing in large arenas, they often leave the audience cold. Like the Prodigy, Shaggy has mastered the art of showmanship — combining great singing with energetic dancing to reach out to his audience. As Shaggy himself has said, "If you don't know me yet, come to a Shaggy concert. I guarantee, when you leave, you'll be a Shaggy fan!"

Shaggy has played to crowds all over the world.

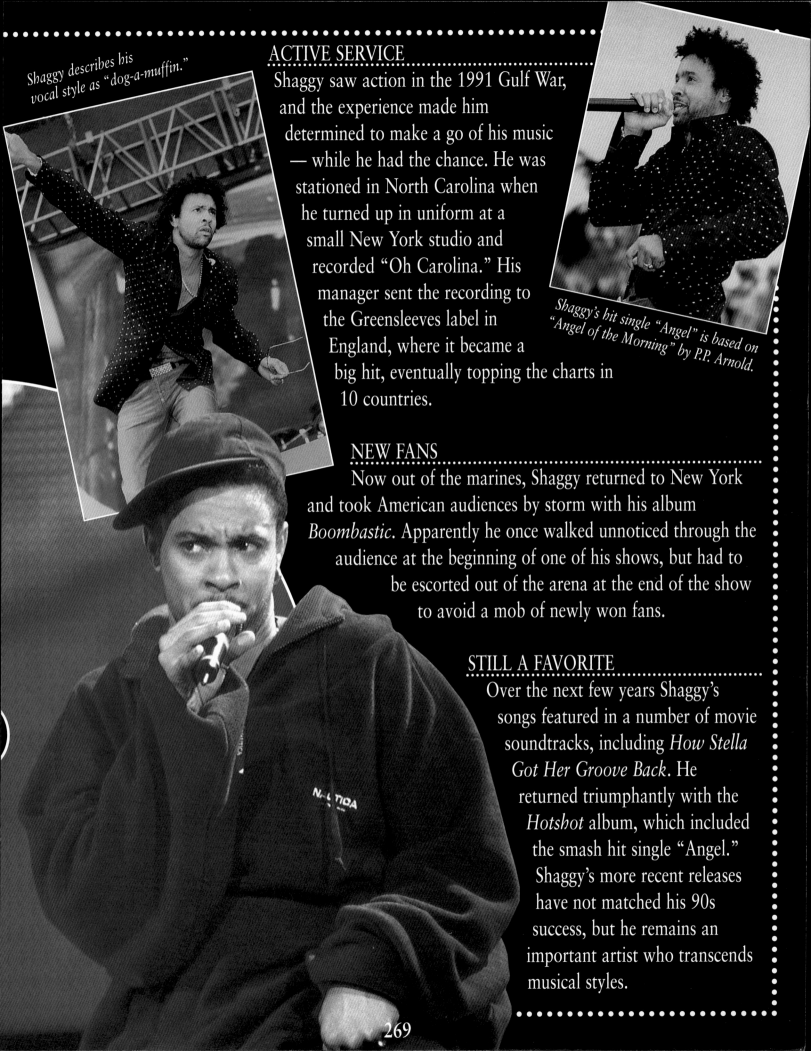

Shaggy describes his vocal style as "dog-a-muffin."

ACTIVE SERVICE

Shaggy saw action in the 1991 Gulf War, and the experience made him determined to make a go of his music — while he had the chance. He was stationed in North Carolina when he turned up in uniform at a small New York studio and recorded "Oh Carolina." His manager sent the recording to the Greensleeves label in England, where it became a big hit, eventually topping the charts in 10 countries.

Shaggy's hit single "Angel" is based on "Angel of the Morning" by P.P. Arnold.

NEW FANS

Now out of the marines, Shaggy returned to New York and took American audiences by storm with his album *Boombastic*. Apparently he once walked unnoticed through the audience at the beginning of one of his shows, but had to be escorted out of the arena at the end of the show to avoid a mob of newly won fans.

STILL A FAVORITE

Over the next few years Shaggy's songs featured in a number of movie soundtracks, including *How Stella Got Her Groove Back*. He returned triumphantly with the *Hotshot* album, which included the smash hit single "Angel." Shaggy's more recent releases have not matched his 90s success, but he remains an important artist who transcends musical styles.

GAZETTEER

Modern musical trends change so quickly that it's sometimes difficult to keep up with them. With so many imitators out there, "alternative rock" is no longer alternative. Time for the trendsetters to start thinking up some new names for the music!

Green Day stole the show at the 1994 Woodstock Festival, which helped sales of their album Dookie.

Chris Frantz and Tina Weymouth of the Tom Tom Club also contribute to Gorillaz.

Feeder's bass guitarist, Taka Hirose (left), was born in Tokyo, Japan.

POST GRUNGE

Green Day was the biggest post-Nirvana grunge band. Their album *Dookie* sold eight million copies. Feeder led the British post-grunge scene with their albums *Polythene* and *Yesterday Went Too Soon.*

Linkin Park shared the stage with Papa Roach at the 2001 Ozzfest festival.

BEHIND THE MASK

Sometimes musicians like to hide from the limelight. Damon Albarn of Blur leaped at the chance to perform in the "virtual hip-hop" act Gorillaz, whose members are computer-animated characters. The first Gorillaz album, *Tomorrow Comes Today,* appeared in 2000, and fans can keep up with the imaginary band on its website. Linkin Park has been dubbed a nu-metal boy band, partly because their first album, *Hybrid Theory*, appealed to young pop fans and contained no swearing.

Nobody could possibly call Slipknot a boy band. Their aggressive, masked stage act has taken rap-metal to new extremes.

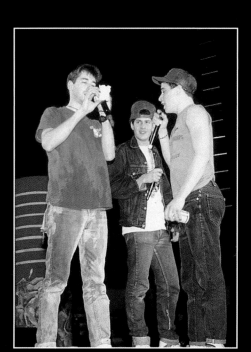

Slipknot's Corey Taylor does his best to scare the pants off his audiences!

GENTLY DOES IT

Placebo's music is often described as "neo-glam," harking back to 1970s acts, such as T. Rex and David Bowie. Their back-to-basics 2001 album *Black Market Music,* won over many mainstream rock fans. Wheatus have also attracted many older fans who have no interest in other post-grunge bands.

Founded by brothers Brendan and Peter Brown, Wheatus released their first album in 2000.

Placebo performed at glam rock star David Bowie's 50th birthday.

RAP'S OLD-TIMERS

The Beastie Boys are veterans of the rap scene. They were the first white rap act to be taken seriously by African-American audiences and rappers. The boys caused outrage when they first appeared in the 1980s, and many countries tried to ban them from their shores. But today the rap veterans are held in great affection as they turn up at rock festivals every summer.

Brendan Brown sings and plays guitar in Wheatus. His brother Peter plays drums.

Licensed to Ill *is one of the Beastie Boys' best-known album.*

Rock 'n' Roll

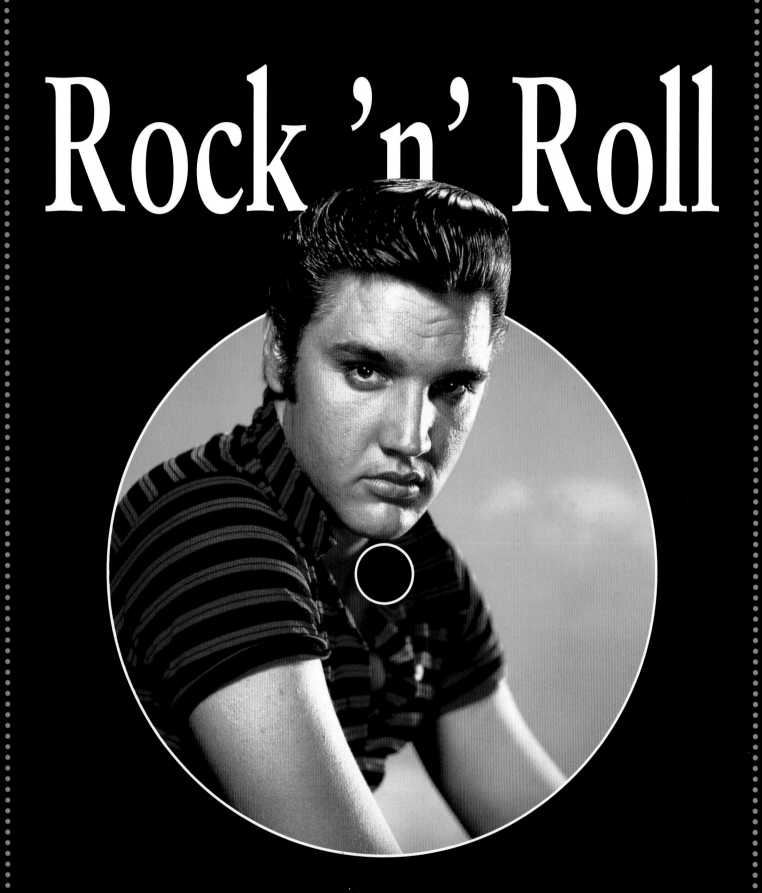

CONTENTS

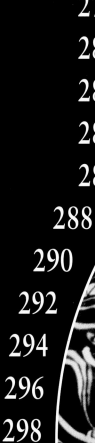

On these disks is a selection of the artists' recordings. Many of these albums are now available on CD and MP3. If they are not, many of the tracks from them can be found on compilations.

Chuck Berry

These boxes give you extra information about the artists and their times.

Some contain anecdotes about the artists themselves or about the people who helped their careers or, occasionally, about those who exploited them.

Others provide historical facts about the music, lifestyles, fans and fashions of the day.

INTRODUCTION

In the mid-1950s a New York disc jockey, Alan Freed, invented the term "rock 'n' roll" for a new, exciting music he was beginning to play on his popular radio station.

Loud, brash, with a very strong beat, rock' n' roll was aimed at a new group of people: teenagers. Before the 1950s young people did not have their own music, clothes and fads but were just younger versions of their parents. That was about to change.

Bill Haley's "Rock Around The Clock" is arguably the best-known anthem of rock 'n' roll music. It has sold over 20 million copies.

Alan Freed and many other disc jockeys started to play music that the grown-ups did not approve of. African-American singers like Chuck Berry, Fats Domino, Little Richard, Bo Diddley and many others were producing music based on their powerful rhythm-and-blues gospel roots. White performers were mixing all those influences with country and western and soul music.

Elvis Presley, Buddy Holly, Gene Vincent, Eddie Cochran and dozens of other performers started to make records for young people. They sang about teenagers' problems — with parents, boyfriends/girlfriends, school, money. In the UK artists like Cliff Richard, Marty Wilde, Billy Fury and Tommy Steele did the same. Rock and roll music is as popular today as when it burst into people's lives over 50 years ago. Parents at the time dismissed it as a five-minute wonder. A long five minutes!

CHUCK BERRY

What sets Chuck Berry apart from most of the rock 'n' roll stars of the 1950s and 60s is that he was a very accomplished songwriter. Performers like Elvis Presley, Little Richard, Buddy Holly and many others relied on professional songwriters to provide them with material to record. Berry wrote his own songs, dealing entertainingly with the problems of relationships, parents, school, cars, cash flow — all the things that teenagers were worrying about.

GETTING STARTED

Born in 1926 in San Jose, California, Charles Edward Berry moved to Saint Louis, Missouri, as a child and sang in his church and school choirs in his teens. He trained as a hairdresser and played for fun with a trio at weekends. In 1955, when he was nearly 30 years old, he recorded a couple of his own songs and moved to Chicago, the center for blues music at the time. He searched out blues legend Muddy Waters, who introduced him to Leonard Chess, owner of the Chess record label. Chess listened to Chuck's two songs and released both of them.

One Dozen Berrys
1958
After School Sessions
1958

The Collection
1988
Chuck Berry Boxed Set
1989

"Maybellene," a witty song about a boy who chases his two-timing girlfriend, went straight to the top of the rhythm-and-blues charts.

THE GUITAR GOES ELECTRIC

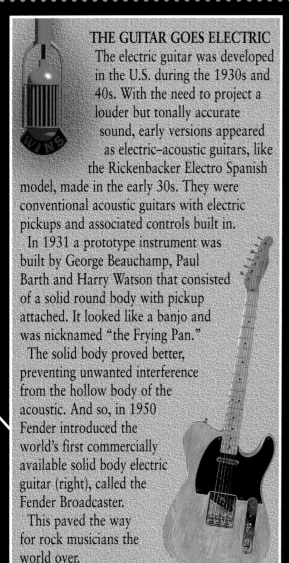

The electric guitar was developed in the U.S. during the 1930s and 40s. With the need to project a louder but tonally accurate sound, early versions appeared as electric–acoustic guitars, like the Rickenbacker Electro Spanish model, made in the early 30s. They were conventional acoustic guitars with electric pickups and associated controls built in.

In 1931 a prototype instrument was built by George Beauchamp, Paul Barth and Harry Watson that consisted of a solid round body with pickup attached. It looked like a banjo and was nicknamed "the Frying Pan."

The solid body proved better, preventing unwanted interference from the hollow body of the acoustic. And so, in 1950 Fender introduced the world's first commercially available solid body electric guitar (right), called the Fender Broadcaster.

This paved the way for rock musicians the world over.

Chuck Berry's career was launched, his music a mixture of blues, country and western, R&B and rock 'n' roll.

Berry in the film, Hail, Hail, Rock 'n' Roll.

SUCCESS

Berry put his finger firmly on the pulse of the worries of a generation. He recorded dozens of his own songs, many of them complete short stories. He was an innovative guitarist and also developed his famous duckwalk — while playing, he would walk across the stage in a peculiar bent-kneed style. He charged promoters extra to perform this maneuver!

The singles "Brown Eyed Handsome Man," "Roll Over Beethoven" (later recorded by the Beatles), "Sweet Little Sixteen," "Too Much Monkey Business," "Johnny B. Good," "School Days" and "No Money Down" made Chuck Berry a popular and wealthy entertainer by the 60s.

BAD TIMES

Too soon it started to go wrong. Berry was imprisoned between 1962 and 64, and despite quickly releasing three more classic singles, "Nadine," "No Particular Place To Go" and "You Can Never Tell," he never regained his earlier level of international success. Berry continued to tour the world, although he sometimes lacked his previous dynamism. In 1972 he achieved his first number one single on both sides of the Atlantic with "Ding A Ling," although the song was certainly not one of his best.

In 1987 Chuck Berry featured in the film documentary *Hail, Hail, Rock 'n' Roll,* in which an exasperated Keith Richards (guitarist in the Rolling Stones) tries to persuade a stubborn Berry to improve his rather sloppy stage performance.

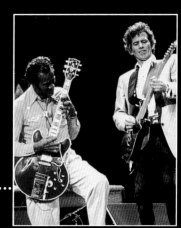

Berry plays with Richards in Hail, Hail, Rock 'n' Roll.

STILL GOING STRONG

Chuck Berry continues to perform some of the very best rock 'n' roll songs ever written — one of the true rock 'n' roll greats.

EDDIE COCHRAN

On April 17, 1960 Eddie Cochran took a taxi from Bristol in order to catch his plane home after his successful UK tour. With him were Gene Vincent and Cochran's girlfriend, Sharon Sheely. A tire blew, the car crashed into a lamppost, and 16 hours later Eddie Cochran died from severe head injuries. Ironically, he had escaped death just one year earlier, when he had turned down the chance of appearing in the Winter Dance Party Tour, featuring Buddy Holly, Ritchie Valens and the Big Bopper. All three died when their light plane crashed shortly after take-off from Iowa on February 3, 1959.

KEEN TEEN

Edward Ray Cochran was born in Oklahoma in 1938. As a teenager he became very interested in music and, after flirting with several instruments, decided the guitar was what he wanted to play. In 1955 he formed the Cochrans with friend Hank Cochran (no relation). A year later Jerry Capeheart joined the duo. They made various records, none of which was commercially successful. Hank left the trio. Eddie and Jerry's first cowritten song, "Skinny Jim," was not a hit — but Eddie Cochran was just about to get his extremely lucky break.

Cochran, with obligatory slicked-back hair, belting out some rock 'n' roll with gusto.

THE BREAK

Cochan was asked to sing "Twenty Flight Rock" in the film, *The Girl Can't Help It*. The film was a great success all over the world. A contract with the very prestigious Liberty record label followed.

In April 1957 Cochran enjoyed his first Top 20 hit in the UK, "Sitting in the Balcony." Two flop singles followed, but in September 1958 Cochran released his all-time classic record "Summertime Blues." A telling song about teenage frustration, it entered the Top 20 charts on both sides of the Atlantic.

UK IDOL

From this point on, Eddie Cochran was more successful in the UK than the U.S. In 1959 "C'm on Everybody" entered the UK Top 10, but it didn't even make the Top 30 in the U.S. Later that year "Somethin' Else" became a big UK hit (both of these singles would be covered by the Sex Pistols 20 years later), as did "Hallelujah I Love Her" in 1960.

Cochran made his UK television debut in 1960 on Jack Good's *Boy Meets Girl* pop show and did a lengthy tour with fellow rockers Gene Vincent, Billy Fury, Joe Brown and Georgie Fame. The tour was so successful that promoter Larry Parnes extended it by two weeks. Finally, a weary Cochran and Vincent climbed into a cab to take them to the airport and their flight home.

SWAN SONG

The poignantly titled "Three Steps to Heaven," was released just after Cochran's death. Eddie Cochran was only 21 when he died — in the country that had adopted him as one of its very favorite rock 'n' roll performers.

JACK GOOD AND LARRY PARNES

TV was important in promoting rock 'n' roll in the UK, and Jack Good produced most of the shows that were compulsory viewing for teenagers in the late 50s. *6.5 Special* was followed by *Oh Boy!* and *Boy Meets Girl* then *Wham!*

Amazingly, Good predicted the rock video: "It will ultimately become standard practice for every artist to make a film of themselves performing their record. These short films will be sent to TV producers for their programs." The year was 1959.

Larry Parnes was the man who "spotted" most of the UK's rock 'n' roll stars. In 1960 he rejected the Beatles as not good enough to back his new find, Billy Fury.

Jack Good was converted to rock 'n' roll when he saw Rock Around the Clock.

Singing to My Baby
1958

The Eddie Cochran Memorial Album
1960

Cherished Memories
1962

The Very Best of Eddie Cochran
1970

BO DIDDLEY

In 1951 Elias McDaniel, aged 21, secured his first professional job as a musician in Chicago's 708 Clubs. Astonishingly, he had already been playing guitar semiprofessionally for over 10 years, although only on the street and at parties and dances. McDaniel had also enjoyed modest success as a boxer. It was while he was boxing that he was nicknamed "Bo Diddley."

MUSIC WINS OUT

Diddley studied classical violin for 12 years and, living in Chicago, had been exposed to the blues style of Muddy Waters who gigged locally. It was hardly surprising that music should take precedence over boxing, and Bo began to write songs and develop his musical skills.

In 1955, along with fellow musicians Jerome Green, Frank Kirkland, Lester Davenport and legendary piano player Otis Spann, Diddley took his songs, "Bo Diddley," "I'm a Man" and "You Don't Love Me," to Chicago's Checker record label, owned by Leonard Chess. "Bo Diddley" was released in June of that year and, with its throbbing jungle rhythm, was an immediate success. An appearance on the prestigious *Ed Sullivan Show* followed, and Diddley was on his way.

Like many other US rock 'n' rollers, he achieved a greater success in the UK than at home.

Diddley is famous for his series of custom-made guitars.

Bo Diddley jams with Ron Wood from the Faces.

However, his singles "Who Do You Love," "Crackin' Up," "Say Man," "Road Runner" and "You Can't Judge a Book by Looking at Its Cover" all did well, making the Top 100.

DIDDLEY IN THE UK

Diddley was becoming a huge influence on some very important UK bands. The Rolling Stones, Manfred Mann, the Yardbirds, the Animals, the Who and many other groups recorded his songs.

In 1963 Diddley arrived in the UK for a tour with the Everly Brothers and the Rolling Stones. His presence helped to put "Pretty Thing" and "Bo Diddley" into the UK charts during that year.

Between 1963 and 69 Diddley spent a great deal of time in the UK, touring and appearing on TV. His albums were now selling better than his singles.

BACK TO BLUES

In 1968 Diddley returned to his blues roots when he recorded the album *The Super Blues Band*, with Muddy Waters and Little Walter. In the late 60s and early 70s Diddley appeared regularly on the Rock 'n' Roll Revival shows with fellow stars Chuck Berry, Little Richard and Jerry Lee Lewis. Few hits followed, but deserved recognition was on its way.

In 1976 Bo Diddley contributed to RCA Records' *The 20th Anniversary of Rock 'n' Roll* with Joe Cocker, Alvin Lee, Keith Moon, Billy Joel, Roger McQuinn and many others.

DIDDLEY ON TV
When it started, rock 'n' roll received so much bad press that Diddley's invitation to appear on the Ed Sullivan Show was good news for the cause. But the rockers didn't always help themselves, and Diddley nearly blew it.

TV superstar Ed Sullivan wanted Diddley to perform "Sixteen Tons." He rehearsed it over and over and the words were written on big cue cards ready for the performance. But as the show went out live, Diddley picked up his guitar, ignored the cue cards (and Ed Sullivan's specific request) and played instead his signature tune, "Bo Diddley."

Diddley plays the Live Aid charity concert in Philadelphia in 1985.

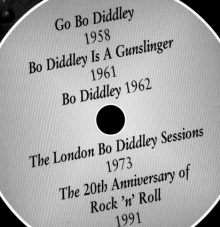

Go Bo Diddley
1958
Bo Diddley Is A Gunslinger
1961
Bo Diddley 1962

The London Bo Diddley Sessions
1973
The 20th Anniversary of
Rock 'n' Roll
1991

FATS DOMINO

Antoine Domino was born in 1926 in New Orleans, Louisiana, the home of many excellent rhythm and blues piano players. Fats Domino is probably the very best of them, and almost certainly the most famous. In 1987 he was honored at the Grammy Awards as "one of the most important links between rhythm and blues and rock 'n' roll, a most influential performer whose style of piano playing and 'down home' singing have led the way for generations of performers." His song "Blueberry Hill" was voted into the Rock 'n' Roll Hall of Fame as one of the best rock 'n' roll songs ever.

FATS HITS THE ROAD

Fats Domino joined Dave Bartholomew's band in 1949 and was soon signed to the Imperial record label. (The nickname "Fats" was given to Domino by his bass player, Billy Diamond, due to Domino's 225-pound (110 kg) bulk.) Domino's song "The Fat Man," sold more than a million copies. Domino hit the road and began his immensely successful career. Hit after hit followed from 1950 to 52.

Domino had married his childhood sweetheart Rose Marie in 1947. He had eight brothers and sisters, he and Rose had eight children. Fats's great love of his family eventually restricted his touring schedule.

Fats Domino
Rock and Rolling!
1956
This Is Fats Domino
1957
Here Stands Fats Domino
1957
My Blue Heaven: The Best of Fats Domino
1991

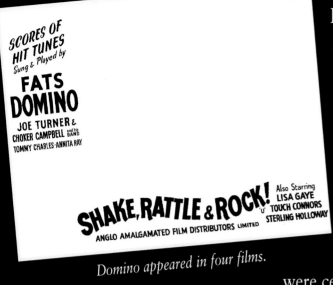

SCORES OF
HIT TUNES
Sung & Played by
FATS
DOMINO
JOE TURNER &
CHOKER CAMPBELL and his BAND
TOMMY CHARLES·ANNITA RAY

SHAKE, RATTLE & ROCK!
Also Starring
LISA GAYE
'U' TOUCH CONNORS
STERLING HOLLOWAY
ANGLO AMALGAMATED FILM DISTRIBUTORS LIMITED

Domino appeared in four films.

Domino had even more hits in 1953 and 54, which allowed him to indulge in the ornate gold and diamond rings he loved. His hands were his living and, adorned, were certainly part of his image. In 1955 Fats won over the new rock 'n' roll audience with a Top 10 hit, "Ain't That a Shame."

THE UK TAKES NOTICE

It wasn't until 1956 that Domino made a real impact in the UK. But once he had made the breakthrough with "I'm in Love Again," "My Blue Heaven" and "Blueberry Hill" he had a steady stream of hits. In 1957 his songs "Honey Chile," "Blue Monday," "I'm Walking" and "Valley of Tears" all entered the UK Top 30. Domino kept writing, kept touring and the hits kept coming.

RICH REWARDS

By the 60s Domino had become a very wealthy man and began to take life just a little easier. Tours became less lengthy, and the gaps between them and between recording sessions became longer. The hit singles petered out. He still appears occasionally on TV and plays selected venues (Las Vegas is a favorite).

Fats Domino can afford to rest upon his laurels. He has produced 36 Top 40 singles and has sold just under 100 million records during his 50-year career.

ALAN FREED

Alan Freed was **the** rock 'n' roll radio DJ of the 50s and, some believe, the man most responsible for rock 'n' roll's success.

In 1958 Freed arranged a concert at the Boston Arena featuring Fats Domino, Jerry Lee Lewis, the Crickets and many others. At that time the notion of black and white artists performing together to a mixed audience was contentious.

When a white girl climbed on stage and grabbed a black performer chaos broke out. The police rushed on the stage, and the audience was pushed outside where more police were beating up the teenagers. Alan Freed climbed on stage and yelled, "The police don't want you to have any fun here."

The only person prosecuted was Freed, for inciting a riot.

Two years later Freed was in trouble again — this time on payola charges (accepting bribes to play records).

Freed (right) had a cameo role in the movie, Don't Knock the Rock.

Domino in concert in Paris at the Halle That Jazz *festival in 1992.*

BILL HALEY

Like so many performers before him, Bill Haley's musical influences were diverse. Born in Michigan in 1925, he came from a musical family. His parents both played and loved country and western music, and Haley himself started his career at the age of 13 with a local country and western band. Two years later he was leading his own band, playing a mixture of country music and western swing, although Haley was also listening hard to the rhythm and blues pouring out of his local radio station. In 1951 he recorded "Rocket 88" and "Rock the Joint." Bill Haley suspected that the heady mix of country music and hard rhythm and blues could be commercially successful, and he was right. In 1952 he recorded the pulsating "Crazy Man Crazy" and two years later "Shake, Rattle and Roll" earned him a gold record, an award for records that sell in excess of one million.

ROCK AROUND THE CLOCK

But the best was yet to come. "Rock Around the Clock," recorded by Haley and the Comets in 1955, is possibly the world's best known rock 'n' roll record, and it eventually sold around 20 million copies. Featured in the film *Blackboard Jungle*, and the inspiration behind Haley's follow-up movie of the same name, "Rock Around the Clock" deserves its status as a rock 'n' roll anthem.

Although "Rock Around the Clock" represents the zenith of Haley's career, the follow-up record, "See You Later Alligator," was also a huge success, and

Haley plays the Albert Hall, London, in May 1968.

another film, *Don't Knock the Clock*, featuring a whole host of rock 'n' rollers, followed fast. In 1957 Bill Haley visited the UK for the first time, to rapturous acclaim. But his popularity was beginning to wane. Haley was 32 years old and competing with a new generation of younger performers. The kiss curl and plaid jacket image was beginning to look very old-fashioned to his young fans.

Although Haley continued to tour the world, earning a very comfortable living, no more hit records were to come. Ill health dogged him, and he died from heart problems in February 1981, aged 55. He left a legacy of some of the most enjoyable rock 'n' roll recordings of all time.

*Haley told the Comets, "Don't just play – **do** something!"*

When "Rock Around the Clock" was rereleased on its 20th anniversary in 1974 it immediately charted again on both sides of the Atlantic.

"One, two, three o'clock, four o'clock rock, five, six, seven o'clock, eight o'clock rock..."

Everybody can sing the next line!

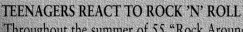

TEENAGERS REACT TO ROCK 'N' ROLL

Throughout the summer of 55 "Rock Around the Clock" was number one — and it had an unprecedented effect on teenagers.

In London a man was fined for "making an abominable noise" playing "Rock Around the Clock" for two and a half hours.

At Princeton University a student played the record, then another joined in and very soon a riot erupted with students singing and burning garbage outside the dorms.

When the film *Blackboard Jungle* was released UK teenagers saw for the first time how to dance to the music. They ended up jiving in the cinema aisles and out into the streets.

In Liverpool police chased 1,000 jiving teenagers a mile across the city center before turning water hoses on them.

Meanwhile teenagers in the U.S. wrecked cinemas as soon as "Rock Around the Clock" was played.

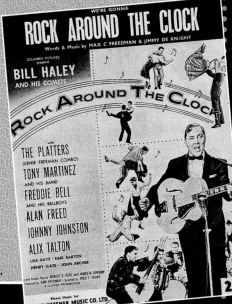

Rock Around the Clock
1956
Rock and Roll Stage Show
1956

The Very Best of Bill Haley
& His Comets
1992

BUDDY HOLLY

On the morning of February 3, 1959 in Clear Lake, Iowa, Buddy Holly climbed aboard a small airplane with fellow rock 'n' roll artists the Big Bopper and Ritchie Valens. Their aim was to avoid yet another long, cold trip on the tour bus, so they could arrive early enough at the next concert venue to do their washing and catch up with some much needed sleep. The Winter Dance Party Tour had been grueling. Minutes after takeoff the tiny Beechcraft Bonanza plunged to the ground near Mason City, Iowa. All aboard died. Buddy Holly was just 22 years old.

The Big Bopper

Ritchie Valens

The wreckage of the plane that crashed with Holly on board.

THE HITS START COMING

A big admirer of Elvis Presley, Chuck Berry and Little Richard, Holly started playing country and western music in 1954. He teamed up with Jerry Allison, Joe Maudlin and Niki Sullivan and met a man who would have a huge influence on his short career, producer and songwriter Norman Petty. "That'll Be the Day" was released in May 1957 and was an instant number one hit on both sides of the Atlantic.

TEENAGERS IN THE 50s

Bespectacled teenagers the world over breathed a huge sigh of relief when Buddy Holly burst on to the scene as a rock 'n' roll star. At last, here was a popular hero who wore glasses!

It was 1957, and for the first time teenagers were no longer just younger versions of their parents. They had their own language, clothes, social scene and music.

Teenagers met in ice cream parlors, drank ice cream sodas and malted milk and ate pizza pie. They went to drive-ins and to the first McDonalds. Boys customized their cars while girls borrowed their parents' cars to cruise and hang out.

Boys had sideburns and their quiffed hair tapered into a point at the back of the neck, called a DA (duck's ass). Their shoes were suede (more often white than blue!).

Girls wore pants that stopped short of the ankle, called pedal pushers (always with a side zip — flies were for boys!), white ankle socks and ponytails.

"Cat," "hip," "chick," "cool" were all part of the new teen-speak and came from language previously used mainly by African-Americans in the 20s.

Cruising past a drive-in movie in the 50s.

Holly himself was an accomplished writer, and hit after hit followed during 1957 and 58. Buddy Holly and the Crickets made a rare and welcome visit to the UK in 1958.

TIRED OF TOURING

Holly's touring schedule was exhausting in the 50s. He fell out with Norman Petty, who demanded a credit and royalties on all of Holly's songs. This and Holly's move to New York were both factors in his split from the Crickets. Now two versions of the band were on tour, Buddy Holly and his new backing group, and the Crickets. Holly was weary of traveling by 1959, but, short of money, he hauled himself on to the road to pay the bills.

He had recorded "It Doesn't Matter Anymore," written by Paul Anka. The song was an ironic and sad posthumous success for Holly, topping the charts in the U.S. and the UK.

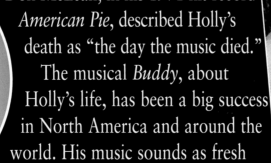

STILL REMEMBERED

Don McLean, in his 1971 hit record *American Pie*, described Holly's death as "the day the music died." The musical *Buddy*, about Holly's life, has been a big success in North America and around the world. His music sounds as fresh today as in 1959.

Buddy Holly
1958

20 Golden Greats
1978
'20 Love Songs
1982

The Crickets in 1958 were (from left to right) Jerry Allison (18), Joe Maudlin (18) and Holly (21).

JERRY LEE LEWIS

Described as the wildest rock 'n' roller bar none, Jerry Lee Lewis's nickname is "The Killer," earned because of his exuberant stage presence. Lewis was born in Louisiana in 1935. He taught himself to play the piano in just two weeks at the age of 13. Three years later he married the first of his six wives. His personal life has been tumultuous: two of his wives died in mysterious circumstances, two of his children died in tragic accidents and two of his marriages were bigamous.

THE BREAKTHROUGH

In 1956, when Jerry was 21 years old, he and his father went to the legendary Sun Studios in Memphis, where Elvis Presley and Carl Perkins had started their recording careers. Lewis persuaded owner Sam Phillips to record his powerful "Whole Lotta Shakin' Goin' On." Banned by many radio stations, it sold a modest amount until Lewis got the break he really needed. He was invited to appear on the nationally broadcast *Steve Allen Show.* Sales of the single immediately escalated. Six million copies later, Lewis found himself at the top of both the rhythm and blues and country and western charts.

MILLION DOLLAR QUARTET

Christmas 1956 saw Jerry Lee Lewis at the Sun Studios in Memphis, where the so-called Million Dollar Quartet were recorded playing together for the first and only time.

Elvis was home for Christmas. (He'd given his and hers cadillacs to his parents.) He went along to Sun Studios where he met up with Lewis, Johnny Cash and Carl Perkins — and the Million Dollar Quartet had their only jamming session.

When the tape of the session was released 25 years later most people agreed that the music was awful!

Lewis is known for his "pumpin' piano" style.

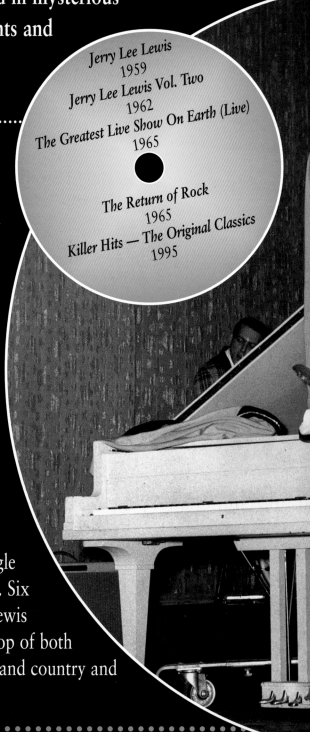

Jerry Lee Lewis
1959
Jerry Lee Lewis Vol. Two
1962
The Greatest Live Show On Earth (Live)
1965
The Return of Rock
1965
Killer Hits — The Original Classics
1995

To cap a highly successful year, he then appeared in a film, with Carl Perkins, Fats Domino and many other R&B stars, entitled *Jamboree*. He toured incessantly but still found the time to marry bigamously his 13-year-old second cousin, Myra Gale Brown, the daughter of his bass player.

THE SCANDAL

In 1958 there was success, but also problems. When Lewis arrived in the UK with his child bride for a major tour, the British media expressed its horror at what it saw as a scandal. The tour was canceled. Lewis's career began to stall on both sides of the Atlantic. He toured the UK again in 1962 and 64, and in 1966 played Iago in Jack Good's musical, *Othello*. By now alcohol and drugs were badly affecting Lewis, and his life was in turmoil.

Lewis and his young wife, Myra, face the cameras in London.

In 1968 Lewis turned to country and western and for the next 20 years had a successful career. Although he never quite left rock 'n' roll behind him, it never dominated his music again.

More divorces and marriages followed, and in 1976 Lewis crashed his Rolls Royce, shot his bass player and was arrested outside Elvis Presley's home, demanding to see Elvis while armed with a gun.

Lewis performs at a C&W festival in Wembley, London, in 1982.

STILL GOING STRONG

A larger than life character, "The Killer" still tours the world at the age of 73, causing mayhem, but richly entertaining thousands of fans.

ROY ORBISON

Roy Orbison's image and stage presence were very subdued for a rock 'n' roll star. Orbison, dressed in black, his eyes concealed by his trademark sunglasses, stayed glued to the center stage. His rather high pitched, quavering voice was unique and seemed almost more suited to light opera than to rock music.

SONGWRITER TURNED SINGER

In 1960, after rather a slow start to his show business career, Orbison wrote and released his first massive hit. A song he had actually written for either Elvis or the Everly Brothers to record, the dramatic "Only the Lonely" was a huge hit for Orbison on both sides of the Atlantic. Its success was quickly repeated. Many more singles made the charts in the U.S. and the UK in the 60s, selling millions of copies.

In 1962 Orbison released "Dream Baby" and, like so many rock 'n' rollers, found that the young people in the UK had taken him to their hearts.

*Orbison appeared **without** his glasses in a movie,* The Fastest Guitar Alive, *in 1966.*

In September 1963 he toured England. "In Dreams" was a big hit in the same year, and it seemed that Roy Orbison was destined to stay in the fast lane.

TRAGEDY AND TOURS

The hits followed, with "Blue Bayou," "It's Over" and possibly his best known release, "Oh Pretty Woman," which sold over seven million copies and made him very wealthy.

But personal tragedy was to strike, not once but twice. In 1966 his wife was killed in an accident while the two of them were riding their motorcycles. Orbison threw himself into a tough touring schedule. He was beginning to recover from this dreadful loss when two of his three children died in a fire at his Nashville home. Devastated, Orbison coped in the same way as he had before — work and more work! He toured the world for the next decade, rarely giving himself a break from his punishing regime.

Orbison collects his award from the Rock 'n' Roll Hall of Fame in 1987.

A TRIBUTE

Orbison's hits dried up, but other artists recorded his excellent songs. In 1987 he was inducted into the Rock 'n' Roll Hall of Fame in New York. A richly deserved TV tribute followed, honoring his 26-year career at the forefront of rock 'n' roll.

In 1988 Orbison joined Bob Dylan, Jeff Lynne, George Harrison and Tom Petty in the Traveling Wilburys. Their debut album entered the Top 20 in both the UK and the U.S. Tragically, Orbison died from a heart attack soon afterwards.

Lonely and Blue
1961
Crying 1962
Roy Orbison's Greatest Hits
1962
In Dreams 1963
The Singles Collection 1965-1973
1989
Golden Decade Boxed Set 1990
The Golden Years 1960-1969
1993

12-BAR BLUES

In blues, a 12-bar structure, three phrases of four bars, soon became the norm. A blues in E, a key popular with guitarists, would be as below:

There are many variations on this sequence, and, of course, not all blues pieces use this structure.

Bar:	1	2	3	4
Chord:	E	E	E	E
	5	6	7	8
	A	A	E	E
	9	10	11	12
	B	A	E	E

If you have a keyboard with automatic rhythms, find a blues or R&B setting and switch on the "single fingered chord" facility. Start the rhythm and play E at the bottom end of the keyboard, counting out four bars of E as follows: E234 E234 E234 E234

Now try the whole 12 bars as written out right:

E234	E234	E234	E234
A234	A234	E234	E234
B234	A234	E234	fill-in*

* Press the fill-in button here.

291

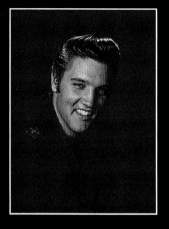

ELVIS PRESLEY

The only survivor of twins, Elvis Aaron Presley was born in Tupelo, Mississippi, on January 8, 1935 and died just over 42 years later in Memphis on August 16, 1977. Elvis Presley drifted through school and had several menial jobs. His family was poor, and Presley was keen to contribute to their finances. He could hardly have dreamt how great that contribution would become.

ELVIS IS SPOTTED

In 1953 Elvis Presley dropped into the Sun Sudios in Memphis to make a record as a present for his mother. Owner Sam Phillips spotted his huge talent. He introduced Presley to three musicians, Scotty Moore, Bill Black and D.J. Fontana, and Presley released five singles on the Sun label. None sold well, but Presley's talent was recognized by RCA Records, a large record company in New York. They paid Sam Phillips $35,000 (worth about $300,000 in today's money!) for Presley's contract and the right to release all future records by him.

Elvis and Priscilla appeared in the movie This is Elvis.

ELVIS SOUNDS BLACK

Rock 'n' roll's roots were in African-American gospel music. Sam Phillips felt he had only to find a white boy who could sing black music and he would have it made. Elvis Presley was that boy. When he was interviewed on local radio Presley was asked which school he had attended — so that the listeners would hear it was a school for whites.

When Presley appeared on the Ed Sullivan TV show in 1956, his gyrating act in front of screaming teenagers caused an outcry. Sullivan later insisted that Elvis be filmed only from the waist up, but the audience still screamed as hard as ever.

CALLED UP

Elvis's career dramatically took off in 1956, when "Heartbreak Hotel" topped the charts for eight weeks. Nine number one hits followed for Presley, but in 1958 his career was rudely interrupted when he was called up by the U.S. Army. Before joining Elvis recorded several songs that were hits while he was away.

*Elvis may be **the** most famous U.S. soldier.*

MOVIES

On March 1, 1961, Elvis returned to civilian life and started a new career as a movie star. Some fans think his talent was wasted over the next decade as he appeared in a stream of mediocre films.

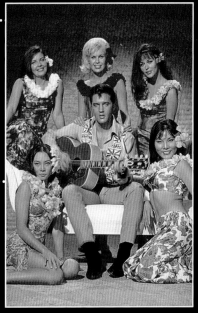

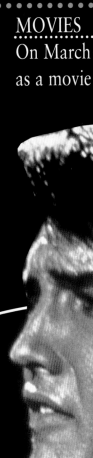

MORE HITS

In 1968, following his marriage to Priscilla and the birth of their daughter, Lisa-Marie, he made a comeback on an NBC TV special. Between 1970 and 73, 11 hit singles followed, and in 1973 Presley performed in a live worldwide TV program from Hawaii. All the proceeds went to charity, and the sound-track album sold over a million copies.

Elvis starred in the movie,
Paradise Hawaiian Style.

DIVORCE, DRUGS, DEATH

Things were going wrong for Elvis in his personal life. He was divorced from Priscilla in 1972. Five years later, due to drug problems and an appallingly unhealthy diet, he died at his home, Graceland.

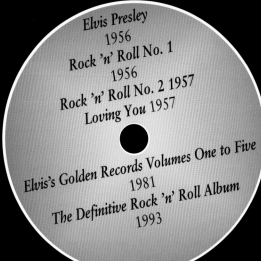

Elvis Presley
1956
Rock 'n' Roll No. 1
1956
Rock 'n' Roll No. 2 1957
Loving You 1957

Elvis's Golden Records Volumes One to Five
1981
The Definitive Rock 'n' Roll Album
1993

CLIFF RICHARD

"It was the most crude exhibitionism ever seen on British TV. Revolting. Hardly the kind of performance any parent would wish his children to witness!" This was how a journalist described the debut television performance of Harry Webb on September 13, 1958. Forty years later, Webb was knighted.

BRITAIN'S ELVIS

Richard started his singing career as Britain's answer to Elvis Presley, and he certainly deserves his place in the annals of rock 'n' roll history, although he didn't remain a rock 'n' roller for very long.

Harry Webb was born in India in 1940 and went to England with his parents when he was eight years old. An uneventful childhood followed, but in 1957 Webb discovered the thrilling sounds of rock 'n' roll! In one of several parallels with the career of his idol, Elvis Presley, Webb recorded a private demonstration disc with his new band, the Drifters. Gigs at London's renowned 21s Coffee Bar followed ,and Harry Webb became Cliff Richard.

In July 1958 Richard and the Drifters won a prestigious talent competition at the Gaumont Cinema in London's Shepherd's Bush, and Richard's agent, George Ganjon, persuaded the major UK

Richard started out playing guitar but soon concentrated on vocals.

Cliff
1952
Cliff Sings
1959
Me and My Shadows 1960

Rock on With Cliff Richard
1987
Cliff Richard:
The Rock 'n' Roll Years
1997

record label EMI to listen to him. EMI's man, Norrie Paramor, liked what he heard, and Richard recorded his first single. The song chosen for Richard to record was called "Schoolboy Crush" — the throwaway B side of the record, "Move It," was written by Drifter Ian Samwell during his bus journey to the recording studio. When the record was released everybody preferred this song. "Move It" is still considered to be one of the most authentic UK rock 'n' roll records ever made.

THE SHADOWS

In October 1958 Richard made his infamous debut on the popular *Oh Boy* TV show. Producer Jack Good molded Richard's image, and his popularity rocketed. Richard recruited a new lineup for his backing band, consisting of guitarists Hank Marvin and Bruce Welch, bass player Jet Harris and drummer Tony Meehan who quickly changed their name from the Drifters to the Shadows. They achieved huge success as an instrumental group, at one stage knocking Richard off the number one spot with "Apache."

The Shadows and Richard, who's holding his gold record for Congratulations *in 1968.*

TEDDY BOYS AND GIRLS

When not tuning in to Radio Luxembourg on their transistor radios, teenagers in the UK met in coffee bars and listened to their music on the new jukeboxes. The most famous coffee bar of all was the 2Is in London's Soho. Many rock 'n' roll stars had their first break there, including Cliff Richard.

Because space was so limited in these bars, the hand jive was born — a dance that was performed seated or standing but only the hands moved!

The "Teddy Boy" look at the time was slicked-back hair with a DA, long jackets, drainpipe pants and heavy, crepe-soled shoes. "Teddy Girls" wore stiletto heels, pencil skirts, turtle necks and had back-combed "beehive" hair. By the mid-50s girls wore big skirts with stiff petticoats — perfect for jiving — or tight, ankle-length pants. All a far cry from the post-war fashions of their parents.

A curious teenager checks out the Teddy Boy look.

CAREER MOVE

Richard had a string of hit records, but by 1960, fearing that Richard's "Elvis" phase would date, Paramor persuaded him to record the more middle-of-the-road "Living Doll." Richard didn't like it, but when the song gave him his first number one hit he realized that a new career, aimed at a much wider age range, would be a smart move.

After a career lasting five decades and countless hit singles, he was right, but many of his original fans felt that Richard's post-rock 'n' roll work lacked the appeal of his early singles. Respectable Sir Cliff he may have become, but perhaps his two-year reign as one of Britain's finest rock 'n' rollers was a little too short!

LITTLE RICHARD

Richard Wayne Penniman hardly warranted his nickname "Little." One of the most flamboyant and egoistic performers on the rock 'n' roll scene, Little Richard enjoyed a spectacular career during the 50s and 60s. Born in 1935 in Macon, Georgia, Little Richard came from a familiar background for a rock 'n' roller. Blues and gospel music greatly influenced him, and his large family (he had eleven brothers and sisters) were all heavily involved in the church, singing and playing spiritual music.

TEENAGE BEGINNINGS

Richard's unique talent as a singer and piano player soon emerged. His first efforts in the RCA Victor recording studios at the tender age of 16 were not successful, but, considering his age, the eight songs he recorded showed a surprising maturity and promise.

In 1954 Little Richard met rock 'n' roll star Lloyd Price who suggested that he send tapes of his songs to Los Angeles record company Specialty Records. In the following year Richard recorded a song for Specialty that would launch his international career, "Tutti Frutti," with one of the most bizarre first lines ever written, "Awop bop a loo bop a lop bam boom, tutti frutti." He sold all publishing and royalty rights to the song for $50. It entered the charts, peaked at number 17 and eventually sold over three million copies!

Little Richard went back into the studio in 1956 with his band of Earl Palmer (drums), Lee Allen (sax), Frank Field (bass) and other renowned New Orleans musicians. Between 1956 and 58 Richard could do no wrong, recording a stream of hugely successful international hits.

Here's Little Richard
1957
Little Richard 2 1958
The Fabulous Little Richard
1959

Little Richard is Back
1965
20 Classic Cuts 1986
The Collection
1989

Richard's appearance in the film, The Girl Can't Help It promoted his outrageous reputation.

TOM EWELL · JAYNE MANSFIELD · EDMOND O'BRIEN
in THE GIRL CAN'T HELP IT
CINEMASCOPE
PICTURE
IN EASTMAN COLOUR
Cert 'U'
with Guest stars JULIE LONDON · RAY ANTHONY · BARRY GORDON and featuring HENRY JONES
Screenplay by FRANK TASHLIN and HERBERT BAKER
Produced and Directed by FRANK TASHLIN

RICHARD AND RELIGION

The world seemed at Little Richard's feet, but a terrifying incident during a European flight pitched him into a completely different direction. An engine fire convinced him that he was going to die, and he pledged that, if saved, he would devote his life to God. He kept his promise. Little Richard went to college, earned a BA and was ordained as a minister of the Seventh Day Adventist Church. He stayed in the church until 1963.

FAME AGAIN

Richard returned to music and spent years touring Europe with the then little-known bands the Rolling Stones and the Beatles, who were very familiar with his material. As both bands became hugely successful in the U.S. in the late 60s, their loud praise of Little Richard had a great spin off for him. Work flooded in, and he hit the road.

ROCK 'N' ROLL BANNED

In the '50s a howling African-American man who wore eye makeup was an unlikely candidate for stardom — but by 1955 Little Richard had made it. The following year radio DJs all over the U.S. were trying to ban rock 'n' roll.

DJ Noble(!) Gravelin of WAMM in Michigan said, "I banned Little Richard's "Lucille" because I feel the lyrics advocate immoral practices ... I did a most praiseworthy thing."

"Long, Tall Sally" fared better. The NBC censor said, "How can I restrict it when I can't even understand it?"

Other DJs smashed all their rock 'n' roll records saying, "It's simply a weeding out of undesirable music," and "There comes a time when human endurance reaches its limit."

British band leader Ted Heath said, "Rock 'n' roll is mainly performed by colored artists for colored people, and is therefore unlikely to ever prove popular in Britain."

Students demonstrate rock 'n' roll's popularity.

Little Richard was successful again, although he never achieved the heady heights he had enjoyed in the 50s and 60s.

Despite a brief return to the church after the death of his brother in the mid-70s, in the 21st century Little Richard is still playing, still recording and still pounding those keyboards all over the world.

GENE VINCENT

Eugene Vincent Craddock was born in Norfolk, Virginia, in 1935. He joined the navy when he was in his teens, lying about his age in order to enlist. When he was 20 years old his leg was seriously injured in a motorcycle accident. Vincent was bored and unable to work, and so, as he had an excellent voice, his mother advised him to become a singer. The huge label Capitol was on the lookout for an artist to compete with Elvis Presley. They held a talent contest, and Vincent won. He promptly recorded two songs, "Women Love" and a song he bought for $25 from his friend, Don Graves, called "Be Bop A Lula."

A FINE START

In 1956 "Women Love" was released as the A side of the record and earned Gene Vincent a $10,000 fine for "public lewdness and obscenity." Nobody cared though, because "Be Bop A Lula" was the song all the DJs chose to play. The record shot to number seven on the charts and went on to sell a million copies.

Between 1956 and 58 Gene Vincent had many more hits and worked with an excellent backing group called the Blue Caps, who were revered in their own right by rock 'n' roll fans. Their first lead guitar player, Cliff Gallup, was extremely talented, and acclaimed British rock guitarist Jeff Beck recorded a tribute to him with the UK band Big Town Playboys. Eventually Vincent was more popular and successful in Europe than in the U.S. "Lotta Lovin," "Race with the Devil,"

Gene Vincent & His
Blue Caps 1957
Gene Vincent Rocks and
the Blue Caps Roll 1957
A Gene Vincent Record Date 1958

Sounds like Gene Vincent
1958
Crazy Times
1960
The Gene Vincent Box Set
1990

Vincent returns to the U.S. after the car crash.

"Blue Jean Bop" and "Dance To The Bop" all did well for him during the late 50s.

COCHRAN'S CRASH

Sadly, during a tour of the UK in 1960 Vincent was badly injured in a serious car accident that killed a fellow rocker, the hugely talented Eddie Cochran. Recovering from his injuries took months. Vincent then chose to make his home in the UK and earned a reasonable living touring there and in Europe. He returned to the U.S. many times, taking part in the regular rock 'n' roll revival shows which were very popular in the 1970s, with fellow heroes Little Richard, Bo Diddley, Jerry Lee Lewis and many other famous rock 'n' roll performers.

Vincent and the Blue Caps rock in the film, The Girl Can't Help It.

BACK HOME

Vincent's serious injuries, his years of alcohol and drug abuse and the strain of constant touring finally took their toll. In 1971, back in the U.S., Vincent was taken to hospital with internal bleeding caused by a perforated stomach ulcer. Gene Vincent died on October 12, 1971, in Newhall, California. He was just 36 years old.

DRINK AND DRUGS

With all the publicity that surrounds drug and alcohol abuse today, it would be reasonable to think that it is a problem of recent years.

Not so.

Back in the 1950s, some of the greatest of the rock 'n' rollers paid the highest penalty for their drug-taking and drinking habits — an early death. So much talent and brilliant music is lost to us as a result. Over the years the drugs may have changed, but, sadly, the end is too often the same. There is a lesson to be learnt from the short lives of these revelers of the past.

Vincent visits a London club just a few months before his death, looking older than his 36 years.

GAZETTEER

Billy Fury

There were many, many rock 'n' roll heroes to be found on both sides of the Atlantic, and no one book could feature them all!

UK ROCK 'N' ROLLERS

In the UK Cliff Richard was not the only credible rock 'n' roller. Ronald Wycherly, a Liverpool tugboat man, talked his way backstage during a Marty Wilde concert to request an audition with promoter Larry Parnes and found himself performing for the rest of the tour, renamed Billy Fury. He recorded "Sound of Fury" which is generally thought to be the finest British rock 'n' roll album ever recorded, plus many hit singles, including the classic, "Half Way to Paradise." Tommy Steele enjoyed a short but spectacular rock 'n' roll career. He soon became a popular all-around entertainer.

Duane Eddy

INSTRUMENTAL GROUPS

During the 1960s there were literally dozens of popular instrumental groups working in the U.S. and the UK. The Ventures ("Walk Don't Run"), the Champs ("Tequila"), Duane Eddy ("Peter Gunn," "Rebel Rouser" and many other hits) and Johnny and the Hurricanes ("Red River Rock") were very successful in the U.S. In the UK one group, the Shadows, dominated the rock 'n' roll scene. Cliff Richard's backing group in the mid-60s, they enjoyed dozens of Top 20 hits in their own right.

Carl Perkins

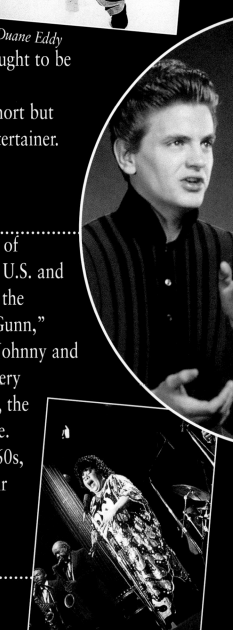

Ruth Brown

BLUE SUEDE SHOES

Arguably the greatest performers were found here in the U.S. The list is almost endless. Carl Perkins wrote and recorded one of the greatest rockabilly songs of all time, "Blue Suede Shoes."

Elvis Presley recorded it later. Perkins was one of the most gifted rock 'n' roll performers, although his career stalled after an awful car crash in the 60s. He died in 1998.

The Ronettes

ROCK 'N' ROLL WOMEN

Many very talented women performers were extremely successful.
Some were solo singers, and others were members of duos or trios. LaVern Baker and Ruth Brown came from spiritual music backgrounds, whereas the Shirelles, the Crystals, the Ronettes, Little Eva, Brenda Lee and Connie Francis were pop stars who strongly demonstrated their rock 'n' roll roots.

Connie Francis

BROTHERS

Other important rock 'n' roll stars included the Everly Brothers, a sublimely talented singing duo who unfortunately couldn't stand each other and for decades stayed in separate hotels during tours. Two other sets of brothers were very popular: the Isley Brothers and the Righteous Brothers, most famous for their beautiful recording of "You've Lost That Loving Feeling."

The Righteous Brothers

Everly brothers

HARMONY GROUPS

Frankie Lymon, Danny and the Juniors and the witty Coasters all proved that there was a place in the charts for harmony groups singing about teenage problems.

Rock 'n' roll was dismissed by the parents of at least two generations of teenagers as a fad that would last for months at the most. More than 50 years on, its appeal is as enduring as ever.

Tommy Steele

Soul

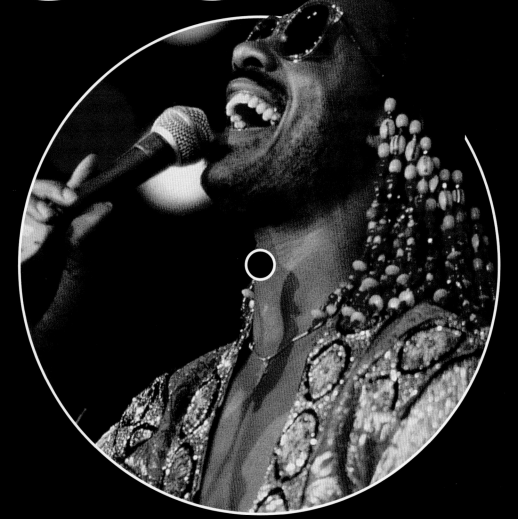

CONTENTS

On these disks is a selection of the artist's recordings. Many of these albums are now available on CD and MP3. If they are not, many of the tracks from them can be found on compilations.

These boxes give you extra information about the artists and their times.

Some contain anecdotes about the artists themselves or about the people who helped their careers or, occasionally, about those who exploited them.

Others provide historical facts about the music, lifestyle, fans, fads and fashions of the day.

INTRODUCTION

"Soul music" is a very broad term, used to describe the popular music of African-Americans that emerged in the late 1950s and early 60s. Its roots were in light jazz and the gospel music that was heard in churches all over the country. Over the next 40 years, soul changed out of all recognition, as pioneers such as Smokey Robinson and Stevie Wonder set new standards with their songwriting and production.

Richard Roundtree (above) starred in the 1971 "blaxploitation" film Shaft. *"Blaxploitation" means the exploitation of black people by producers of black-oriented films. Soul star Isaac Hayes (left) won an Oscar for the title song.*

There were four major soul labels in the 1960s and 70s, each of which had a unique sound. The most famous was Motown in Detroit, which still exists today, but as a small part of a much larger company. Motown mostly recruited local talent, but Atlantic, in New York, searched far and wide to find stars such as Aretha Franklin and Ray Charles. Stax, in the southern city of Memphis, was always associated with the funky, good-time sound of Booker T. and the MGs and Isaac Hayes. Philadelphia International Records (PIR) was as important to soul in the 1970s as Motown had been in the 60s. PIR had Teddy Pendergrass, the O'Jays and the Three Degrees on its books.

But soul was not all about having fun. It gave a voice to a new generation of African-Americans, who were angry at the way they were treated but proud of their heritage. Compared to jazz or blues, soul is a young form of music. Who knows how it will develop over the next 40 years?

JAMES BROWN

The Godfather of Soul, Mr. Dynamite, Soul Brother Number One, The Hardest-Working Man in Show Business — just some of the descriptions given to James Brown, the singer whose career spanned half a century. But for all his drive, business-sense and the praise heaped upon him, Brown was always an unpredictable genius, who often fell foul of the law.

Please, Please, Please 1959
Live at the Apollo 1963
Sex Machine 1970
Hot Pants 1971
There It Is 1972

Payback 1973
Black Caesar 1973
Hell 1974
In The Jungle Mood 1986
Soul Jubilee 1999
Legends Collection 2001

JUVENILE DELINQUENT

Born in South Carolina in 1933, Brown was already in trouble in his teens, doing time in a corrective institution for armed robbery. The family of singer Bobby Byrd helped to gain him parole, and Brown and Byrd started a gospel group. The group changed direction to rhythm and blues, called themselves the Famous Flames, signed to the Federal label and had a hit with "Please, Please, Please." It looked like the band was destined for stardom, but their next nine records flopped.

James's performances were physically draining.

HARD WORK PAYS OFF

But Brown showed superhuman determination, touring relentlessly, sharpening his act and keeping an eye on changing trends. After no hits for two years, Federal was about to drop the band when "Try Me" hit number one in the R&B charts in 1958. Now the focal point of the band, Brown took a large group of musicians on the road. His shows were a mixture of hysteria and musical precision, and as the 1960s dawned, Brown's R&B became harder, as he tried out Latin and jazz rhythms.

306

THE APOLLO

The Apollo Theater in Harlem, New York, has been a center for musical talent since 1913. Originally it was called Hurtig and Seamon's New (Burlesque) Theater, and it provided variety entertainment for mainly white audiences. Since 1935 the Apollo has been host to almost every major African-American performer, including James Brown, jazz singer Ella Fitzgerald, blues legend Bessie Smith, rock star Prince and the soul musicians listed in the picture below.

The city of New York has listed the interior and exterior of the Apollo Theater as designated landmarks.

By 1963 Brown was well-known for his tortured, screaming voice and manic stage shows, but it was only in June of that year that he became a superstar. That month saw the release of his *Live at the Apollo* album, recorded at the famous Harlem venue the previous year. The record managed to capture the excitement and intensity of a James Brown performance, and it hit number two in the pop charts — an astonishing feat for a heavy soul album.

A NEW GENERATION OF FANS

Brown built on the success of *Live at the Apollo* with a string of hits that defined 1960s soul — "Papa's Got a Brand New Bag," "I Got You (I Feel Good)" and "Say It Loud — I'm Black and I'm Proud." The hits were drying up by the mid-1970s, but he found new fans in the 80s and 90s, when dozens of rap and hip-hop artists sampled his earlier work. Brown died from complications from pneumonia on December 25, 2006.

James Brown is well-known for his flamboyant stage outfits.

RAY CHARLES

At the dawn of the 1960s, the expression "soul music" had not been invented. Ray Charles probably did more to develop the music than any other musician. He combined the high-powered R&B of the 50s with elements of gospel music, country, jazz and blues to create a fresh and exciting new sound.

The Genius Of Ray Charles 1959
The Genius Hits The Road 1960
Modern Sounds in Country and Western Music 1962
Sweet & Sour Tears 1964

Live 1973
Anthology 1989
Very Best of Ray Charles, Vols 1 & 2 2000
Cocktail Hour 2001
Confession Blues 2001

A DIFFICULT START

Ray Charles Robinson had a tough childhood. He went blind at the age of six, and by the time he was 17 both his parents were dead. But Charles had studied composition and had learned to play a number of instruments at the St. Augustine School for the Deaf and the Blind. So, despite being orphaned at an early age, he was able to fend for himself and start a career as a musician. In 1949, aged 18, he signed to Downbeat Records.

Ray Charles was sometimes accused of being a showbiz sell-out.

SIGNED BY ATLANTIC

Charles's biggest influence was the gentle crooner and pianist Nat "King" Cole, and his early recordings never hint at the rough, emotional style he would later adopt. In 1952 his recording contract was bought out by Atlantic Records. Charles hit number seven in the R&B charts with "It Should Have Been Me," the first in a string of hits for Atlantic, where his sound got harder. And the hits kept on coming: "What'd I Say," "Georgia On My Mind" and Ray's first number one on the pop charts, "Hit the Road, Jack," in 1961.

INTERNATIONAL STAR

By the mid-1960s Charles was a major star with another number one to his name, "I Can't Stop Loving You." He was introducing hints of gospel music to his work and inventing his own brand of soul. His triumphant career was only interrupted by an arrest for drug possession in 1966 — a medical checkup showing him to be drug-free kept him out of jail. For the next 38 years, until his death at the age of 74, Ray proved himself to have one of the most distinctive voices in soul music.

ATLANTIC RECORDS

Along with Stax, Motown and Philadelphia International, Atlantic was one of the big-four soul record labels. Ahmet Ertegun, son of a former Turkish ambassador to the United States, borrowed $10,000 from his dentist to start the New York-based label in 1947. The investment soon paid off — along with Ray Charles, Atlantic had the Coasters, Aretha Franklin, Wilson Pickett and Solomon Burke on its books. From the 1960s Atlantic branched out into rock music, signing Led Zeppelin and AC/DC.

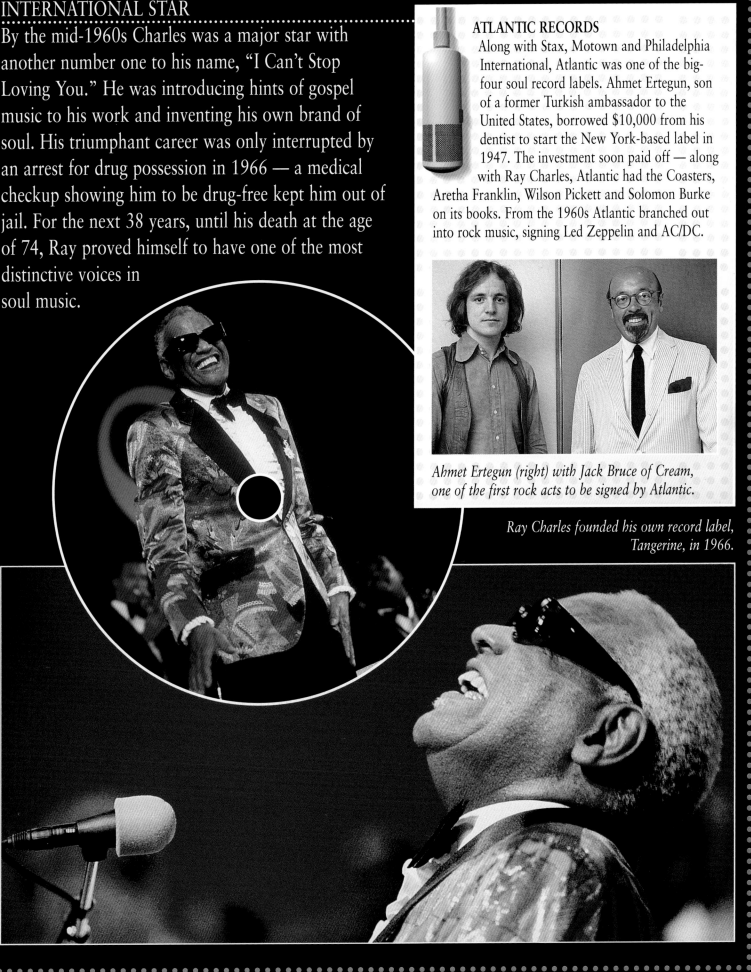

Ahmet Ertegun (right) with Jack Bruce of Cream, one of the first rock acts to be signed by Atlantic.

Ray Charles founded his own record label, Tangerine, in 1966.

ARETHA FRANKLIN

Aretha Franklin, the Queen of Soul, is arguably the most exciting singer to have burst on to the soul scene in the 1960s. Her powerful and emotional vocal range has made her the most recognizable female singer in African-American music. It was in church that she discovered her voice.

GOSPEL BEGINNINGS

Franklin was the fourth child of the Reverend C.L. Franklin, pastor of the New Bethel Church in Detroit, who was the most famous gospel preacher of the 1950s. He spotted his daughter's potential and promoted her as a soloist in the choir, turning young Aretha into a local celebrity. She made her first gospel recordings at the age of 14. This brought Franklin to the attention of Columbia Records, who signed her when she was 18, in 1960.

Aretha Arrives 1967
Lady Soul 1968
Aretha Now 1968
Soul '69 1969
Spirit in the Dark 1970

Young, Gifted and Black 1971
Amazing Grace 1972
Who's Zoomin' Who? 1985
A Rose Is Still a Rose 1998
Love Songs 2001

310

ARETHA ARRIVES

Franklin was unhappy with the way she was treated by Columbia, and when her contract expired in 1966 she was snapped up by Atlantic. Producer Jerry Wexler was the first person to capture the true Aretha Franklin sound, and success arrived at last. "I Never Loved a Man (The Way I Love You)" topped the R&B charts for nine weeks, and "Respect" was number one in the pop charts for a month. "Think" and "I Say a Little Prayer" sealed Franklin's reputation as the purest voice in soul.

Franklin sang with Al Green in 1995.

AMAZING GRACE

After several years of recording non-religious material, Franklin returned to her gospel roots in 1972. The result was the inspiring double album *Amazing Grace*, recorded in a Los Angeles church. Franklin spent the next 30 years balancing gospel with raw soul music and collected over a dozen Grammy Awards and countless gold records along the way. Tragedy struck in 1985, when Aretha's father was shot during a civil rights campaign. He survived but remained in a coma until his death in 1987, just as Franklin was enjoying her last U.S. and UK number one — "I Knew You Were Waiting (For Me)," a duet with George Michael.

GOSPEL MUSIC

It's a testament to Aretha Franklin's extraordinary talent that she became a gospel star at such a young age. Gospel music is a huge movement among African-Americans, so to stand out from the crowd you need to offer something very special. Gospel services are joyous, celebratory and noisy events! Choirs praise the Lord through their music, with its striking harmonies and driving rhythms, usually accompanied by piano and percussion instruments.

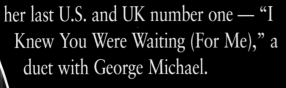

Franklin has sung with James Brown, Elton John, Whitney Houston, George Benson and Eurythmics.

Gospel music is an important part of the soul sound.

MARVIN GAYE

The Detroit-based company Motown launched some of the most talented, enduring and inspirational singers of the 20th century. No artist was more closely associated with that legendary label than Marvin Gaye, not least because he married the boss's sister! But neither Gaye's marriage nor his tenure at Motown were destined to last.

FRIENDS IN HIGH PLACES

Like Aretha Franklin, Marvin Pentz Gay was born into a church family (he added the "e" to his surname in adulthood, emulating his hero Sam Cooke). A shy boy, Gaye was brought up strictly by his father, who was a church minister. He found comfort in music, showing a talent for piano and drums, as well as singing. In 1960 Gaye and his friend Harvey Fuqua left their group, the Moonglows, and moved to Detroit. Fuqua became involved with Motown and recruited Gaye as a session drummer for the label. Within a year, Gaye had married Anna Gordy, the sister of Motown's founder, Berry Gordy.

What's Going On 1971
Let's Get It On 1973
Here My Dear 1978
Midnight Love 1982

Every Great Motown Hit of Marvin Gaye 1983
Anthology 1995
Forever Yours 1997
The Final Concert 2000

Gaye recorded "Ain't No Mountain High Enough" with Tammi Terrell.

IT TAKES TWO

Gaye teamed up with a string of singing partners. After hits with Mary Wells and Kim Weston, he found his musical soulmate in Tammi Terrell. Nobody knows if he and Terrell became lovers, but their intense musical intimacy is beyond doubt. Sadly, Terrell was dogged by ill-health, and she collapsed into Gaye's arms on stage. When she died in 1970, Gaye was so devastated that he became a recluse, and was rarely seen for the next year. His marriage to Anna was also crumbling at this time.

Gaye returned with a triumphant album, *What's Going On*, which he orchestrated and produced himself. There would be more hits in the 70s, but financial difficulties forced him out of the U.S. — he had debts of $7 million by 1978. He settled in Ostend, Belgium, where he attempted to rebuild his life.

A VIOLENT END

Gaye was tempted back to the U.S. by a contract with Columbia in 1982. The result was the album "Midnight Love" and the award-winning single "(Sexual) Healing." But this renewed success was short-lived. Years of drug abuse had left Gaye with paranoid delusions. He often threatened suicide and once had a gun forcibly removed from him. In 1984, the day before his 45th birthday, Gaye had a bitter argument with his father, whom he knew to be armed. The preacher shot his son dead and was later sentenced to five years' imprisonment for manslaughter.

CIVIL RIGHTS

Soul music is closely linked to the civil rights movement. In the 1960s, African-Americans supposedly had the same rights as white people, but there was still fierce racism and segregation, and many African-Americans suffered a poor standard of living. Also, thousands of young Americans were being killed in the controversial Vietnam War. This led to anger and protest. Marvin Gaye reacted with a plea for tolerance and peace in songs such as "What's Going On" and "What's Happening Brother."

Martin Luther King was a civil rights campaigner. Marvin Gaye celebrated him in his song "Abraham, Martin and John." His birthday is now a national holiday.

Gaye sometimes played keyboards on stage.

"I Heard It Through the Grapevine" is Gaye's best-known hit.

WHITNEY HOUSTON

Some people have all the luck. Whitney Houston is blessed with beauty, determination and an extraordinary vocal range. She was also born into a family with a matchless musical pedigree.

Whitney Houston
1985
Whitney
1987
I'm Your Baby Tonight
1990

My Love Is Your Love
1998
Greatest Hits
2000

RUNNING IN THE FAMILY

Whitney's mother is the soul singer Cissy Houston. Her cousin is another, more famous, vocalist, Dionne Warwick, so it was only natural that young Whitney should start singing from an early age. Her career began in a gospel setting — the New Hope Baptist Junior Choir. As a teenager, Whitney was already singing backing vocals for Chaka Khan and Lou Rawls and developing a solo stage act.

"I Will Always Love You" won several Grammy Awards.

SNAPPED UP

Houston also pursued a modeling career, which saw her on the covers of several magazines. This brought her to the attention of the head of Arista Records, who offered her a contract. Aided by some major songwriters, her first album sold an amazing 14 million copies.

RECORD-BREAKER

The follow-up, *Whitney* shattered all records by providing no fewer than seven number one singles. It was difficult to avoid Whitney Houston in the 1980s — her music was on the radio, her videos were on television and her face was in every magazine. In 1992 Houston added another string to her bow by starring in an action film, *The Bodyguard*. The love theme from the movie gave Whitney her biggest hit, "I Will Always Love You," which spent 13 weeks at the top of the Billboard chart.

OVERDOING IT?

Many critics have accused Houston of "over-singing" — she rarely uses one note when five will do. But her fans don't seem to mind. Houston's career slowed down in the 2000s, as she was plagued by troubles in her marriage and rumors of drug abuse. However, following her divorce from Bobby Brown in 2007, she returned to the studio and released a new album in August 2009.

Houston re-signed with Arista for $100 million in 2001.

DIONNE WARWICK

Whitney Houston's cousin Dionne Warwick was one of the most famous singers of the 1960s and the most successful interpreter of the songs of Burt Bacharach and Hal David. Warwick had hits with "Walk On By," "You'll Never Get To Heaven (If You Break My Heart)" and "Do You Know the Way to San José." She enjoyed a chart comeback in 1983 with the hit album *Heartbreaker*.

Dionne topped the pop chart with "That's What Friends Are For" in 1985, with Elton John, Stevie Wonder and Gladys Knight.

Houston married singer Bobby Brown in 1992.

315

The JACKSONS

One of the last great acts to appear on the Motown label was a group of five brothers from Gary, Indiana. In the early 1970s the Jackson 5 were so huge that they even had their own TV cartoon series. Jackie, Tito, Jermaine and Marlon reunited in 2001 to play some concerts with their youngest brother, Michael — one of the biggest and most controversial stars in popular music, who sold hundreds of millions of records.

BIRTH OF A LEGEND

The group first performed together in 1964, spurred on by their ambitious parents, who had spotted six-year-old Michael practicing dance moves in front of a mirror. They gained a strong live reputation and won a number of talent contests. In 1969 they were signed by Motown boss Berry Gordy, Jr., who moved them to Hollywood. "I Want You Back," "The Love You Save" and "I'll Be There" were all number one hits. Meanwhile, Michael started a successful solo career, while still a teenager.

SOLO SUCCESS

A move to Epic Records saw the band change their name to the Jacksons, with brother Randy replacing Jermaine. In 1979 Michael released his biggest hit to date, the album *Off the Wall*, which sold over 10 million copies. His follow-up was an even bigger hit — for nearly 20 years *Thriller* held the record as the biggest-selling album of all time. It also gave Michael the hit singles "Billie Jean" and "Beat It," 12 Grammy nominations and a record 37 weeks at the top of the US chart. But how do you follow a success like that? Michael's answer was to regroup with his brothers for the Victory tour and album in 1984.

Michael Jackson was famous for his love of animals.

316

AN ECCENTRIC STAR

Michael nearly matched the sales of *Thriller* with his 1987 album *Bad*, but as he grew older, his behaviour won him more headlines than his music. Eccentric to some, just plain weird to others, Michael surrounded himself with a variety of exotic pets at his lavish California mansion, complete with an amusement park in the backyard! He had also undergone extensive plastic surgery, which has drastically altered his appearance, and even the color of his skin seemed to have changed. Michael caused an outcry at the 1996 Brit Awards in London, England, when he appeared to be emulating Jesus Christ in his stage act. Back in 2001 with *Invincible*, his first album of new material for many years, Michael topped the charts, all over the world. Sadly, he died unexpectedly on June 25, 2009.

THE GIRLS

Janet Jackson is the youngest of the nine Jackson children. She was too young to join her brothers in the group, though she did occasionally appear on stage with them during the 1970s. Janet's first album appeared in 1982, when she was 16 years old. She was soon a star in her own right, renegotiating her contract for a record millions of dollars. Her sister LaToya is the bad girl of the family. When her singing career stalled, LaToya wrote a controversial book, full of revelations about life in the Jackson household.

Janet Jackson is one of the biggest soul stars of the past 20 years.

Jarvis Cocker of Pulp was so enraged by Michael Jackson's performance at the 1996 Brit Awards that he invaded the stage, disrupting Jackson's act.

The Jacksons:
Diana Ross Presents the Jackson 5 1970
A B C 1970
Jackson 5 Christmas Album 1970
Victory 1984

Michael Jackson:
Off the Wall 1979
Thriller 1982
Bad 1987
Dangerous 1992
Invincible 2001

WILSON PICKETT

The "Wicked Pickett" was in the premier league of male soul singers, along with James Brown, Marvin Gaye and Otis Redding. He was the essence of macho, strutting, hip-grinding 1960s soul.

Pickett was signed to the Double L label by its founder, the singer Lloyd Price.

In the Midnight Hour
1965
The Exciting Wilson Pickett
1966

Greatest Hits
1976
A Man and a Half
1992
It's Harder Now
1999

PAYING HIS DUES

Wilson Pickett was born in Prattville, Alabama, in 1941, and first came to prominence as the leader of the Detroit-based act the Falcons. Wilson was quickly signed as a solo artist by the small Double L label, and he had a handful of minor hits there. But his talents were spotted by the much larger Atlantic Records, and they bought out his contract.

MOVER AND SHAKER

Atlantic hooked Wilson up with ace producer Jerry Wexler, who took him to Stax studios in Memphis to record with the soul band Booker T. and the MGs. The result was "In the Midnight Hour," which became a soul classic covered by dozens of artists. "634-5789" followed in 1966 and spent seven weeks at the top of the R&B chart. Meanwhile, Wilson was honing his wild stage act with a large revue of musicians. The hits kept coming through the 1960s, including "Mustang Sally" and a cover of the Beatles' "Hey Jude."

A BAD MOVE

Many soul artists found that when they left Atlantic or Motown the hits started to dry up. Wilson Pickett was no exception, and a move to RCA in 1973 saw a downturn in his fortunes. His aggressive stage persona was matched by a fiery temperament off-stage, which was fueled by his passion for alcohol. In 1974 Wilson was arrested for pulling a gun during an argument. But for the next few years he carried on doing what he knew best — leaping around on stage, growling and shrieking in a suggestive manner. Wilson signed to Motown for a time and had some modest success, but his greatest achievements were in the 1960s and early 70s, all now beautifully preserved.

THE COMMITMENTS

Set in Dublin, *The Commitments* is a movie about a group of young Irish musicians. Believing that the Irish have the same social standing in Europe as African-Americans, they decide to start a soul band. This hilarious film follows the trials and tribulations they experience. The soundtrack album was almost as successful as the film. Lead-singer Andrew Strong belts out several soul classics, including the Wilson Pickett hits "Mustang Sally" and "In The Midnight Hour."

Andrew Strong (third from right) was tipped for stardom after his role in The Commitments.

Wilson Pickett toured constantly through the 1970s.

OTIS REDDING

In 1967 a small private plane inexplicably dived into a lake in Wisconsin. Amongst the dead was soul singer Otis Redding, the greatest star to record for Stax.

"(Sittin' on) The Dock of The Bay" was a worldwide hit and won two Grammy Awards.

STAX BECKONS

Like so many other blues and soul performers, Redding started his career by winning talent competitions — not the ones in the famous Apollo Theater in Harlem, but in the Douglas Theater in Macon, Georgia. Through a school friend, Redding was introduced to his heroes Johnny Jenkins and the Pinetoppers, and he happily accepted a job with them as a general assistant and occasional singer. In 1962 Redding drove the band to a session at the legendary Stax studios in Memphis. With some studio time left over, Otis persuaded Stax owner Jim Stewart to let him record two of his own compositions. Stewart was so impressed with the results that he released the first Otis Redding single, "These Arms Of Mine," which hit number 20 on the R&B chart.

A SECOND HOME IN HARLEM

On the strength of his first few hits, Redding was offered a regular slot at the Apollo Theater in Harlem and was paid $400 per week — a fortune at the time. Redding continued to record and built up a reputation as a fine songwriter — Aretha Franklin took his song "Respect" to the top of the charts in 1967. In 1965 he released *Otis Blue*, one of the greatest soul albums ever.

Pain in My Heart 1964
The Great Otis Redding Sings Soul Ballads 1965
Otis Blue 1965
Dock of the Bay 1968
Otis Redding In Person at the Whiskey A Go-Go 1968
Dreams to Remember — The Otis Redding Anthology 1998

Redding astonished everyone at the June 1967 Monterey Pop Festival. His performance was seen as a deliberate attempt to capture the white rock audience. Otis was the only soul singer on a bill featuring rock acts such as Jimi Hendrix and the Who, but the hippy audience was knocked out by his energy and verve.

POSTHUMOUS LEGEND

On December 7, 1967, Redding entered Stax studios to record his biggest hit, "(Sittin' on) The Dock of the Bay," a relaxing ballad. But he would not live to see its success — just three days later he was dead. By the end of the decade Redding's brand of gentle soul was out of fashion, but a loyal core of fans and a string of reissues have kept his music alive. Today Redding's records sound as fresh as the day they were recorded.

THE MEMPHIS SOUND

Memphis, Tennessee, was the home of Stax Records, one of the four major soul labels. Jim Stewart and his sister Estelle Axton were the owners of a Memphis record store and decided to start their own label, Satellite, in 1959. Their first releases were records of country music, but because they were located in an African-American area of town, they soon switched to heavy R&B and soul. They changed their name to Stax in 1961 and had Sam and Dave, Eddie Floyd, Isaac Hayes and William Bell on their books.

Booker T. and the MGs were Stax's resident session band.

Otis was only 26 when he died.

SMOKEY ROBINSON

William "Smokey" Robinson would have been remembered as one of the chief figures in soul music even if he had never sung a note. His writing for Motown acts, such as the Temptations, Marvin Gaye and Mary Wells, led Bob Dylan to name him "America's greatest living folk poet." But Smokey also possesses one of the most emotional voices in music.

The Motortown Revue featured Martha and the Vandellas, the Supremes and Stevie Wonder, as well as the Miracles, with Smokey on lead vocals (above).

MOTOWN'S FINEST

Smokey Robinson and the Miracles were spotted by Motown boss Berry Gordy, Jr., in 1957. For the next decade they recorded some of Motown's greatest hits, including "I Second That Emotion," "Tracks of My Tears" and "Tears of a Clown." All this time, Smokey was establishing himself as a highly sophisticated songwriter, whose blend of poignant lyrics and intricate melody provided hits for a string of artists. Smokey and the Miracles toured the world during the 60s and were even hailed as the Beatles' favorite band.

ELECTED TO THE BOARD

In 1971 Smokey left the Miracles to concentrate on his position as vice-president of Motown, in charge of nurturing new talent. He claimed that he had no wish for a solo career as he contined to produce the Miracles and write for other artists. But Smokey's "retirement" did not last for long. His records in the 1970s tended to be more reflective and experimental than his earlier work, and though they rarely reached the heights of his 60s hits, they confirmed Smokey's reputation as soul's most thoughtful and intelligent artist.

BACK IN THE CHARTS AGAIN

It looked as though Smokey was going to gently ease into middle age, but it was not to be. In 1981 he scored a huge surprise hit with "Being With You," which hit number one nearly 25 years after he started in showbusiness. Smokey left Motown in 1990, but he still releases occasional records and plays to adoring fans all over America.

THE DETROIT SOUND

Motown is the best known of all the major soul labels. It got its name from its home, Detroit, the center of the American car industry — motor town. Berry Gordy, Jr., worked in a car factory in the mid-1950s, but he supplemented his income by writing songs and producing records. He launched Motown in 1960, and its subsidiary Tamla shortly afterward. Motown's roster of artists included the Four Tops, the Marvelettes, Gladys Knight and the Pips, the Isley Brothers and the Supremes. Gordy also wrote several songs with Smokey Robinson.

Berry Gordy, Jr., moved Motown to Los Angeles in 1970.

Smokey toured less frequently during the 1970s.

A Quiet Storm
1975
Whatever Makes You Happy
1993
Ultimate Collection
1997

Intimate
1999
Along Came Love
1999
Our Very Best Christmas
1999

DIANA ROSS

Singing groups come and go in pop music. Once they have gone their separate ways, it's rare for group members to repeat their earlier success. But when Diana Ross left the Supremes, the most popular girl group of the 1960s, she went on to a triumphant solo career and became the biggest African-American female star of all time.

MAKING OF A DIVA

Diana Ross had already enjoyed 12 number one singles with the Supremes when she left the group in 1970. She had been the focal point of the Supremes, and Motown boss Berry Gordy, Jr., had wisely been grooming her for solo stardom for some time. Ross made her debut solo performance just seven weeks after leaving the group. Six months later she had her first solo number one, a rearrangement of "Ain't No Mountain High Enough," which had been a hit for Marvin Gaye and Tammi Terrell. Ross kept up a frantic recording schedule, and by the end of 1973 she had no fewer than seven hit albums to her name. Ross's records in the 1970s were usually richly arranged ballads, which were typical of the 1970s Motown sound.

The Supremes often toured and recorded with their Motown label-mates the Temptations.

LADY SINGS THE BLUES

During her early solo years, Diana Ross also forged a career as a a an actress. She starred in *Mahogany*, for which she designed her own costumes — all 50 of them! She also appeared in *The Wiz*, a remake of the classic movie *The Wizard of Oz*. But her most acclaimed performance was in *Lady Sings the Blues* in 1972. Ross was nominated for an Oscar for her portrayal of Billie Holiday, the singer whose life was tragically cut short by addictions to drugs and alcohol.

Billie Holiday, "Lady Day," was only 44 when she died in hospital, under police guard for drugs offences.

STAYING ONE STEP AHEAD

Ross's music was always at the forefront of changing fashions in the 1970s. Her albums *The Boss* and *Diana* were heavily influenced by disco. As she entered the third decade of her career, Ross was still at the top end of the charts with "Upside Down," "My Old Piano" and "It's My Turn." Her final single for Motown was also the biggest hit the label had ever had — "Endless Love," a duet with Lionel Richie.

Diana Ross 1970
Everything Is Everything 1971
Lady Sings the Blues 1973
The Boss 1979
Diana 1980

Why Do Fools Fall in Love 1981
Swept Away 1984
Take Me Higher 1995
Every Day Is a New Day 1999
Love From Diana Ross 2001

Diana Ross is the mother of five children.

Motown invested $100,000 in Ross's solo career.

THE BOSS TAKES CONTROL

The move from Motown in 1981 gave Diana a lucrative new recording contract. "Why Do Fools Fall In Love," "Chain Reaction" and "Muscles" sold millions, but Ross's music was moving away from soul and into the realms of pure pop music. Today Diana is admired as much for her elegance and keen business-sense as for her singing. She remains the undisputed First Lady of Soul.

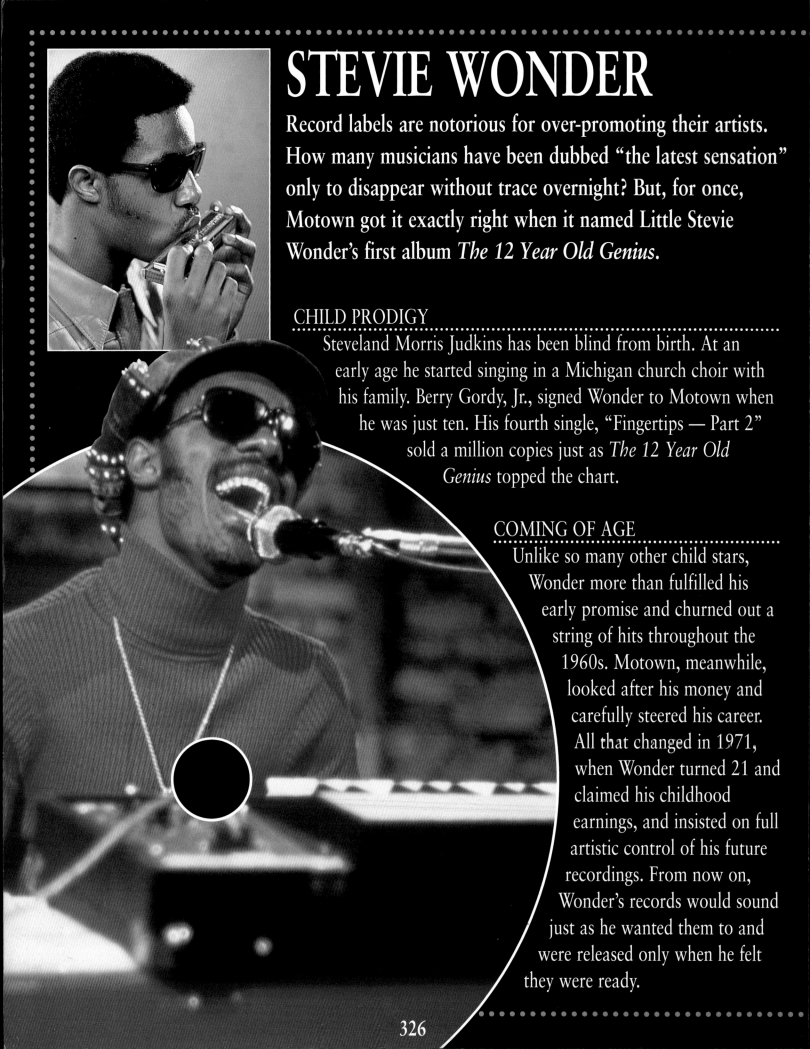

STEVIE WONDER

Record labels are notorious for over-promoting their artists. How many musicians have been dubbed "the latest sensation" only to disappear without trace overnight? But, for once, Motown got it exactly right when it named Little Stevie Wonder's first album *The 12 Year Old Genius*.

CHILD PRODIGY

Steveland Morris Judkins has been blind from birth. At an early age he started singing in a Michigan church choir with his family. Berry Gordy, Jr., signed Wonder to Motown when he was just ten. His fourth single, "Fingertips — Part 2" sold a million copies just as *The 12 Year Old Genius* topped the chart.

COMING OF AGE

Unlike so many other child stars, Wonder more than fulfilled his early promise and churned out a string of hits throughout the 1960s. Motown, meanwhile, looked after his money and carefully steered his career. All that changed in 1971, when Wonder turned 21 and claimed his childhood earnings, and insisted on full artistic control of his future recordings. From now on, Wonder's records would sound just as he wanted them to and were released only when he felt they were ready.

Stevie is a harmonica- and keyboard-player, as well as a singer.

In late 1984 the Irish singer Bob Geldof was shocked by TV pictures of the devastating Ethiopian famine. He gathered the top British musicians of the day and recorded a charity single to raise money for the victims. The U.S. quickly followed suit with "We Are the World," by USA for Africa, a collection of performers that included Harry Belafonte and Stevie Wonder. Both singles raised millions for the starving.

Lionel Richie, Dionne Warwick, Bob Dylan and many others sang "We Are the World" at the Live Aid concert in July 1985.

TAKING THE REINS

Despite Motown's misgivings, Wonder delivered some of the classic soul recordings of the 1970s and embraced the latest electronic technology. "You Are the Sunshine of My Life," "He's Misstra Know It All," "I Wish" and "Sir Duke" have been covered by dozens of artists.

For Once in My Life 1968
My Cherie Amour 1969
Signed, Sealed & Delivered 1970
Music of My Mind 1972
Talking Book 1972

Innervisions 1973
Songs in the Key of Life 1976
Hotter than July 1980
In Square Circle 1985
At the Close of a Century 1999

MUSIC WITH A CONSCIENCE

Wonder was closely involved with disability and civil rights issues. His duet with Paul McCartney, "Ebony and Ivory" celebrated racial harmony, and "Happy Birthday" helped to persuade the American government to recognize Martin Luther King, Jr.'s birthday as a national holiday. New releases from Stevie Wonder are increasingly rare, but this genius still has plenty to offer his fans.

Wonder won an Oscar for "I Just Called to Say I Love You" from the 1984 movie The Woman In Red.

GAZETTEER

The huge success of soul stars such as Stevie Wonder and Whitney Houston sometimes overshadows the achievements of other, equally important, musicians. And great soul was not only confined to the big four labels — Buddah, ABC Paramount, Vee-Jay, Mercury and Casablanca all produced some classic soul records.

The Isleys added two more brothers and a cousin to make a five-piece band in 1969.

Curtis Mayfield founded his own Curtom label in 1968.

BROTHERLY LOVE

The Isley Brothers were one of the most successful and longest-lived soul groups. The original Isleys, Rudolph, Ronald and O'Kelly, started singing gospel music in Cincinnati in the mid-1950s. But it was only in the late 60s and 70s that they achieved international success, with songs such as "Behind a Painted Smile" and "Harvest for the World." The Four Tops have lasted even longer. The group formed in Detroit in 1953, and they are still together over half a century later, their first lineup change happening only in 1997, upon the death of Lawrence Payton. The Impressions were formed in 1957 and still perform today. Their leader, Curtis Mayfield, left the group in 1970 and recorded the soundtrack to the "blaxploitation" movie *Superfly*. It topped the charts for a month.

Hundreds of fans rioted at Sam Cooke's funeral in Chicago.

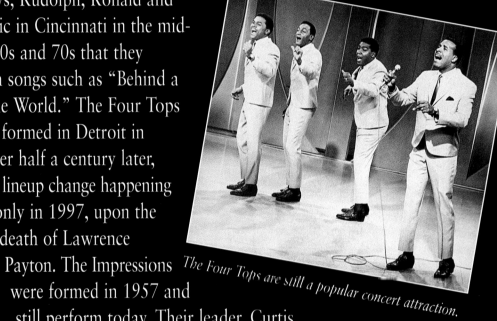

The Four Tops are still a popular concert attraction.

INSPIRATIONAL SINGER

Sam Cooke had one of the most romantic and wistful voices in soul. "Only Sixteen," "Wonderful World" and "Cupid" enchanted a generation of listeners. Tragically, Cooke was shot dead in 1964 in mysterious circumstances.

Like James Brown, Barry White served time in a corrective institution as a youth.

FEMALE SINGERS

Gladys Knight and the Pips were the first act to have a hit with "I Heard It Through the Grapevine," later covered by Marvin Gaye. Singer Randy Crawford has made little impression in her native U.S., but in the UK and Europe her records have sold millions, and her concerts never fail to sell out.

Randy Crawford's Secret Combination album spent over a year on the UK chart.

SOUL GIANT

Barry White is a huge star in more ways than one! Barry's rich bass voice perfectly complements his bulky physique, and his versions of "You're the First, the Last, My Everything" and "Just the Way You Are" had audiences swooning in the 70s.

Gladys Knight won $2,000 in a TV talent contest at the age of eight!

AWARD-WINNING SONGWRITER

The Commodores were one of Motown's most valuable acts in the 1970s. They owed much of their success to the singing and songwriting of Lionel Richie, who gave them "Easy" and "Three Times a Lady." Lionel launched a solo career in 1982, and was king of the dancefloor with "All Night Long" and the album *Dancing On The Ceiling*.

The Commodores carried on after Lionel Richie (bottom center) left the group.

World Music

CONTENTS

On these disks is a selection of the artist's recordings. Many of these albums are now available on CD and MP3. If they are not, many of the tracks from them can be found on compilations.

These boxes give you extra information about the artists and their times. Some contain anecdotes about the artists themselves or about the people who helped their careers or, occasionally, about those who exploited them. Others provide historical facts about the music, lifestyle, fans, fads and fashions of the day.

Rock star David Byrne (right) has used African and Latin American sounds on his albums.

INTRODUCTION

One of the biggest changes in listening habits over the last couple of decades has been the huge growth in world music. Of course, the expression "world music" is an over-simplification. All music is world music — where else could it come from?

Like it or not, popular music in the 20th century was largely dominated by North American and British musicians, whose songs can be heard on the radio almost everywhere. Traditional music from other parts of the world (world music) was in danger of dying out as Western acts had a stranglehold. But today world music is alive and well and a massive global industry, and much of its heritage has been preserved.

Sting (center) has also embraced world music. He interrupted his career to concentrate on preserving the Brazilian rain forest. He's pictured here with native Brazilian Chief Raoni on a tour of the rain forest.

There are several reasons for this revival. Talented individuals, such as Ravi Shankar and Youssou N'Dour, have gained millions of fans through their associations with Western rock musicians. Also, people's ears have been opened by the ease of modern travel. Previously inaccessible places are now popular tourist destinations, and music fans often bring home some of the local culture, in musical form. Simple, modern recording technology has not only preserved world music — it has enabled it to grow. And world music is not all pipes and drums these days. It's just as likely to be performed using drum machines, synthesizers and electric guitars.

KING SUNNY ADE

Nigeria is a sweltering and often violent republic on Africa's west coast. Today it has a modern economy based on oil exports, but Nigeria maintains its proud tribal traditions, which stretch back hundreds of years. There are over 250 tribal groups, each with its own culture. Juju music and dance originated in Yoruba, one of the principal African kingdoms.

Juju Music 1982
Synchro System 1983
Live Juju 1988

E Dide (Get Up) 1995
Odu 1998
Seven Degrees North 2000

AFRICAN ARISTOCRAT

Sunday Adeniyi was born into a branch of the royal family of Ondo, a town in the south of the country. He started to play the guitar at an early age, and in 1966 he started his first band, the Green Spots. Changing his name to King Sunny Ade, to highlight his royal connections, he had some success with the Green Spots, and in 1974 he formed his own record label, Sunny Alade. With his eye on the international audience, Ade changed the name of the band to the African Beats and found local fame with the albums *The Royal Sound* and *The Late General Murtala Muhammed*, a tribute to Nigeria's least unpopular military dictator.

HANDS ACROSS THE WATER

In 1977 Island Records, based in Jamaica, were looking for another tropical star to add to their roster of artists, which included the reggae singer Bob Marley. That year journalists had named Ade the "King of Juju Music," and Island were quick to sign him to a global contract. Juju is a lively music and dance style, almost entirely sung in native languages, mainly Yoruba. It is dominated by driving percussion and joyous vocals, and the guitar lineup of Ade's band, plus his own stage charisma, looked set to win him worldwide stardom. That came with the albums *Juju Music* and *Synchro System* in the early 1980s.

King Sunny Ade is known as "Wizard of the Guitar."

ON THE ROPES

But the juju boom did not survive Ade's third Island release, *Aura*. Island dropped him, and his band walked out mid-tour. Discouraged by political repression in Nigeria, Ade withdrew from the limelight, and it looked like his career was all but over. But in 1998 he was approached by Andy Frankel, a manager based in Seattle, who arranged some shows in Europe and America. To the delight of juju fans, Ade was back in top form.

Ade has often had to deny rumors of his death.

Ade is the father of 12 children.

CIVIL STRIFE
Much of Africa has been blighted by war and corruption, and Nigeria is no exception. One of the most bloody conflicts was in the late 1960s, when the eastern part of the country formed the breakaway Republic of Biafra. The war and resulting famine caused untold misery. Biafra bowed to Nigeria's greater might in 1970.

Nigeria has been dominated by military rule.

BUENA VISTA SOCIAL CLUB

The American blues guitarist Ry Cooder has successfully collaborated with many international musicians over the years. In 1996 he set out for Cuba to record traditional *son* music before it died out.

SAVIOUR OF SON

Son can be played by small acoustic bands or larger and louder brass ensembles. Opening verses are usually followed by improvized phrases from a solo singer and chorus. But until Ry Cooder's intervention, its traditions were in danger of being lost. He brought together for the first time Cuba's most experienced musicians and recorded them under the name Buena Vista Social Club.

The resulting album perfectly captured the world music mood of the 1990s and was a legendary success for the group known locally as *los superabuelos* (the supergrandfathers).

Omara Portuondo (left) provides vocals for the Buena Vista Social Club.

Buena Vista Social Club
1997
Buena Vista Social Club
Presents Ibrahim Ferrer
1999

Buena Vista Social Club
Presents Omara Portuondo
2000
Buena Vista Social Club at Carnegie Hall
2008

Ry Cooder (below right) has also worked with musicians from India and Mali.

CASTRO'S CUBA

Many people say that the republic of Cuba, in the Caribbean, is stuck in a time warp. General Fidel Castro led a revolution in 1959 and established a hard-line communist state. This was viewed with deep suspicion by the United States, its neighbor, which imposed trade sanctions. As a result, Cuba has had to fend for itself rather than rely on imports: 50-year-old cars, like the one below, still cruise the streets because new ones are mostly unavailable.

General Castro announced he would step down as Cuba's leader in 2008, after 50 years in power.

CUBAN OLD TIMERS

The main composer and guitarist, Compay Segundo, was 89 at the time of the recording. Singer Ibrahim Ferrer, at 70, had not performed for years. The other stars were pianist Rúben González, 77, and the baby of the band, Eliades Ochoa, who was 49.

The German filmmaker Wim Wenders made a documentary about the musicians, which featured archive footage and performances at their sellout concerts in Amsterdam and New York's prestigious Carnegie Hall.

Ry Cooder produced a solo album by singer Ibrahim Ferrer (below).

UPDATES

The following members have died: Compay Segundo (in 2003), Ibrahim Ferrer (2005) and Ruben Gonzales (2003). New members have come on board, and the Buena Vista Social Club is still touring.

THE GIPSY KINGS

The wandering Gipsy people of southern France and northern Spain have a legend about how their musical traditions have survived. When an old singer or guitarist is about to die, he will perform in front of a pregnant woman. Her unborn child will then inherit his talent.

"Volare" was a Gipsy Kings' hit.

KEEPING IT IN THE FAMILY

José Reyes was a famous flamenco singer who fled Spain for France during the Spanish Civil War in the 1930s. It's not known whether dying musicians played for his wife, but his sons Nicolas, André and Paul formed a group called Los Reyes ("the Kings") in the Gipsy areas of Arles and Montpellier, where they grew up. In 1982 they hooked up with their cousins the Baliardos (the guitarists) to form the Gipsy Kings, playing a lively version of "rumba" music, featuring driving rhythms and rich vocals.

Nicolas Reyes has a rough-sounding voice.

FAMOUS FRIENDS

The film star Brigitte Bardot is said to have spotted the band busking in Saint-Tropez, and she invited them to perform at a party full of her celebrity friends.

Within months they had a host of famous fans, including rock guitarist Eric Clapton and even Princess Diana. With that sort of endorsement some major concerts were arranged, as well as recording dates.

BAMBOLEO

The pinnacle came with their 1988 self-titled album, which featured the hit single "Bamboleo." Until the arrival of *The Buena Vista Social Club*, *The Gipsy Kings* was the best-selling album of world music to date. Since then the group has recorded another dozen albums, complete with horns, strings, accordions and even electronic instruments.

FLAMENCO

Flamenco music and dance originated on the streets of Spain in about 1750. The music is highly rhythmical and emotional, and dancers need to have immense discipline and poise as they twirl their frilled dresses, revealing agile ankles and feet. Much flamenco dance is improvized to the sound of the accompanying guitar. Dancers hold small wooden castanets between their fingers, which they click vigorously in time to the music. Flamenco has enjoyed a recent surge of publicity, thanks to the popularity of the young dancer Joaquín Cortes.

Flamenco is as popular today as it has ever been.

The Gipsy Kings 1988
Allegria 1989
Mosaique 1989
Este Mundo 1991
Live 1992

Love & Liberté 1994
Tierra Gitana 1996
Compas 1997
Cantos de Amor 1998
Somos Gitanos 2001

The Gipsy Kings recorded a version of the Frank Sinatra hit "My Way" ("A Mi Manera").

OFRA HAZA

Jewish people all over the world have rich traditions of music and culture, none more so than the Yemenite Jews. But Yemen is a Muslim country, and for centuries the Jewish population suffered great persecution, until almost all of them were evacuated to Israel between 1948 and 1950.

Yemenite Songs
1985
Shaday
1988

Desert Wind
1989
Kirya
1992

A SAFE HAVEN

Ofra Haza's parents were forced to flee Yemen on foot and eventually arrived in Tel Aviv. Haza was born in 1957, and as a child she was steeped in the Yemenite songs that the Jewish people would sing to suit every occasion — at times of celebration and grief, at work and at prayer. In her teens she joined a theater group, but her performing career was interrupted by a compulsory two years in the Israeli army. Out of uniform in 1979, she returned to singing and quickly became a star.

VERSATILE STAR

Haza's local success was not that surprising — Yemenite Jews are among the most popular artists in Israel today. What was remarkable was her popularity in neighboring Arab countries, which have been locked in conflict with Israel for decades. Haza was a prolific recording artist, and she released a huge body of albums, encompassing styles as varied as disco and goth music. In 1983 she was chosen to represent her country in the Eurovision Song Contest.

Haza's songs were turned into dance tracks by club DJs.

YEMENITE SONGS

Haza returned to her musical roots with *Yemenite Songs*, which was inspired by the age-old melodies she had learned from her mother. The songs are accompanied by the clattering of metal: the Jews in Yemen had been forbidden musical instruments and played on oil drums and trays instead. Haza's dignified, pure and velvety voice turned the album into a triumphant success. Tragically, her career was cut short by her early and unexpected death in February 2000.

PROTEST MUSIC

Despite the ban on instruments, the Yemenite Jews still managed to preserve their musical heritage. All over the world, oppressive regimes have tried to stifle the traditions of minority peoples. The aboriginal peoples of Australia suffered harsh treatment under European settlers, but many of their survival skills, languages and legends are being rediscovered. Aboriginal ceremonial dances, or "corroborees" are popular tourist attractions all over Australia these days.

Aboriginals play a long wooden pipe called a didgeridoo.

Haza died from an AIDS-related disease.

JAJOUKA

The foothills of the Rif mountains in Morocco are home to the Berber people. Despite its proud history, this Muslim race and its music were virtually unknown in the West until a few decades ago.

MUSICAL BROTHERHOOD

The Master Musicians of Jajouka are Berber musicians who have been playing for generations. The Master Musicians make up a close brotherhood, the leadership of which is passed down from father to son — the present leader, Bachir Attar, inherited the title when his father died in 1982. They produce "trance music," a hypnotic mixture of driving rhythms on double-headed drums and the droning sound of the *ghaita*, a double-reed pipe, similar to an oboe.

EAST MEETS WEST

The Moroccan city of Tangier was a haven for artists, actors and writers in the 1960s. In 1968 several members of the Rolling Stones paid a visit, and their guitarist Brian Jones was intrigued to meet the Master Musicians, who had never been heard in the West. Jones made a number of simple recordings of the group and mixed the tapes on his return to London, adding all sorts of electronic special effects.

A rare color photograph of the Master Musicians in about 1911.

CONTINENTAL DRIFT

Brian Jones died before the results were released, but the Rolling Stones issued the album as a tribute to him in 1971. For many years this was the only record of Moroccan music available in the West. Nevertheless, the Master Musicians remained in relative obscurity until the Stones paid another visit in 1989. The Master Musicians contributed to the song "Continental Drift" which opened concerts on the Stones' next massive world tour.

FAME AT LAST

Since then, the Master Musicians have recorded albums and have played at important festivals all over the world. There have been reports of bad blood with another band, who also claim to be the Master Musicians. But Bachir Attar's Master Musicians of Jajouka are true ambassadors for the Berber people.

WORLDLY ROCK MUSICIANS

Brian Jones (right) helped to open Western ears to world music, when it was usually only heard in foreign films or in restaurants. Perhaps Jones was influenced by George Harrison, who had introduced Indian sounds on the Beatles' records. Other rock musicians who have embraced world music are Peter Gabriel, who founded the Real World label, and David Byrne, who has championed African and South American music on his Luaka Bop label.

Brian Jones
Joujouka

Brian Jones was a multi-instrumentalist who played the Indian sitar and African marimba.

Brian Jones Presents
the Pipes of Pan at Jajouka
1971
Apocalypse Across the Sky
1992

Jajouka Between the Mountains
1996
Master Musicians of Jajouka
2000

The Master Musicians play Moroccan drums, the ghaita and the lira, a bamboo flute.

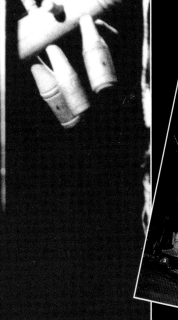

Bachir Attar (left) plays the guimbri, *a three-stringed instrument.*

ANTONIO CARLOS JOBIM

What's the latest craze this year? Perhaps a new hip-hop act has taken the charts by storm or a boy band has invented a new dance routine. Back in the late 1950s, the coolest sound on the radio was bossa nova, a gentle style of music originally based around a singer and solo guitar. It emerged from the vast South American country of Brazil, and it was the invention of one man, Antonio Carlos Jobim.

BIRTH OF BOSSA NOVA

It's very rare that a single person can take credit for coming up with a new musical style, but Jobim certainly deserved to be called the father of bossa nova. The coastal city of Rio de Janeiro has always been the musical capital of Brazil. It was the birthplace of samba, an energetic and highly rhythmical accompaniment to the Rio Carnaval, a huge street party that takes over the city every year. Jobim was a classically trained guitarist who liked to spend time in the chic beach neighborhood of Ipanema during the day and in Rio's lively bars and clubs at night. His idea was to develop relaxed, laid-back but samba-based music. Bossa nova was born.

Antonio Carlos Jobim's nickname was Tom

344

João Gilberto (right) is the ultimate bossa nova performer.

CARNAVAL

All countries colonized by Catholics have celebrations in the days leading up to Ash Wednesday, the first day of Lent, but Brazil goes a lot further. The entire country shuts down for five days from the previous Friday, and almost everybody joins in the biggest party in the world. Each year the Carnaval songs have to be new, so during the previous weeks, music fills the airwaves as dozens of musicians compete to create that year's biggest Carnaval hit.

OUT OF TUNE

The first bossa nova song was called "Desafinado," which means "out of tune." Penned by Jobim, and sung by João Gilberto, it was an instant smash in 1957. Gilberto's wife, Astrud, sang an English version of Jobim's "The Girl from Ipanema," which became Brazil's biggest ever international hit. By then, bossa nova was being embraced by famous American jazz musicians, such as Stan Getz, as the ultimate in smooth musical sophistication.

The Man from Ipanema
1963
Wave
1967
Urubu
1976

Terra Brasilis
1980
Live at the Free Jazz Festival
1993
Antonio Brasileiro
1995

Samba music came out of the Carnaval.

Jobim died in 1996, aged 67.

BORN AGAIN

Like all crazes, bossa nova had a limited life span, and it could not survive the rock and pop explosion of the 1960s. But in Brazil it lived on, and Jobim became a highly respected figure on the local pop music scene. Bossa nova enjoyed a revival in New York clubs a few years ago, where the Brazilian producer Arto Lindsay mixed drum 'n' bass rhythms with the bossa nova singing of Vinicius Cantuária.

NUSRAT FATEH ALI KHAN

The Sufi Muslim people of Pakistan believe that music has spiritual qualities, which can transport the performer and listener closer to God. *Qawwali* is the Sufi music of love and peace, which has traditions stretching back 800 years. Its singers are called *qawwals*, and Nusrat Fateh Ali Khan was the most famous *qawwal* who has ever lived.

MUSICAL DYNASTY

Khan was born in Faisalabad in 1948 into a family that has produced *qawwali* singers for six centuries — his father was a well-known classical musician and *qawwal*. Groups of *qawwals* are varied and can consist of any number of people, but they are always based around a lead singer, one or two backing singers who also play the harmonium and a percussionist. Every group member joins in the singing, accompanied by fierce clapping. In a tradition-al performance, the *qawwal* repeats lyrics about holy love over and over again, and Khan could make his shrill voice soar over the accompanists. Even Khan's Western audiences, who were unaware of the spiritual meaning of *qawwali*, could be mesmerized by the sheer power and beauty of his voice.

Khan recorded for Peter Gabriel's Real World label.

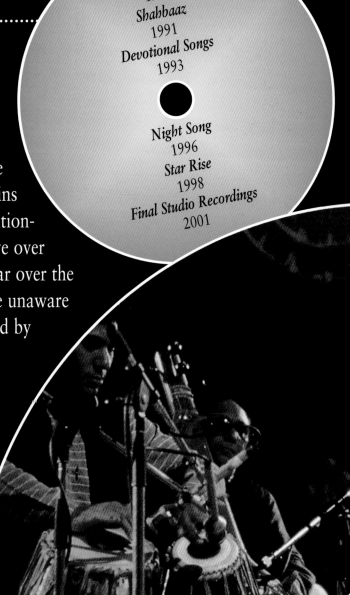

Musst Musst
1990
Shahbaaz
1991
Devotional Songs
1993

Night Song
1996
Star Rise
1998
Final Studio Recordings
2001

SOUNDTRACKER

Khan was already a superstar on the Indian subcontinent when the English rock star Peter Gabriel invited him to sing on the sound-track of the film *The Last Temptation of Christ*. Sufi is a tolerant branch of Islam, and although he was a devout man, Khan was willing to explore other cultures. He went on to appear on several more soundtracks, including the violent American movie *Natural Born Killers*. Qawwali is very accessible to Western ears and lends itself easily to dance remixes. Nitin Sawhney, Joi and Asian Dub Foundation remixed Khan's music for the album *Star Rise*, a club hit in 1997.

Talvin Singh (above) has remixed Nusrat's music.

BHANGRA

The style of music called "bhangra" started out as a folk dance, which celebrated the harvest in the Punjab region over 200 years ago. Led by the *dhol*, a loud wooden drum, bhangra can easily be adapted to fit electronic dance rhythms, particularly house and hip-hop beats. Bhangra is yet another style of music that has gained an audience in our multicultural society.

Cornershop (above) is one of the most popular bhangra groups.

MASSIVE HIT

The dance/rap outfit Massive Attack remixed the title track from Khan's *Musst Musst* album, and it turned into an international hit when Coca Cola used it in a TV commercial. If it seemed strange that this deeply religious music should be used to advertise a soft drink, Khan didn't mind. His job as a *qawwal* was to move as many people as possible closer to God, and millions of people watch TV!

Nusrat Fateh Ali Khan died in 1997.

FELA KUTI

Along with King Sunny Ade, Fela Kuti was one of the most important artists to emerge from West Africa. Like Ade, Kuti was born into the Yoruba tribe of Nigeria, and he invented Afro-beat, a heady mixture of thunderous percussion, brass and vocals sung in pidgin, a simple type of English. Kuti's politics won him few friends among the Nigerian authorities.

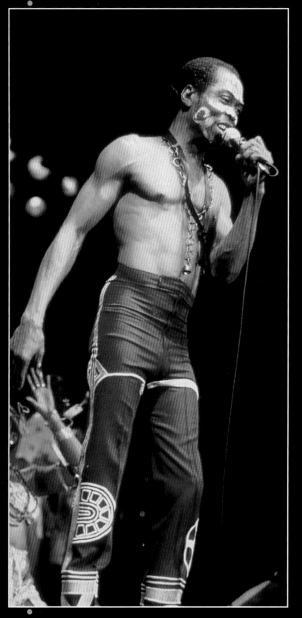

Kuti was often photographed without his shirt!

UNLIKELY DOCTOR

Kuti was born in 1938, the son of a Protestant minister who hoped that his son would become a doctor. Instead, Fela traveled to London's Trinity College of Music, where he studied trumpet and started his first band, Koola Lobitos, in 1961. During a trip to the U.S., Fela fell in with the militant civil rights campaigners the Black Panthers and was deeply influenced by American jazz and funk music. Back home, he blended these styles with African music in his huge Afro-beat band Africa 70, which included 20 female dancers and singers.

Teacher Don't
Teach Me Nonsense
1987
The Best Best of Fela Kuti
1999
Coffin for Head of State
2000

Shuffering and Shmiling
2000
Monkey Banana
2001
Zombie
2001

A BRAVE MUSICIAN

Kuti's records often attacked the incompetence and corruption of the Nigerian regime. His wit and satire appealed to ordinary people, but he was constantly hounded by the government. In 1977 about 1,000 soldiers attacked and burnt his home and threw his 82-year-old mother out of a window. But Kuti refused to change his ideas and continued to taunt the authorities with his music.

BANGED UP

In 1984 Kuti was sent to prison on a false smuggling charge. In typically eccentric fashion, Kuti divorced all 28 of his wives on the same day while he was inside. Worldwide protest eventually helped to secure his release in 1987, and he returned triumphantly with a new band, Egypt 80, and yet more protest records. But in the 90s, Kuti's hard lifestyle was catching up with him. He died in 1997 from an AIDS-related illness. To the disgust of the authorities, around a million mourners attended his funeral.

KUTI JUNIOR

Fela Kuti's son Femi has enjoyed a successful career since the late 1980s, with his group the Positive Force. The Nigerian people have taken Femi to their hearts, especially since his father's death. Femi Kuti is recognizably his father's son in his voice, lyrics and muscular physique. And like his father, he only wears clothes when strictly necessary!

Femi Kuti is signed to the large Polygram label.

Fela Kuti sang in pidgin, which is used by merchants who don't speak the same language.

Kuti switched from trumpet to tenor saxophone.

LADYSMITH BLACK MAMBAZO

Like Nusrat Fateh Ali Khan, Ladysmith Black Mambazo enjoyed unexpected success courtesy of a TV commercial, in their case for baked beans! The catchy "Inkanyezi Nezazi" reached the UK Top 20 in 1997, but the group's international fame goes back a lot further than that.

Ulwandle Oluncgwele
1985
Shaka Zulu
1988
Two Worlds One Heart
1991

Gift of the Tortoise
1994
Liph' Iquiniso
1994
Live at the Royal Albert Hall
1999

MUSIC TO TIPTOE TO

Ladysmith Black Mambazo is a South African Zulu choir, which sings in soft harmonies called *iscathamiya*. This Zulu word means "to step softly." When Zulu men left their villages to work in factories and mines, they stayed in all-male hostels, where rowdy singing and stomping were unwelcome, so they developed a quiet song and dance style.

CUT OFF FROM THE WORLD

The group was formed by Joseph Shabalala in the early 1960s in the town of Ladysmith. The lineup has changed over the years but has always been based around three families — four of Joseph's sons are current members. The took the name *mambazo*, which means ax, because the group boasted that they cut down all their rivals in early singing competitions. Their first album, *Amabutho*, was released in 1973, but South Africa was ruled by an apartheid system in those days — black people and those of mixed race were denied basic rights by the white minority. As a result, many nations imposed trade and cultural sanctions against South Africa, and Zulu music was rarely heard in the West. All that changed in 1986, when the rock musician Paul Simon ignored the ban and recorded in South Africa.

Ladysmith Black Mambazo at London's Royal Albert Hall.

350

A clenched fist is a symbol of black power.

GRACELAND

Paul Simon argued that the cultural ban was stifling
the very people it was meant to help. His album
Graceland, featuring Ladysmith Black Mambazo,
was an enormous hit, and he took them on tour
around the world. It was the first time the choir had
sung to racially mixed audiences. In 1988 he
produced the group's award-winning album *Shaka
Zulu*. Since then Ladysmith Black Mambazo has
collaborated with many western musicians,
including Des'ree and the Lighthouse
Family. But the
group is at its
best singing the
pure and soft
harmonies of
the proud
Zulu
people.

APARTHEID

Under apartheid, black South Africans
were not allowed to vote, enter parlia-
ment, go to white beaches, and white
and black children were educated in separate schools. Nelson Mandela fought
against the South African government
and its racist policies. He was imprisoned for political offenses in 1964
and became a symbol of black
resistance. South Africa finally
reformed its government in the
early 1990s, and Nelson
Mandela went on to
become his country's
first black President.

*Nelson Mandela
on his release
from prison
in 1990.*

*The group's
harmonies are
both complex
and uplifting.*

351

YOUSSOU N'DOUR

Music is a vital part of everyday life in West Africa. Everywhere children imitate the dancing and drumming of their elders, while women sing work songs to the rhythm of pounding pestles and mortars. Professional musicians are a vital part of religious ceremonies. In the past this role was reserved for those born into the "griot" caste.

Youssou recorded "In Your Eyes" with Peter Gabriel.

EVER THE GRIOT

Youssou N'Dour is the son of a mechanic, and he received little formal education when he was growing up in the small country of Senegal. But N'Dour was born into the griot caste and took his duties very seriously from a young age, learning by heart a vast repertoire of traditional songs. To this day N'Dour considers himself a griot, singing songs that offer religious advice and warnings. Although griots are admired and sometimes held in awe by their fellow citizens, they do not rank highly on the social scale, and this partly explains N'Dour's huge popularity among the ordinary people of Senegal. He started his first band, Étoile de Dakar, in 1979, playing rhythmic *mbalax* music, with a Cuban-style brass section.

LIVE ATTRACTION

N'Dour attracted the attention of the English rock star Peter Gabriel, who helped him to land a contract with Virgin Records. N'Dour also joined Gabriel, Bruce Springsteen and Sting on the 1988 Human Rights Now! charity tour and was given a rousing welcome by Western rock fans. But despite his live reputation, N'Dour's records failed to sell in large quantities, and Virgin dropped him after two albums.

MAN OF THE PEOPLE

N'Dour's fortunes took an upturn in 1994, when he signed with Sony. His single "7 Seconds" cracked the *Billboard* Hot 100 and it propelled his album *The Guide* to global success. Today N'Dour is the biggest star of African music, and even listeners with no particular interest in world music know his name. But N'Dour remains true to his roots — he produces at least two albums for the Senegalese market each year and has built recording facilities to promote African music independently from large Western record companies. N'Dour also keeps his loyal fans happy by performing each week at a small club in Dakar. Can you imagine a Western rock star doing the same?

N'Dour created the Jololi label to promote African music.

The Lion
1989
Set
1990
Eyes Open
1992
The Guide (Wommat)
1994

Grand Bal
2000
Joko
2000
Lii!
2000
Birth of a Star
2001

BAABA MAAL

Youssou N'Dour only has one rival for the title of Senegal's biggest musical star — Baaba Maal. In fact, their styles are very different. While N'Dour lives in the capital Dakar, Maal comes from the remote north of the country, on the fringes of the vast Sahara desert. His music is influenced by the Islamic nomads who inhabit this inhospitable area. On his 1998 album *Nomad Soul* Baaba collaborated with western stars Brian Eno and Sinéad O'Connor.

Baaba Maal performed for the South African statesman Nelson Mandela in 2001.

RAVI SHANKAR

One man has done more than anyone to popularize not just Indian music, but all world music — Ravi Shankar. Even before the expression "world music" had been invented, Ravi was enchanting Western listeners with his sensitive and virtuoso mastery of the sitar, one of the world's most difficult instruments to learn.

Live at Monterey — 1967
1967
Three Ragas
1967
Transmigration Macabre
1973

Concerto for Sitar and Orchestra
1986
Concert for Peace
1995
Ragas and Talas
2000

SITAR HERO

The sitar is a long-necked instrument, similar to the guitar but with two sets of finely tuned strings, played in a cross-legged position. Ravi Shankar was born in the province of Uttar Pradesh, close to India's modern capital city, New Delhi, in 1920. He showed early promise on the sitar — he gave his first professional performance at the age of 13 and studied nonstop to develop his skills.

WESTERN FRIENDS

Ravi Shankar made his first concert appearances in Europe and America in the late 1950s and early 60s. These shows had an enormous impact on Western musicians, many of whom knew little of the rich traditions of Indian classical music. The violinist Yehudi Menuhin collaborated with Shankar on an award-winning album in 1966, but it was his association with the Beatles that won him worldwide fame.

A NEW GENERATION OF FANS

The Beatles were the biggest pop group in the world when their guitarist George Harrison tuned into Indian music. Shankar gave Harrison strict lessons, not just about sitar technique, but about respect for the instrument and its traditions. The Beatles' track "Norwegian Wood" was the first use of sitar in a pop song. Shankar wowed hippy fans with his performance at the 1967 Monterey Pop Festival and opened a star lineup at the benefit concerts for the suffering people of Bangladesh in 1971. Ravi Shankar spent more than 30 years touring the world, proving himself to be arguably the finest musician on the planet.

Shankar recorded "West Meets East" with Yehudi Menuhin (below left).

Ravi Shankar on stage with his daughter Anoushka.

POINTS EAST

World music doesn't stop at India — it goes even further East than that. The traditional music of eastern Russia, Siberia, China and Japan still thrives, even though those countries are yet to give the world superstars like those from India, Africa, South America and the Middle East. Japan has given us *enka*, often compared to American soul music, as well as folk, classical and noisy rock music. In China the traditional music is usually based around simple wind and percussion instruments, which have been played for centuries.

In Tuva, southern Siberia, Sailyk Ommun and Yat-Kha blend traditional and rock music.

George Harrison (below left) described Ravi Shankar as the "Godfather of World Music."

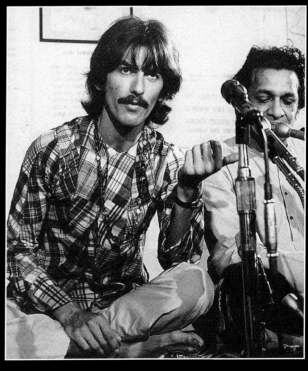

ALAN STIVELL

Today Celtic people live all over the world. From New York to New Zealand, the descendents of Irish, Scottish, Welsh, Cornish and Breton people cling proudly to their traditions. But one part of Celtic heritage nearly died out a few years ago — the Breton harp, from Brittany in northwestern France.

HARP WORK

Alan Stivell is a true star, who played a major role in the invention of folk-rock music in the 1970s and put traditional Breton and Celtic music in the charts. But his greatest achievement was to pull the Breton harp back from the brink of extinction and revive a unique part of Celtic heritage. But Stivell was not working alone — he was carrying on the work of his father.

Stivell's harp accompanies his singing.

FOLLOWING IN HIS FATHER'S FOOTSTEPS

Alan Cochevelou was born in Brittany, the son of a harp maker. Alan's father had rediscovered the Breton harp, but his efforts at promoting the instrument went largely ignored. It was only when Alan started performing at the age of 11 that people began to take notice of this endangered instrument. In his teens, Cochevelou studied all aspects of Celtic music, including the Irish flute, tin whistle and the bagpipes, for which he won awards in Scottish national championships.

Renaissance of the Celtic Harp 1972
Journée a la maison 1978
Celtic Symphony 1979
Harpes du nouvel age 1986

The Mist of Avalon 1991
Zoom 1997
1 Douar 1998
Back to Breizh 2000

SOURCE OF INSPIRATION

During the 1960s, Cochevelou changed his surname to Stivell, the Breton word for "fountain," or "spring." In 1972 he released the classic album *Renaissance of the Celtic Harp* which prompted hundreds of players to take up the instrument, when 20 years before there had been none. Cochevelou has also mastered harps from Ireland, Scotland and Wales on his albums and has collaborated with rock musicians, such as Kate Bush. The Celtic harp is alive and well once more, its hauntingly beautiful sound preserved forever — and all thanks to Alan Stivell.

EASTERN EUROPE

The Celtic music of Alan Stivell originates from the most westerly points of Europe. Far in the east of Europe the musical traditions are just as rich. *La Mystère des voix bulgares* (The mystery of Bulgarian voices) is one of the most successful recent albums of European music. The record started a wave of interest in Bulgarian music, in particular the intricate harmonies and arrangements sung by choirs of female singers, who have a vocal range of just one octave. In total, the ensemble has released four albums of its unique music.

La Mystère des voix bulgares has been performed all over the world.

Celtic music is often improvized at informal gatherings called ceilidhs.

GAZETTEER

By its very nature, world music is a global phenomenon. Of course, there isn't room here to examine in detail every recording artist, or style of music, but the following have all made a major contribution to the music of the world.

Ricky Martin is a huge star.

Caetano Veloso also paints, writes poetry and directs his own videos.

MUSIC FROM THE TROPICS

Caetano Veloso has been at the forefront of Brazilian music for over 40 years. He sings in the *tropicalismo* style, as does Gilberto Gil, who spent many years in London because of his opposition to the Brazilian military regime.

The Afro-Celt Sound System combines Irish folk music with techno in their live act.

Gilberto Gil is influenced by reggae and rock music.

Tito Puente died in Puerto Rico in 1973.

CARIBBEAN STARS

The Caribbean island of Puerto Rico has given the world two huge, but very different, stars. Tito Puente was a larger-than-life bandleader who found fame in New York, playing mambo music in the 1950s.

Ricky Martin crossed over from world music into the pop

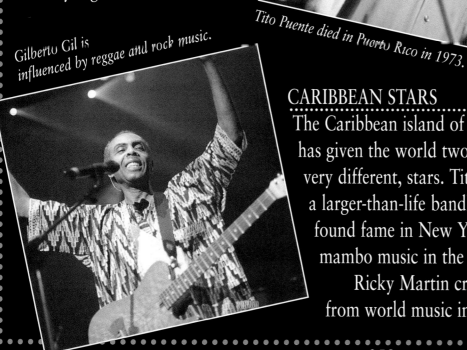

The Mighty Sparrow has recorded over 100 albums.

charts in the
late 90s. Martin has blended the
salsa himself millions of fans. The Mighty Sparrow from
nearby Trinidad is a popular figure throughout the
Caribbean. His witty songs sum up the calypso style.

SOUNDS OF AFRICA

Salif Keita comes from Mali, a huge landlocked country in western
Africa. He overcame poor eyesight and the social stigma of being born
with white skin to become Mali's most popular singer. Further north, in
Algeria, Khaled is the superstar of *rai* singing.
He has enjoyed astounding success at home,
in France and, perhaps surprisingly, in India.

Khaled started his career under the name Cheb Khaled.

UNIQUE MIXTURE

The Afro-Celt Sound System surprised
many people with their unlikely blend of
West African and Celtic instruments, with
electronic dance beats thrown in. Their
records and live shows have been a huge
success since 1996, a fine example of
different cultures coming together to
create something new and exciting.

Salif Keita's noble family opposed his choice of career.

INDEX

Index continued

PHOTO CREDITS

Abbreviations:
t — top, m — middle, b — bottom,
r — right, l — left, c — center.

20th Century Fox (courtesy of Kobal): 282–283.

Adrian Boot/Islandlife: 217m; 218b; 221b; 222 (both); 223t; 229b; 231b; 233t; 234b; 235b; 240ml, b.

Amanda Edwards/Redferns: 97tr.

Amos Zezmer/Redferns: 345m.

Andrew Putler/Redferns: 356 (both).

A. Putler/Redferns: 83l, 160b, 164–165, 165t, 202bl, 240t.

Barbara Steinwehe/Redferns: 103ml, 116bl, 121ml.

Benedict Johnson/Redferns: 244–245, 270mr.

Beryl Bryden/Redferns: 196bl.

B. King/Redferns: 82t, 90t.

Bob Brunning: 7.

Bob King/Redferns: 111ml, 139br, 199b, 338tl.

Bob Willoughby/Redferns: 187tr.

B.P./Redferns: 8b, 9, 18b, 29t.

Brigitte Eugl/Redferns: 347tl.

C.A./Redferns: 51t, 320tl.

Carey Brandon/Redferns: 101tl.

Cherie Nutting: 342 both, 342–343b.

Chuck Boyd/Redferns: 318tl, 355br.

Chuck Stewart/Redferns: 191br, 202tl, 309mr.

Cinergi Pictures (courtesy of Kobal): 74br.

Corbis: 12m, 13m, 30–31.

Corbis/Bettman: 281b, 285t, 286 all, 287m, 288–289, 295m, 297mr, 299tl.

Crixpix/Redferns: 318r.

C. Stewart/Redferns: 163t.

Cyrus Andrews/Redferns: 27–29, 30m, 31tr.

C. Zlotnik/Redferns: 86b.

Danny Gignoux/Redferns: 193tl.

Dave Ellis/Redferns: 139ml, 193tr.

David Farrel/Redferns: 355ml.

David Redfern/Redferns: 6–7; 10b; 10–11; 12b; 14–15; 16t; 16–17; 17 (all); 20–21; 22–23; 213b; 24t; 30t, b; 31tl; 125tr; 127mr; 128bl; 129mr; 130mr, bl; 131br; 134br; 138br; 139tl; 140mr; 140–141; 141br; 144tl; 144 145; 115tr; 146br; 148 (both); 150bl; 187tl, br; 188 (both); 189 (both); 192br; 193br; 195br; 197tr; 199mr; 203tr; 204mr; 208mr; 209mr; 210–211t; 211 (all); 216–217; 217b; 220t; 228–229t; 234t; 236–237; 237b; 238b; 303; 307bl; 309ml; 310b; 311br; 312tl; 313bl , br; 315br; 322br; 322–23; 327tl; 329tl; 337br; 350tl; 356–357; 359tl, tr.

D. Cronin/Redferns: 218–219, 239b.

Delilah/Universal (courtesy of Kobal): 277.

D. Ellis/Redferns: 48t, 48–49, 49t, 58r.

Deltahaze/Redferns: 136tl, 137tr.

Des Willie/Redferns: 108m, 230, 265mr.

Diana Scrimgeour/Redferns: 120tr, 325r.

Dover Books: 184–185.

D. Redfern/Redferns: 67m; 68b; 70b; 80t; 84t; 91tl.

Ebet Roberts/Redferns: 110tl; 111tr; 121bl; 183;

200–201; 232b; 233b; 236; 241tl, mr; 243; 267tr; 271bl; 311tr; 319tl; 336 (both); 337br; 348bl; 352tl.

E. Echenberg/Redferns: 56br, 527t, 155tl.

E. Landy/Redferns: 55t.

Elliott Landy/Redferns: 14t.

Embassy Films (courtesy of Kobal Collection): 175r.

EMI films (courtesy of Kobal): 41m.

E. Reberts/Redferns: 156bl, 157l, 158tl, 164m, 168–169, 171b, 172, 179b.

Erica Echenberg/Redferns: 103br.

E. Roberts/Redferns: 40t; 45b; 46l; 53b; 60m; 63; 66 (both); 69b; 70t; 72t; 74t, bl; 75l; 76b; 76–77; 77b; 78t, m; 83r; 84m; 86t; 86–87; 91m, br;.

F. Costello/Redferns: 60b, 157r, 159m, 161 both, 164t, 169 both, 174tl, 176t, 176–177, 177t, 178t, 179t, 180b, 181t,.

Fin Costello/Redferns: 214–215, 218t, 219, 227mr, 316bl.

F.L. Lange/Redferns: 314bl.

Frank Spooner Pictures: 71t, 78–79, 173t, 280–281, 281t, 283b.

G. Baker/Redferns: 72t.

G. Davis/Redferns: 70t.

G. DeSota/Redferns: 172–173.

Gems/Redferns: 44t, 135br, 160t, 202br, 328tr.

George Chin/Redferns: 98tl, 247mr, 248b, 255bl, 340bl, 348tl.

Gered Mankowitz/Redferns: 106tl, 117b.

Gerrit Schilp/Redferns: 123; 126 (both); 127tl; br.

Giovanni De Bei/Redferns: 94–95.

Glen A Baker Archives/Redferns: 36t, 38 (both), 49b, 54t, 58l, 133br, 135bl, 147b.

Glenn A. Baker/Redferns: 208tl, 305tr, 329tr, 344tl.

Glen Baker/Redferns: 11t, 223b, 241tr.

Glenn Miles/Redferns: 99tr.

Graham Baker/Redferns 228b.

Grant Davis/Redferns: 105t, 113tl, 121tr, 251mr, 253tm, 257br, 261b, 271tl, 316mr.

Greg Mankowitz/Redferns: 239t.

G. Wiltshire/Redferns: 43m.

Harry Goodwin/Redferns: 316tl.

H. Baum/Redferns: 67b.

Henrietta Butler/Redferns: 200m, 339tr.

Hulton Archive: 142tl, 143mr, 335br.

Hulton Getty Collection: 16b; 21b; 25m, b; 275; 279; 282; 284 (both); 284–285; 287b; 288t; 289 (both); 292m; 294 (both); 294–295; 295b; 299b; 301b.

Ian Dickenson/Redferns: 221t, 225mr.

I. Dickenson/Redferns: 80t, 88b, 89t, 90m.

I. Dickson: 170b.

Island Records: 229m, 232t.

James Dittiger/Redferns: 113bl.

J. Marshall: 47t.

JM International/Redferns: 100m; 115tr; 249bl; 264bl, mr; 314tl.

John Kirk/Redferns: 222–223, 241b.

John Marshall/Redferns: 97b.

Jon Lusk/Redferns: 349mr, 355tr

Jon Super/Redferns: 97t, 103mr, 104b, 147mr, 315tr, 317tr, 331, 353br.

K. Doherty/Redferns: 78b.

Keith Morris/Redferns: 139bl, 163m.

Kieran Doherty/Redferns: 93, 98m, 98–99, 107ml, 114bl, 115br, 119tl, 316–317.

K. Morris/Redferns: 59bl.

Kobal Collection: 151tl; 207mr; 273; 292t, b; 292–293; 19mr.

Krasner/Trebitz/Redferns: 200tl, 201br.

Leon Morris/Redferns: 129bl; 311bl; 335l, tr; 349br; 357br; 359br.

Mark Young/Redferns: 69t.

Martina Raddat/Redferns: 110br.

Max Jones Files/Redferns: 143br; 150tl; 150br; 186bl; 194tl; 203b; 205br; 210tl; tr, b.

M. Cameron/Redferns: 85b.

Me Company: 95tr.

M. Hutson/Redferns: 35; 40br; 42t; 43b; 89m, b; 153; 156m; 158bl; 158–159; 162t, br; 166b; 168b; 175l; 177b; 178br; 180t; 181mr, b.

Michael Finn/Redferns: 113mr, 314–315.

Michael Ochs Archive/Redferns: 8t; 8–9; 18t; 31m; 31b; 36–37; 42b; 43t; 54–55; 105brl 124–125; 128tl; 134tl; 136b; 137ml; 138tl; 140tl; 141tl; 142–143; 143tl; 145bl; 146tl, ml; 149mr; 151mr; 163b; 185tr; 186tl; 190tl; 192tl; 195tl; 196tl; 198tl; 198–199; 201mr; 204tl, bl; 206tl; 207br; 210bl; 222–223; 304–305; 306 (both); 307tr; 308 (both); 310tl; 312bl; 313mr; 320r; 321mr, bl; 322tl, ml; 324br; 328tl, br; 329br; 340tl; 341r; 344b; 345b.

Michel Linssen/Redferns: 118tl, 266tl.

Mick Hutson/Redferns: 18–19; 96bl; 101b; 102b; 108bl; 109 (both); 110–111; 112tl; 114–115; 116tl; 129tl; 216; 241b; 250 (both); 251b, br; 252br; 253br; 254 (both); 255m, mr; 256 (both); 257tm; 258 (both); 260bl; 261tr; 262 (both); 263 (both); 266m; 268 (both); 268–269b; 270br; 327bl; 338b; 347r; 352tr; 353tl; 358tr.

Mike Cameron/Redferns: 215t.

Mike Prior/Redferns: 208r, 209bl.

M. Linssen/Redferns: 173m.

N.E./Redferns: 91m, bl.

N.E./Reporta/Redferns: 319br.

Neville Elder/Redferns: 108tl.

Nicky J. Sims/Redferns: 131t, 246tl, 247br; 249tr; 258–259b; 260tl; 266br; 269 (both); 271tr, br; 351tl; 354tl; 354–355b; 358–359b.

Nigel Crane/Redferns: 247tm.

Norman Granz/Redferns: 197br.

Paramount Pictures (courtesy of Kobal): 39b, 87b, 293.

Patrick Ford/Redferns: 99br, 106bl, 107tr, 114tr, 120br, 121br, 151bl, 248tl, 358bl.

Paul Bergen/Redferns: 101mr; 106–107b; 113r; 120tl, bl; 249tr; 253tr; 259br; 309b; 336–337.

Paul Fenton/Redferns: 264tl.

Paul J. Hoeffler/Redferns: 195mr.

P. Cronin/Redferns: 174m.

Peter Cronin/Redferns: 117mr.

Peter Sanders/Redferns: 21m.

P. Ford: 36b, 156tl, 181ml,.

Pictorial Press: 24–25.

Popperfoto/Reuters: 351.

R. Aaron/Redferns: 64–65; 72–73; 73b; 82m, b; 154–155; 162bl.

Rafael Macia/Redferns: 240mr, 334tl.

Rashied Ali: 191tr.

Ray Johnson/Redferns: 102tl.

R.B./Redferns: 39t, 41b, 44–45, 50t, 52t, 57br, 60t, 136–137; 321br; 323mr; 324tl, ml; 325bl; 326 (both); 328bl; 329m.

Redferns: 5; 11b; 20b; 25t; 27l; 37 (both); 40bl; 41t; 48b; 49m; 50–51; 51b; 52–53; 55b; 59br; 61m, b; 118–119; 119br; 132tl; 149bl; 165b; 171tl, tr; 180m; 190br; 191bl.

Retna: 12t; 13b; 15 (both); 46r; 47b; 213; 224t, br; 226t; 227t, br; 230–21; 231m; 238t.

Retna Pictures: 274–275, 276t, 276–277, 278 (both), 286–287, 288b, 290 (both), 290–291, 291; 298t, 300 (all), 300–301, 301 (all).

Rex Features: 71b.

Richie Aaron/Redferns: 29tl; 34–35; 35; 38–39; 53; 56t, bl; 57bl; 59t; 100tl; 133ml; 145ml; 224bl; 327mr.

Rico D'Rozario/Redferns: 346bl.

Roberta Parkin/Redferns: 350br, 351br, 358tl

Robert Knight/Redferns: 130tl, 132ml, 132–133, 150tr, 270tl.

Robin Little/Redferns: 307tl.

Rogan Coles/Redferns: 226m, 341bl.

Ronald Grant Archive: 12–13; 23tl, tr; 27b; 225ml; 228t; 237b; 278–279; 283t & m; 285b; 296 (both); 297ml; 298–299.

R. Parkin/Redferns: 45t, 47m.

S. & G./Redferns: 52b; 88t.

Salifu Idriss/Redferns: 265br, 24bl.

S. Cunningham: 77t.

S. Gibbons/Redferns: 173b.

Simon Ivan/Redferns: 246bl.

Simon King/Redferns: 245tr.

Simon Ritter/Redferns: 117ml, 227bl, 235t, 358m.

S. Ritter/Redferns: 160m.

Steve Gillett/Redferns: 343br.

Steve Rose/Redferns: 118br.

Stigwood/Hemdale (courtesy of Kobal): 28b; 73t.

Sue Cunningham/Redferns: 333tr.

Sue Schneider/Redferns: 96tl, 104tl, 105bl, 252tl, 267b.

Suzi Gibbons/Redferns: 68c, 80, 357r.

T. Hall/Redferns: 68t.

T. Hanley: 84b.

Tim Hall/Redferns: 19; 220b; 332–333; 334br; 338m; 338–339b; 346tl; 346–47; 349l.

Toby Wales/Redferns: 345tl.

Tommy Hanley/Redferns: 10t, 170t.

Warner Bros. (courtesy of Kobal): 79, 85t.

Warner/Goldcrest (courtesy of Kobal): 67t.

William Gottlieb/Library of Congress/Redferns: 194bl, 198bl, 206br.

William Gottlieb/Redferns: 196–197, 205l, 257bl.